TRACING THE ROOTS OF CHINESE CHARACTERS: 500 CASES

Written and sketched by Li Leyi
Translated by Wang Chengzhi

BEIJING LANGUAGE AND
CULTURE UNIVERSITY PRESS

北京语言文化大学出版社

First Edition 1993
Third Printing 1997
ISBN 7-5619-0204-2/H • 149

Published by Beijing Language and Culture University Press
15 Xueyuan Road, Beijing 100083, China
Distributed by China International Book Trading Corporation
35 Chegongzhuang Xilu, P.O. Box 399
Beijing 100044, China
Printed in the People's Republic of China

CONTENTS

Preface

With a history of approximately six thousand years, the Chinese characters is one of the earliest forms of written language in the world. Throughout its evolution, it has made great contributions to the development of China's long cultural history. Even now, more than one -fourth of the world's population are still using it. As an art form, Chinese calligraphy is an indispensable part of the cultural and artistic legacy of the Chinese people.

The past several thousands of years have witnessed the evolution of Chinese characters, of which the main forms are as follows:

I. *Jia Gu Wen:* **Oracle Bone Inscriptions**

As the earliest form of the Chinese written language, *jia gu wen* refers to the writings inscribed on the carapaces of tortoises and on mammal bones during the Shang Dynasty (c. 16th — 11th century B. C.). It recorded the art of divination commonly practiced by the ancient people, so it is also called *bu ci*, divination writings, and *qi wen*, inscribed writings. As the inscribed oracle bones were first discovered in the Yin ruins (the capital ruins from the end of Shang Dynasty, now the Xiaotun Village, Anyang County, Henan Province), they also became known as "Yin ruins' characters." One thousand or more of the over four thousand characters inscribed on the collected oracle bones can be deciphered and understood. Although to some extent this ancient script is a set language, many strokes and radicals are not in a final fixed form. In the early Zhou Dynasty (c. 11th century-256 B.C.) some oracle bones were already unearthed.

II. *Jin Wen*: **Bronze Inscriptions**

The characters cast or inscribed on the bronze articles of the Shang and Zhou Dynasties are known as *jin wen*, or *zhong ding wen* (lit: writings on bronze bells or tripods). The earliest was similar to the oracle bone inscriptions, some in the form of the early pictographs. The latest were closer in form to their discendants, *xiao zhuan*, small seal characters. Half of the six thousand or so characters cast or inscribed on bronze objects can be deciphered and understood. Their form and structure show a much greater maturity than their predecessors. The text inscribed on one bronze object in the Zhou Dynasty runs as long as five hundred characters.

III. *Xiao Zhuan:* **Small Seal Characters**

It is the written language popularly used in Qin Dynasty (221-207 B. C.). It is also known as *Qin zhuan*, Qin Dynasty characters. During the Warring States Period (475-221B.C.), differenf writings were in use in different parts of the land. Following the conquest and unification of the country, the first emperor of the Qin Dynasty simplified and unified the written language. The surviving form was *xiao zhuan*, based on *da zhuan*, big seal characters, which was also called *zhou wen*, characters popularly used in the Qin State during the Spring and Autumn (770-476 B.C.) and the Warring States periods. The unification of the written language in Qin Dynasty contributed significantly to the standardization of Chinese characters.

IV. *Li Shu:* **Official Script**

As a formal written language in the Han Dynasty (206 B.C. – 220 A.D.), this form began to be used at the end of the Qin Dynasty, and lasted to Three Kingdoms Period (220 – 280 A.D.). It is also called *Han li*, Han Dynasty script, among other names. In the early version of official script, traces of small seal characters can be observed. In the later version, curved and broken strokes were added. As a sound foundation laid for the coming standardization of Chinese characters, official script symbolized a turning point in the evolution history of Chinese characters. Since that time, Chinese characters moved from an ancient to a modern stage of development.

V. *Kai Shu:* **Regular Script**

Appearing at the end of the Han Dynasty, *kai shu* has been in vogue to the present day and is still in common use. It is characterized by a straight and upright character form, and thus is also named *zhengshu*, square script, and *zhen shu*, realistic script. In history, many calligraphers are famous for their use of *kai shu* in their artistic creations.

VI. *Cao Shu:* **Cursive Writing or Grass Stroke Characters**

Appearing first at the beginning of Han Dynasty, *cao shu* was actually a much earlier form than *kai shu*. The earliest cursive writings were variants of the cursively written forms of official script, and they were called *cao li*, cursive official script. Later, they became known as *zhang cao*, cursive seal characters. Since the end of the Han Dynasty, the strokes became slightly linked and the radicals mutually interchangeable, with the traces retained in the cursive seal characters no longer visible. Hence, *jin cao*, contemporary cursive script, emerged, which later evolved into *kuang cao*, "extreme" cursive script, in the Tang Dynasty with strokes becoming more unorthodox and some characters even illegible. The cursive calligraphy used at the present day is generally in the form of *jin cao*.

VII. Xing Shu: **Freehand Cursive**

As a writing style somewhere between the geometrical *kai shu* and the curvy, unrestrained *cao shu*, it appeared and became popular during the Three Kingdoms Period (200 – 280 A.D.) and Jin Dynasty (265 – 420 A.D.). Such a form is more convenient to write than *kai shu* and easier to read than *cao shu*, so it became the preferred writing style of people. *xing shu* can also be divided into two categories: *xing kai* and *xing cao*. The former is composed of more orthodox strokes, while the latter tends more toward employing more cursive style strokes. Their difference, however, is not readily apparent.

In addition, since the birth of the Chinese written language a great number of simplified versions of characters emerged for the convenience of usage. They are called *su zi*, common characters, *shou tou zi*, "handy" characters, among other names. In the developing process of Chinese characters, there existed tendencies both to complicate and to simplify, of which the latter was the main current. In the 1950s, Chinese scholars researched simplified characters popular throughout Chinese history. Their efforts gave birth to the several waves of "simplified Characters" which have established themselves as the norm in mainland China today.

Aiming at promoting the general reader's understanding of the evolution of Chinese characters and traditional Chinese culture as well, this book is written and compiled with the following features:

1. Since it is a book for the average reader, each Chinese character is presented with a vivid picture and a simple explanation describing its evolution.

2. Each of the 500 selected Chinese characters (660 characters or more if one includes the interchangeable words, loan words, etc.) is presented in each of its seven forms: oracle bone inscription, bronze inscription, small seal character, official script, regular script, grass stroke character, and freehand cursive writing (some have been simplified, and the simplified versions are added). Rare characters or characters which are incomplete of the seven forms are not in the collection, except for some characters whose bronze inscriptions are replaced by *zhou wen* or Warring States Period characters.

3. Some Chinese characters in certain forms can be written in a multitude of ways. Examples selected in this book are the comparatively typical and commonly used ones.

4. The philological explanation is based on the generally accepted conclusions of philologists, the conclusions of some schools of thought, and the author's views as well. Due to the limited capacity of this book, the explanations are not fully elaborated and the source books are not listed.

5. The texts are arranged in the alphabetical order based on the *pinyin* system (characters with more than one pronunciation are arranged based on their more common usage).

Index of strokes

(arranged according to the number of strokes and 一丨丿丶乛)

5 strokes

6 strokes

7 strokes

8 strokes

9 strokes

10 strokes

11 strokes

12 strokes

13 strokes

14 strokes

15 strokes

16 strokes

安 ān

In a silent house, with her hands folded on her bosom a woman (see Case 女) kneels calmly on a straw mat as the ancient people used to do. Hence, its original meaning was "stable," "comfortable" and "safe."

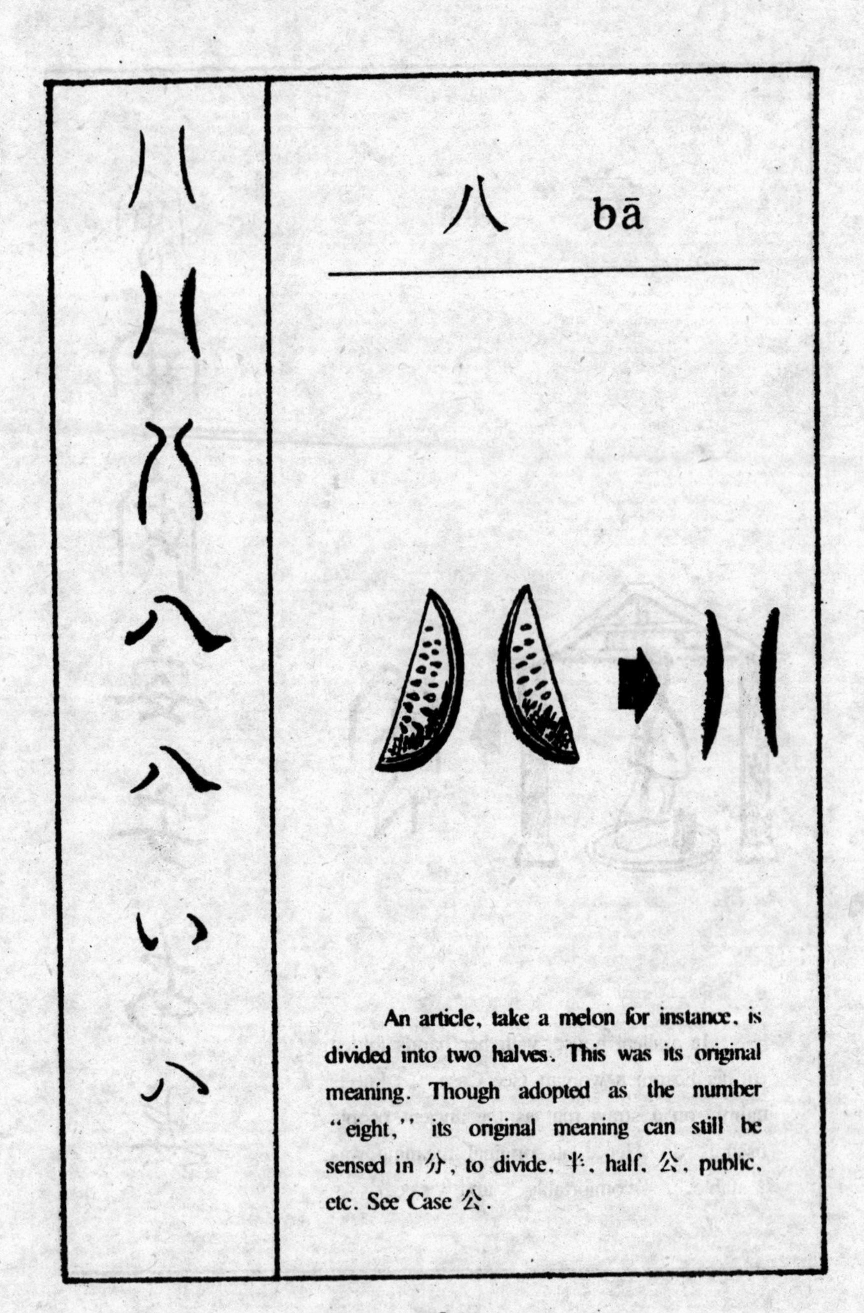

八 bā

An article, take a melon for instance, is divided into two halves. This was its original meaning. Though adopted as the number "eight," its original meaning can still be sensed in 分, to divide, 半, half, 公, public, etc. See Case 公.

〔附〕 伯

Originally, it was the form of a burning candle. Its original meaning was "bright" or "clear." Later, it evolved into "white." In jīa gǔ wén (oracle bone inscriptions) and jīn wén (bronze inscriptions), it was loaned for use in 伯, uncle.

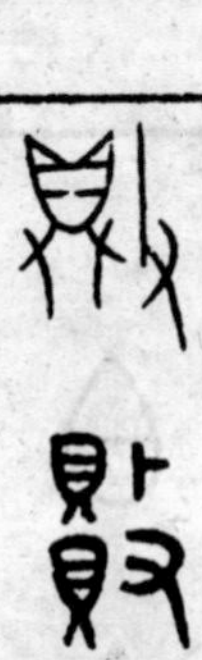

败(敗)bài

In oracle bone inscriptions, it was like a hand (see Case 又) with a stick beating the ding (tripod, an ancient three-legged cooking vessel, see Case 鼎). In bronze inscriptions, the radical 鼎 took form of 貝, shellfish (see Case 貝). Hence, its original meaning was "to destroy."

般 bān

〔附〕 盘

It is the original form of 盘, of which the complex version is 盤. In oracle bone inscriptions, it was like a spoon in a hand fetching food from a tray.

邦

邦

邦 bāng

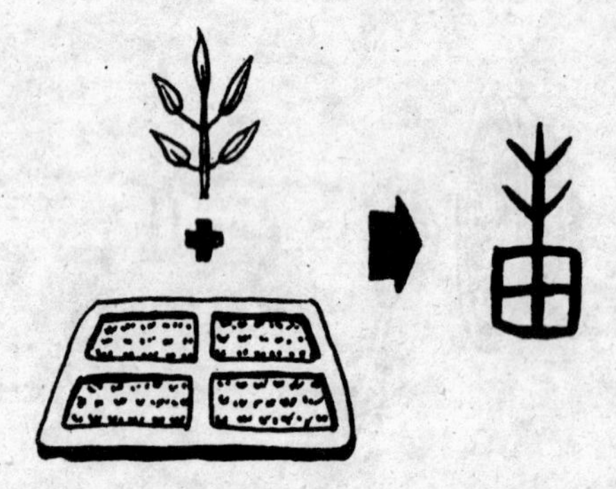

Its original meaning was 国, nation. In oracle bone inscriptions, it was composed of 田, field, and 丰, abundant, of which the former is the place on which people can live and the latter is the phonetic symbol (田 and 丰 are pronounced in the same way in ancient times). In bronze inscriptions, 邑 replaced 田, meaning the place where people live in a compact community.

保 bǎo

〔附〕褓 堡

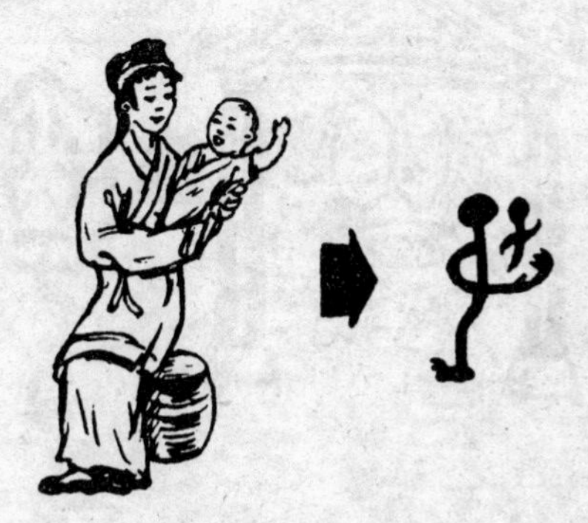

Graphically, a grown-up holds a baby dressed in swaddling clothes in her arms. Hence, its original meaning was "to bring up," "to cultivate," etc. It extends to mean "to protect," "to bless," etc. In ancient books, it was interchangeable with 褓 and 堡.

宝(寶)bǎo

There are "shellfish" (symbolizing richness) and "jade"(symbolizing jewelry) in a house. 缶 (a container, indicating household utensils) is added to some forms of this character. As all of them were considered treasures, its original meaning was "valuable or precious items."

北 běi

〔附〕 背

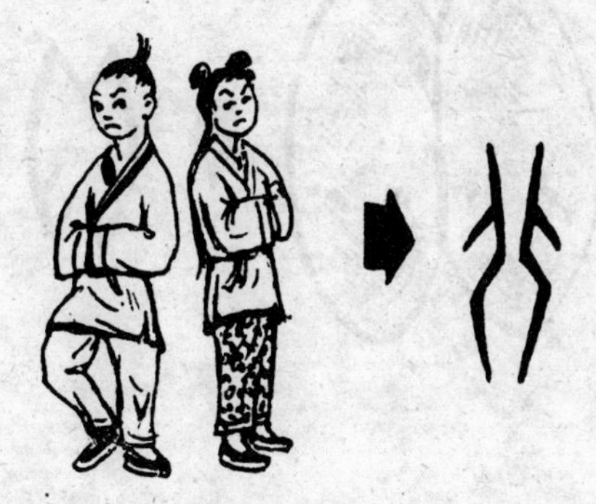

It is the original form of 背, back. Two persons standing back to back forms the initial shape of this character. After it was loaned to mean "north," the new character 背 was invented to take on the meaning of "back."

贝（貝）bèi

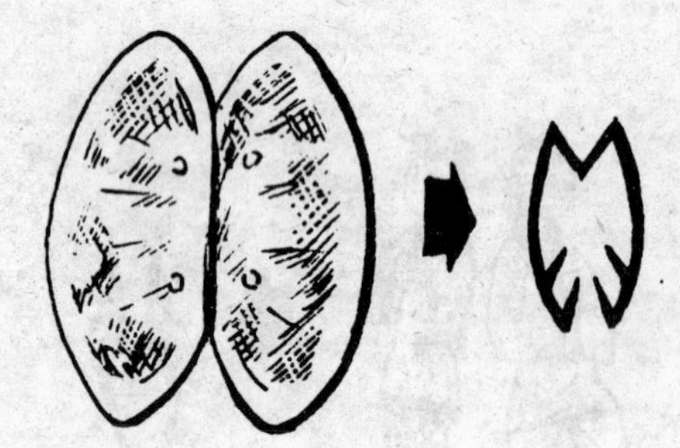

贝，cowrie，refers to a mollusk. Its form is like a shellfish with its two shells open . Ancient people accepted cowries as currency, therefore, characters with the radical 贝 generally have a meaning pertaining to wealth.

比　bǐ

Graphically, two persons stand one in front of the other. Hence, its original meaning was "to juxtapose." Its extended meaning is "to be close to."

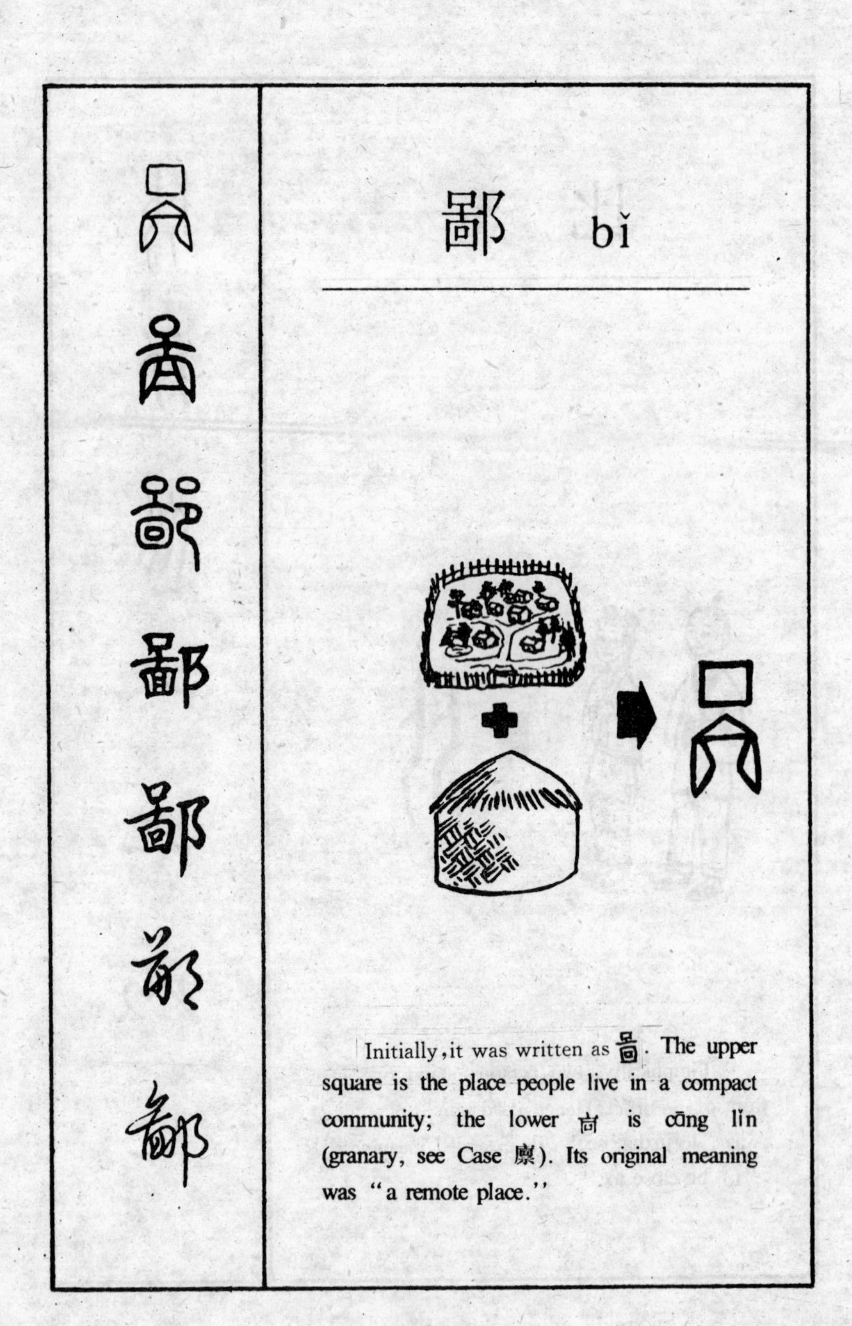

鄙 bǐ

Initially, it was written as 啚. The upper square is the place people live in a compact community; the lower 㐭 is cōng lǐn (granary, see Case 廪). Its original meaning was "a remote place."

毕(畢)bì

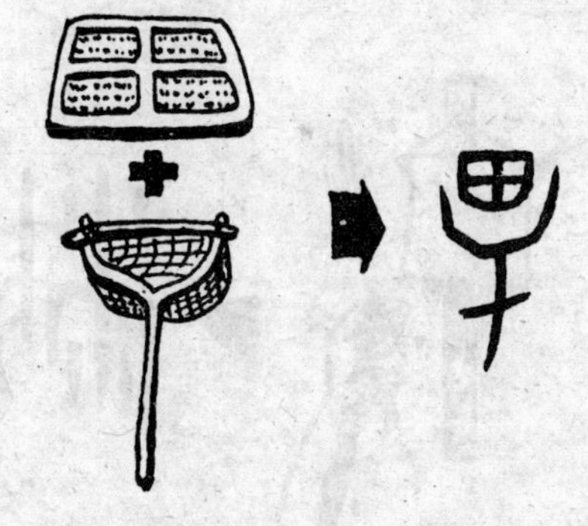

Originally, it was a big net with long shaft to capture birds and animals. The upper 田, field, indicates the place where captured birds and animals are stored.

敝 bì

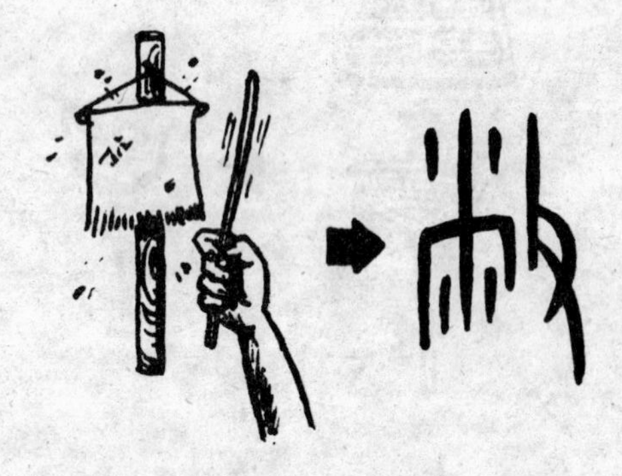

Its left part is a piece of cloth (巾, sheet), which is dirty with dust. The right side is a hand (又, hand) with a club striking the piece of cloth. Its original meaning was "bad" or "worn-out."

必 bì

〔附〕 柲

It is the original form of 柲, shaft. In oracle bone inscriptions, it was like a spoon with long shaft and scattered drops of water. The slanting stroke is the selfexplanatory symbol of the shaft.

宾(賓)bīn

In oracle bone inscriptions, graphically it was a man coming into the house. The radical 足 was added to some forms of this character. In bronze inscriptions, 贝, shellfish and 鼎, tripod, were added to indicate the presents brought by guests.

兵 bīng

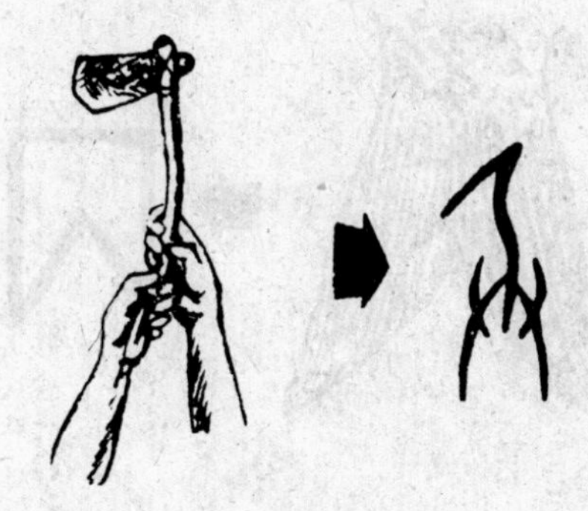

Its original meaning was 兵器, weapon. Later it extended to mean "soldier." Graphically, its upper part is 斤, an ax-shaped weapon (see Case 斤); its lower part is two hands holding the weapon.

丙 bǐng

Initially, it indicated the caudal fin of a fish. With its original meaning no longer existent, today it usually indicates the third of the ten Heavenly Stems.

秉 bǐng

Graphically, a hand holding cereal crops, its original meaning was simply a handful of cereal crops. It also means "to hold."

并(並，併)bìng

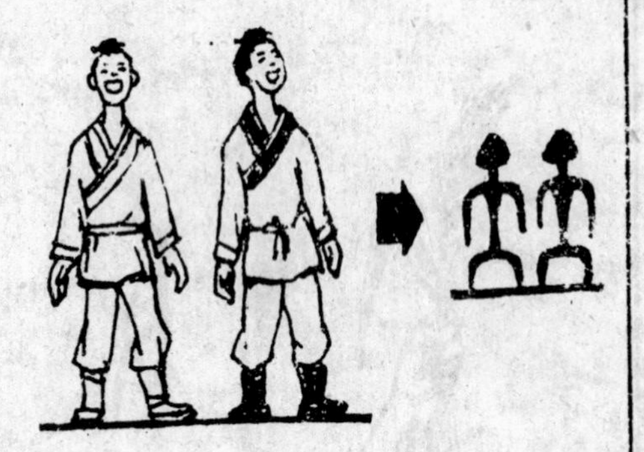

Originally, it was 並, (also 竝), meaning "standing together" "side by side," for its form is two persons standing next to one another Today, 並, 幷, and 倂 are combined and simplified to 并.

卜 bǔ

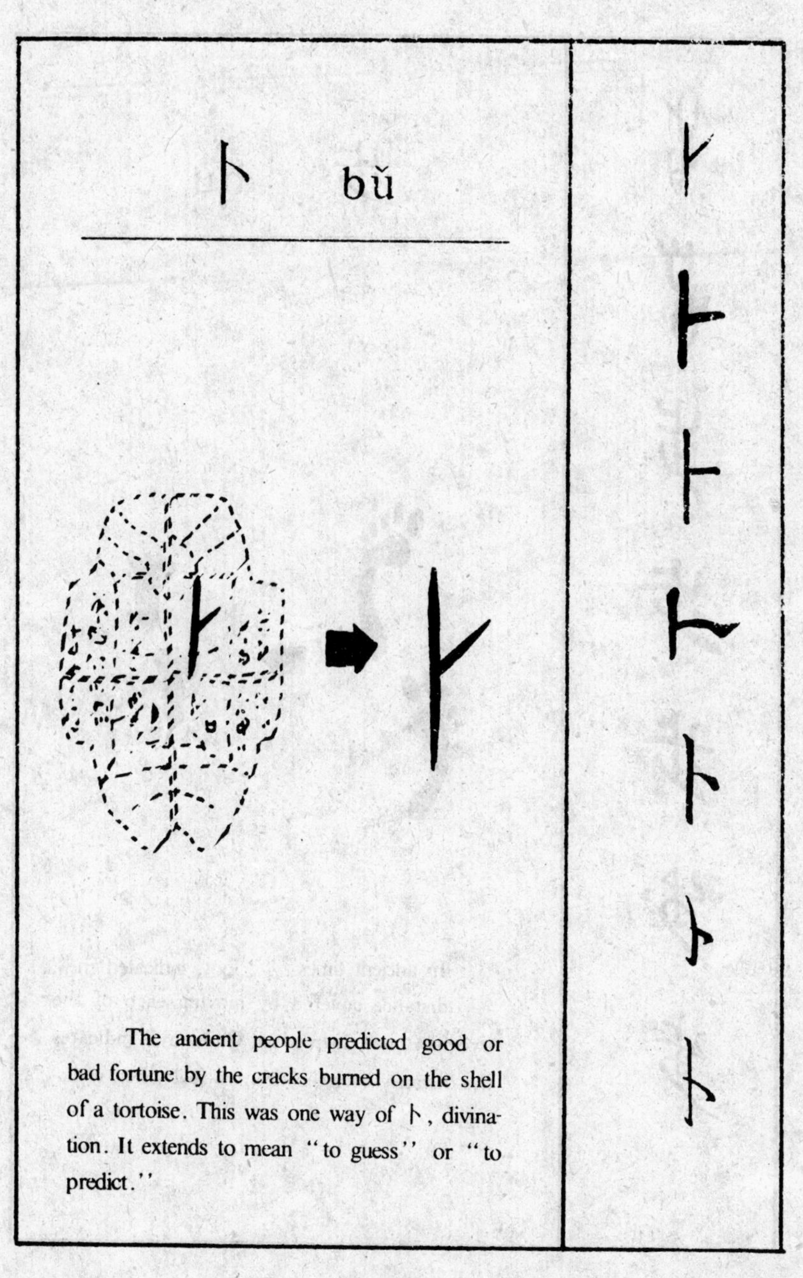

The ancient people predicted good or bad fortune by the cracks burned on the shell of a tortoise. This was one way of 卜, divination. It extends to mean "to guess" or "to predict."

步 bù

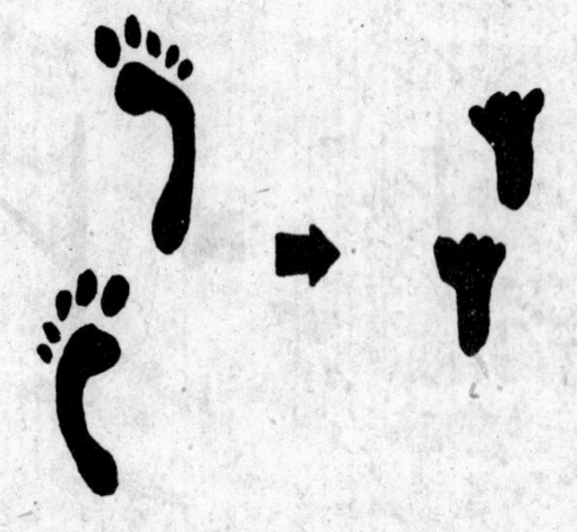

In ancient times, 步, foot, indicated the distance covered by moving each of the two feet once. In modern Chinese, it indicates the distance between the two feet when walking.

不 bù

〔附〕 胚 丕 否

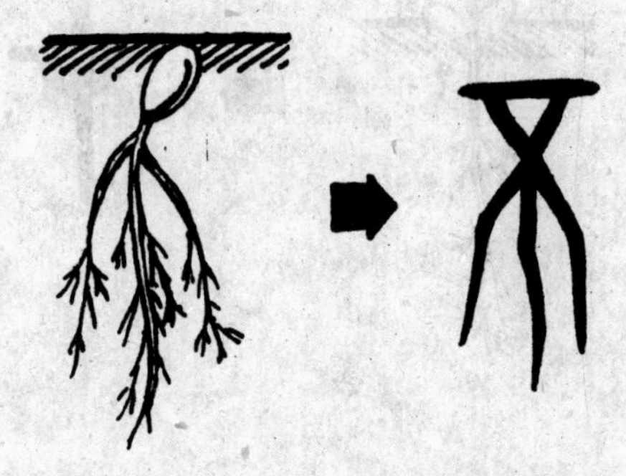

Its original form was 胚. In oracle bone inscriptions, the horizontal plane of this character symbolized the surface, while the tassel-like strokes symbolized the fibrous roots of the seed when it first began to germinate. Later, it was loaned for use in 丕, 不 and 否.

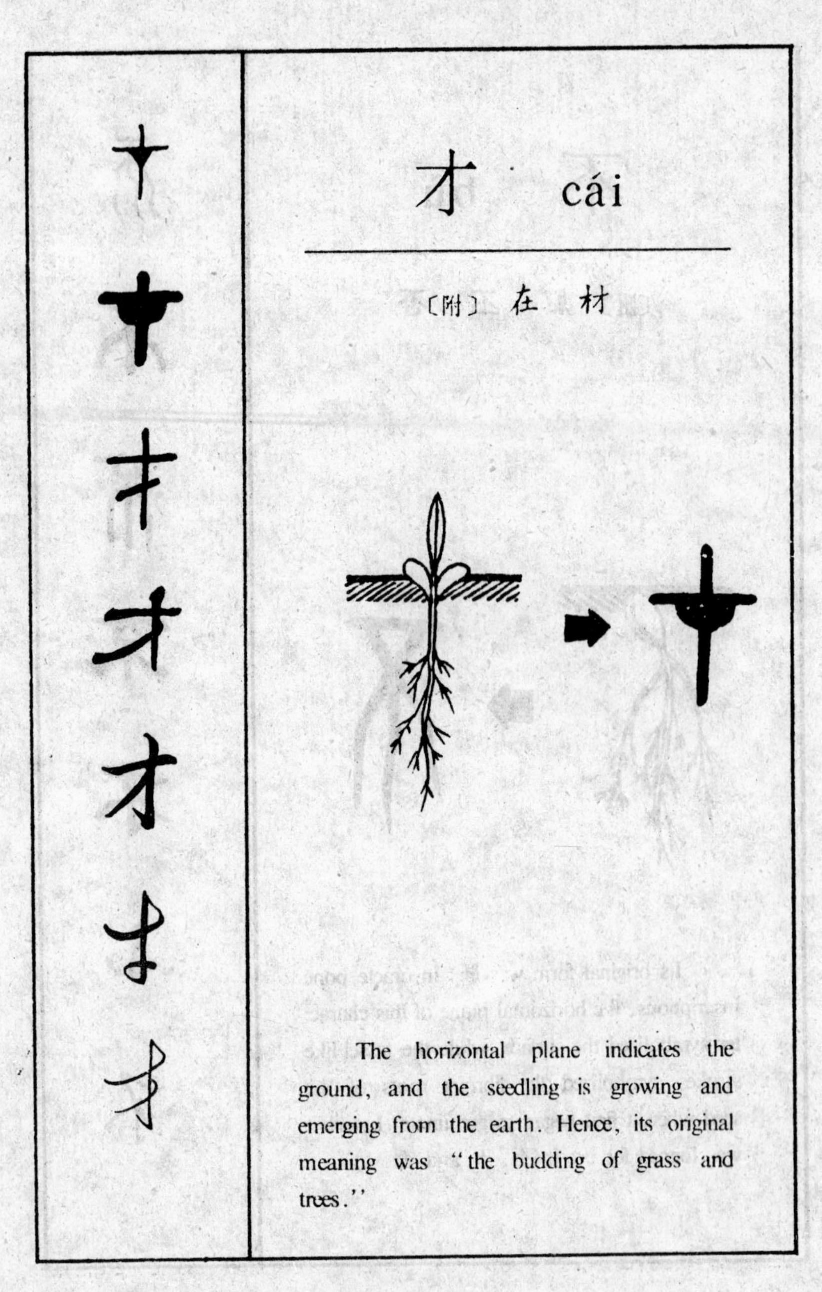

才 cái

〔附〕在 材

The horizontal plane indicates the ground, and the seedling is growing and emerging from the earth. Hence, its original meaning was "the budding of grass and trees."

采(採)cǎi

〔附〕 彩

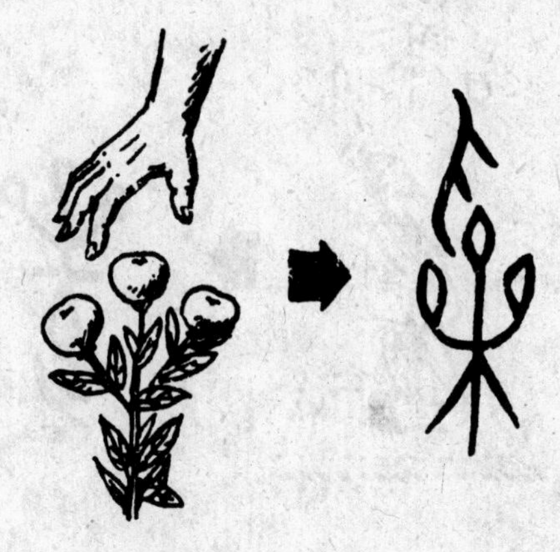

It is the original form of 采. In oracle bone inscriptions, it was a hand plucking fruits. In ancient books, it was interchangeable with 彩, color.

采

採

採

採

采

参(參)cān, shēn

Originally, it was the name for a constellation, then pronounced shēn. Its form is a man with stars above his head. Gradually, three slanting strokes were added to symbolize the light of the stars.

仓(倉)cāng

〔附〕舱　苍　沧

Its original meaning was a granary. Its upper part is the roof, the middle a door and the lower the corner stone. In ancient books, it was loaned for use in 舱, 苍, 沧, etc.

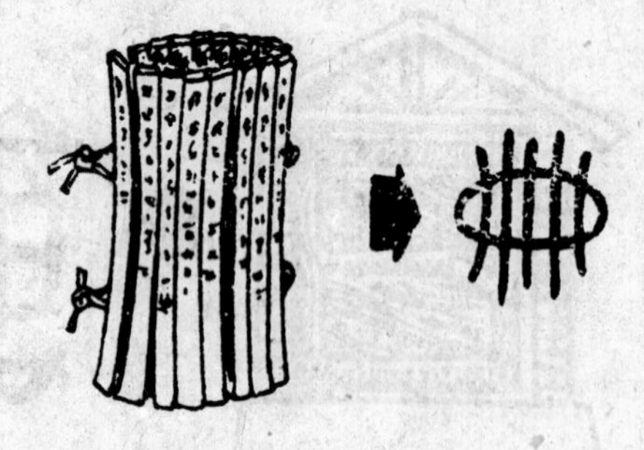

The strips of bamboo written on by primitive people is called jiǎn cè (bamboo strip book). The vertical strokes and horizontal planes in oracle bone and bronze inscriptions symbolized the bamboo strips and the binding leather rope respectively.

长(長)cháng ,zhǎng

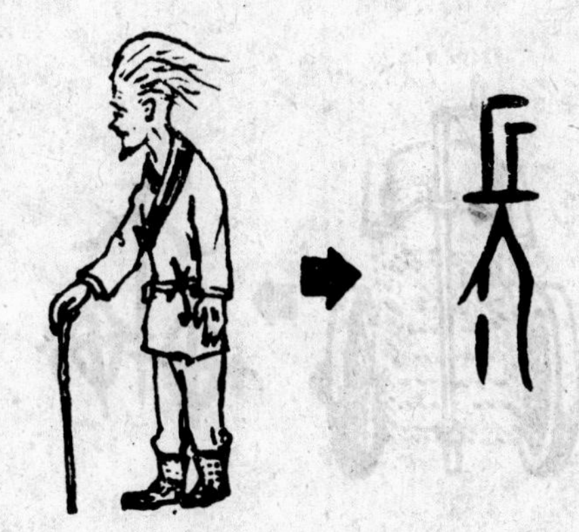

In oracle bone inscriptions, it indicated the long hair on a person's head. For the sake of carving convenience, people preferred the short horizontal planes to the long. It is the same case with 天, heaven, 元, first, and other characters.

车(車)chē

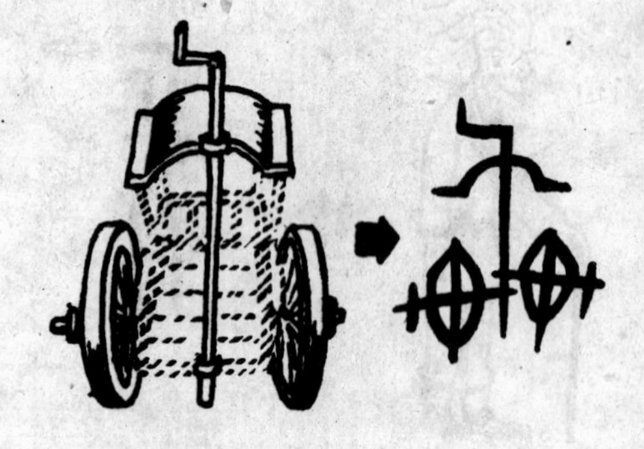

As a typical pictographic character, this character meaning "vehicle" was vividly carved in oracle bone and bronze inscriptions depicting a carriage, two shafts and two wheels. Later, it was simplified to have only one wheel.

臣 chén

Its original meaning was "slave." Slaves are bowing their heads before their master. When a slave lowers his head, the master may find that his eye seems vertical. Hence, the ancient people made use of the vertical eye to give the meaning of "loyal minister."

辰 chén

〔附〕 蜃 晨

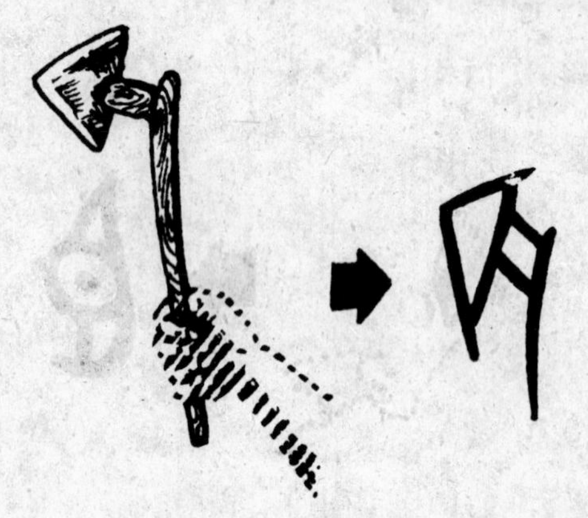

Originally, it indicated a weeding instrument made of sharpened clamshells. It was also adopted as 蜃 and was interchangeable with 晨, dawn.

成 chéng

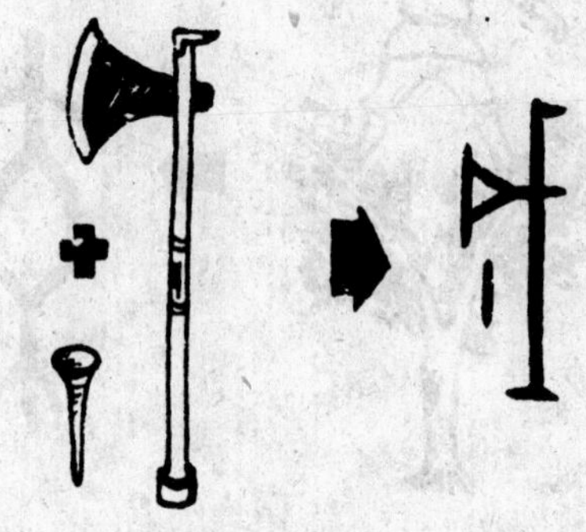

Its original meaning was "to suppress." It also means "to make peace." Since its meanings all have something to do with warfare, this pictophonetic character is composed of 戊, wǔ (see Case 戊) indicating meaning and 丁 indicating the sound.

乘 chéng ,shèng

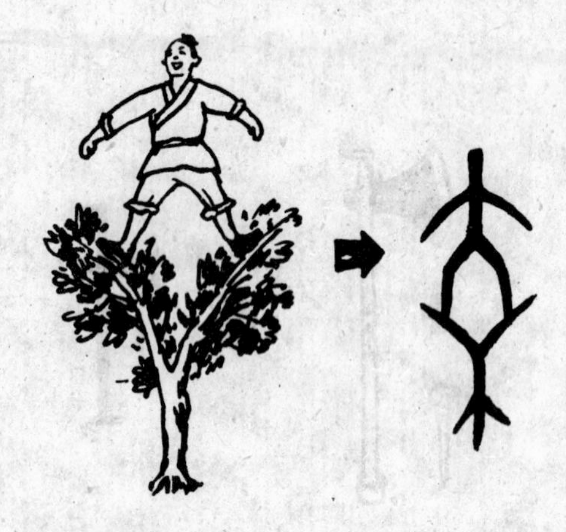

A person climbing up a tree, its original meaning was "to ascend." Later, it took on the meanings of "to sit" and "to drive," with its pronunciation as chèng. It can also be pronounced as shèng with the meaning of "vehicle," e.g. 十乘, shí shèng, means "ten vehicles."

丞 chéng

〔附〕拯

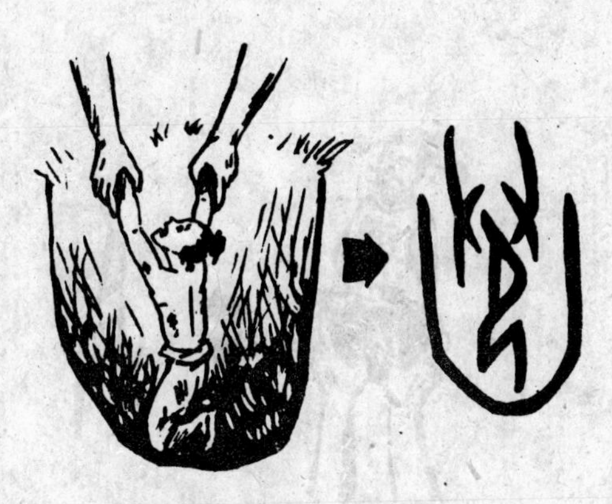

Graphically, a person happens to fall into a deep hole, two helping hands are extended to him. Hence, its original meaning was "to save." Later, it was used for an official title, and another form 拯 was invented to indicate the original meaning.

承 chéng

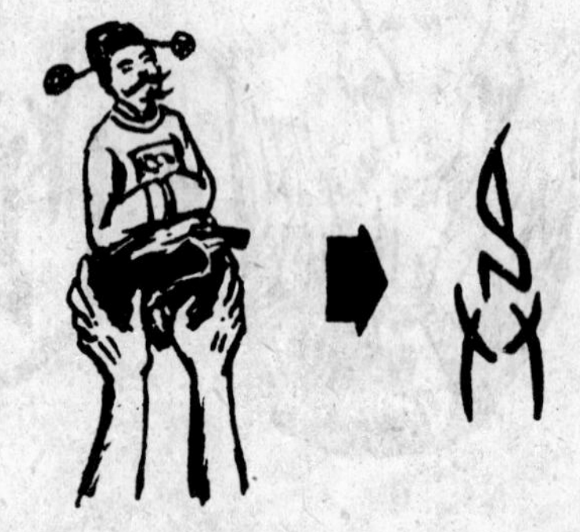

Its original meaning was "to present respectfully" and "to raise with two hands." In oracle bone and bronze inscriptions, it was carved to be a person with two raised hands. In xiǎo zhuàn (small seal characters), another hand was added. Its extended meanings are "obedient," "to accept," "to inherit," etc. It is interchangeable with 丞.

称(稱)chēng ,chèng

〔附〕 偁

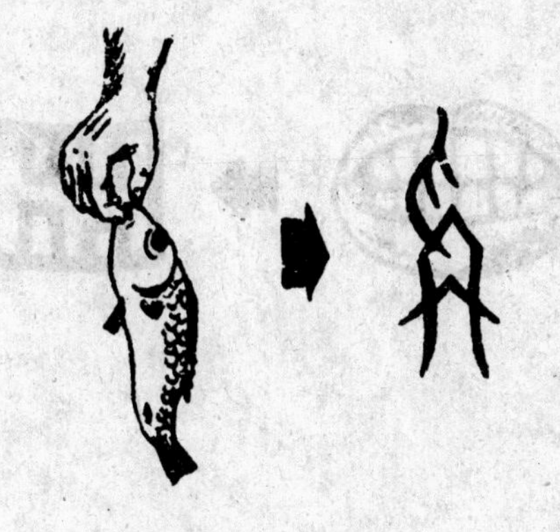

稱
稱
稱
称

Initially, it was 爯 meaning "to weigh on a balance." Graphically, a hand is lifting a fish to determine its weight. In ancient books, when used to mean "to acclaim." "to praise" and "appellation" it was written as 偁 or 稱. Today it is written as

齿(齒)chǐ

Illustrating several teeth in a mouth, it is very vividly delineated in oracle bone inscriptions. In bronze inscriptions, the radical 止 was added to indicate the sound. Since a pony grows a tooth each year, 齿 can be the metaphor for "age."

赤 chì

Originally, it was composed of 大, big and 火, fire. Its original meaning was "red," derived from the color of fire. Today, it also means "empty," "whole-hearted" and "uncovered."

舂 chōng

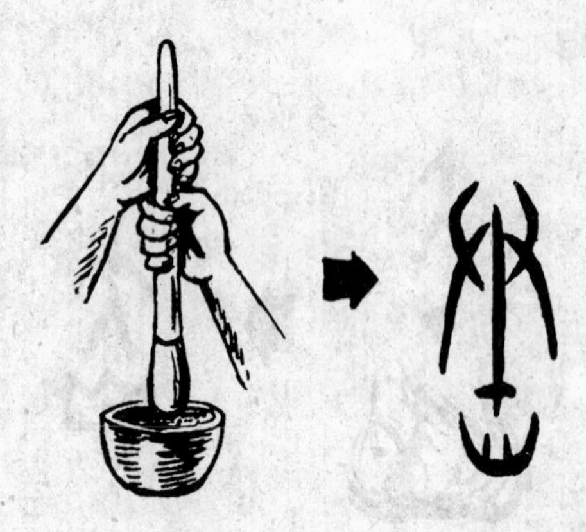

Graphically, two hands hold a pestle and husk the rice in a mortar. Hence, it means "to husk" or "to pound."

虫(蟲)chóng

〔附〕 虺

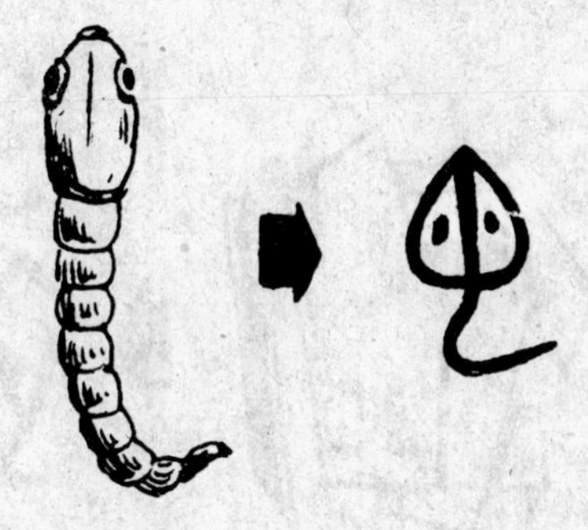

It is the original form of 虺, hui, meaning "viper." Graphically, it is the shape of a worm: Its upper part is the pointed head sometimes drawn with two eyes, its lower part is the crooked body. Later, it indicated the ordinary worm.

初 chū

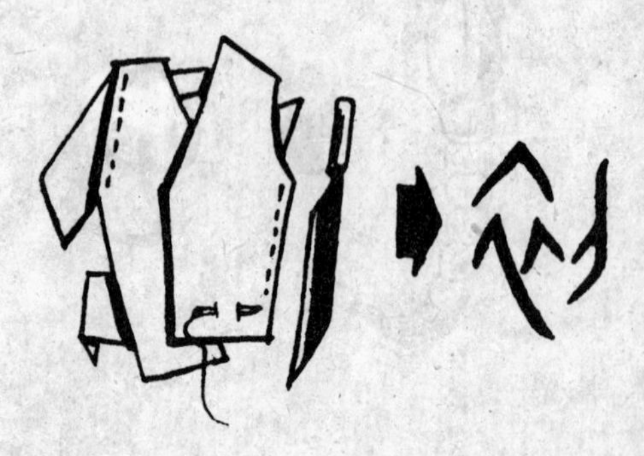

This character is composed of 衣, clothes, and 刀, knife, indicating the time when people began making clothes with knives. Hence, its original meaning was "beginning." Its extended meaning is "original," "past," etc.

出 chū

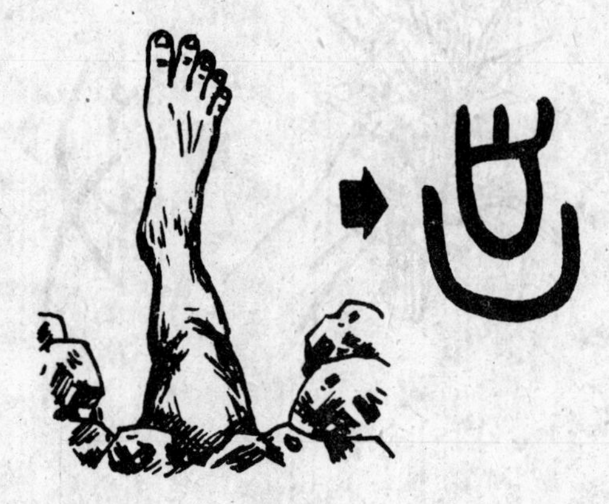

Primitive man lived in caves. When he let one foot out of the cave, he indicated he was going out. Hence, its original meaning was "to go outside." It extends to mean "to expend," "to exceed," etc.

刍(芻)chú

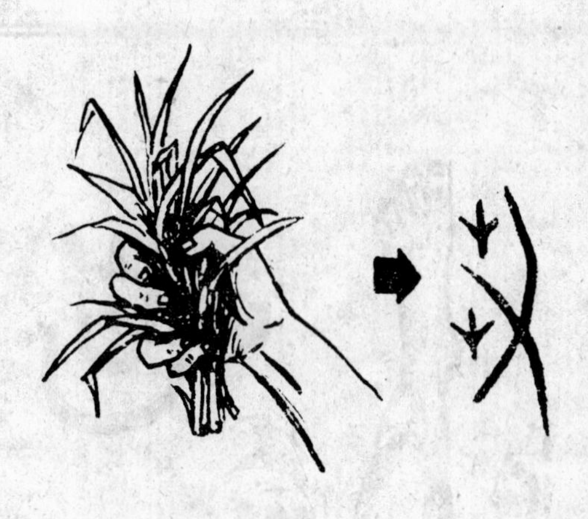

Graphically, a hand is pulling up weeds to feed livestock, hence its original meaning was "to weed" or "to mow." It also means "the grass to feed livestock."

楚 chǔ

In oracle bone inscriptions, the middle part of this character was a square symbolizing the place people live in a community, while the lower part was 止, meaning people's footprints. As it is surrounded by woods 林, its original meaning was a kind of shrub.

川 chuān

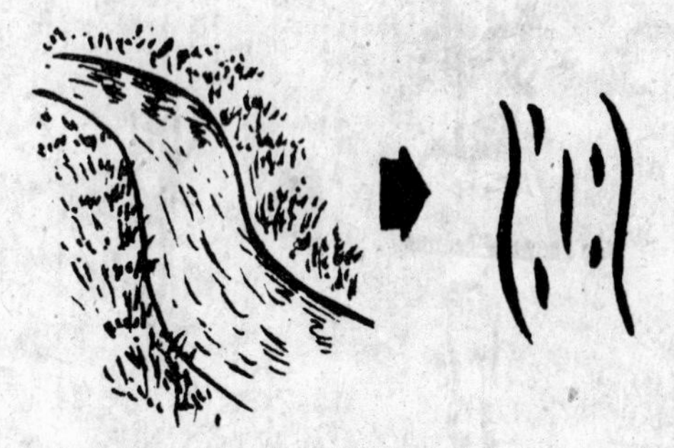

In oracle bone inscriptions, it looked like a river sometimes with wave-shaped carvings. Hence, its original meaning was "river." Later, it also indicated "the low flat land among mountains and highlands."

吹 chuī

It is composed of 口, mouth, and 欠, yawn, (see Case 欠). The 口 is added to mean "exhale with mouth nearly closed." It also means "to blow."

春 chūn

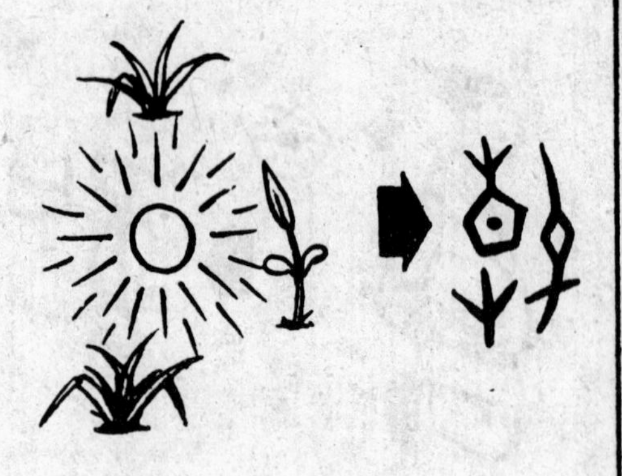

It was composed of 日, sun, 艸, grass and 屯, at its earliest writing (see Case 屯). The sun and the spring grass symbolize that spring has returned.

此 cǐ

The right part is a man and the left part is 止, a foot. It symbolizes "the place a man stands on." Hence, its original meaning was "here" or "this place." 止 also indicates the sound.

从(從)cóng

〔附〕 纵

Graphically, a man was walking and another man is following him. Its original meaning was "to follow." Later, this character added 彳 and 止 indicating walking. In ancient books, it was interchangeable with 纵, jump.

大 dà

〔附〕 太

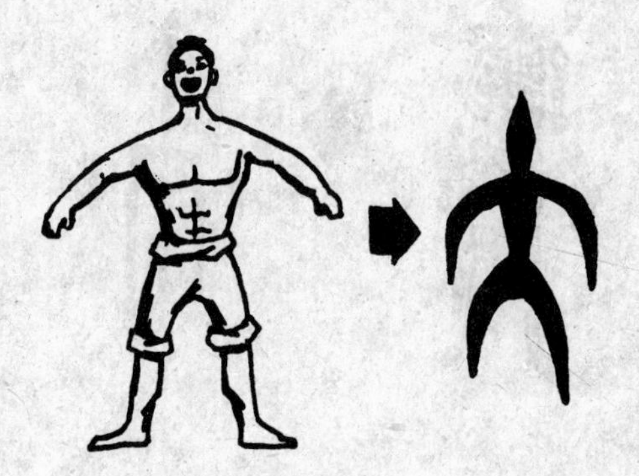

Graphically, a man standing straight with his arms extended outward means "big." In ancient times, people regarded man to be the greatest of all creatures, so his image is used to express "bigness." In oracle bone and bronze inscriptions, it was interchangeable with 太, taì, very.

歹 dǎi

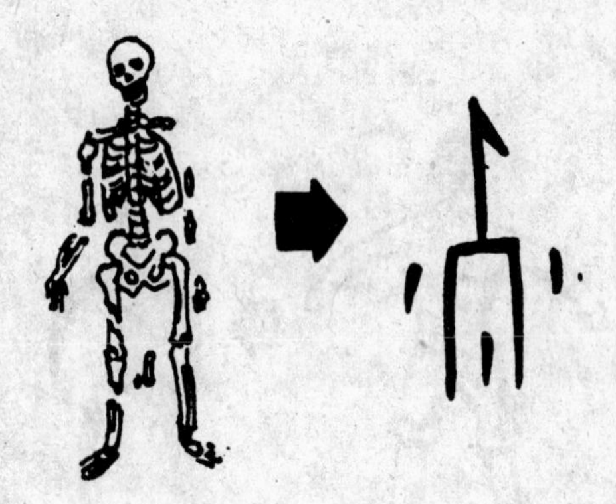

Graphically, it looks like the remains of a dead man. Characters with the radical 歹 usually have the meaning of "death" or "bad," e.g. 死, death, 葬, interment, 残, incomplete, 殡, funeral, 殆, end, 殁 kill, and 殃, affect, to name a few.

丹 dān

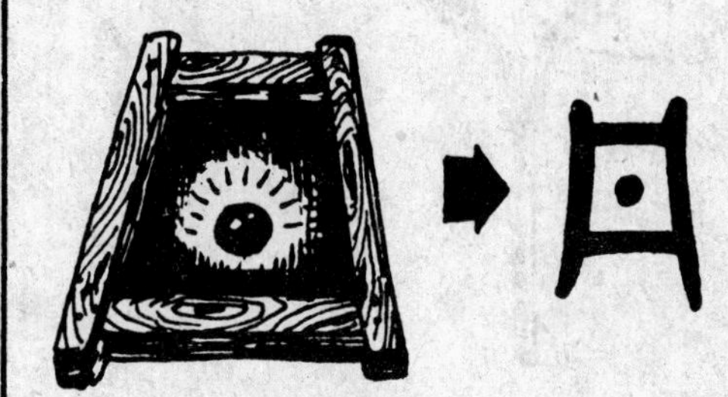

Its original meaning was "cinnabar" extracted from a mine. So, in oracle bone and bronze inscriptions a dot was added in the mineshaped structure. Its extended meanings are "red" (not as deep a red as 赤, chì) and "medicine refined from minerals."

单(單)dān

〔附〕 战

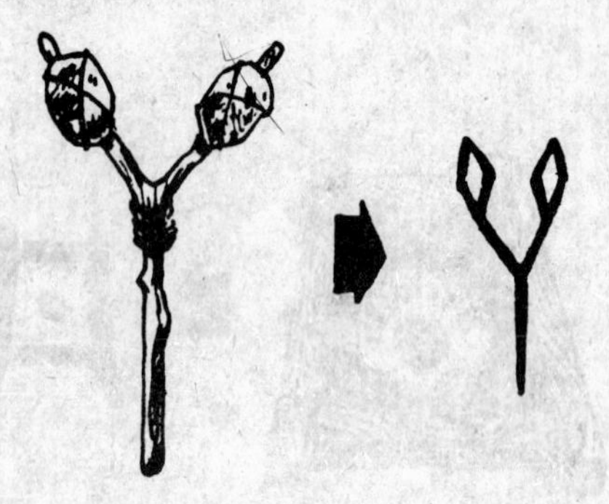

Originally, it was a primeval weapon, made up of the fork of a tree branch and two stones bound on the two ends of the fork. In bronze inscriptions, it was interchangeable with 戰, zhàn, to fight.

旦 dàn

Its original meanings were "dawn" and "morning." Graphically, the sun is rising in the horizon, vividly depicting the morning scene. Later, the horizon was changed to a horizontal plane under the sun.

刀 dāo

The form of the character is like a knife, the upper part as the handle and the lower part as the blade. In ancient times, there was a knife-like coin, it was also called dāo.

稻　dào

In oracle bone inscriptions, it was composed of 米 (rice, see Case 米) as the upper part and rice basket as the lower part. In bronze inscriptions, a flag was added on the upper part to indicate the rice being beaten in the wind and a hand was added to husk the rice. In small seal characters, it evolved to become a pictophonetic character.

德 ·dé

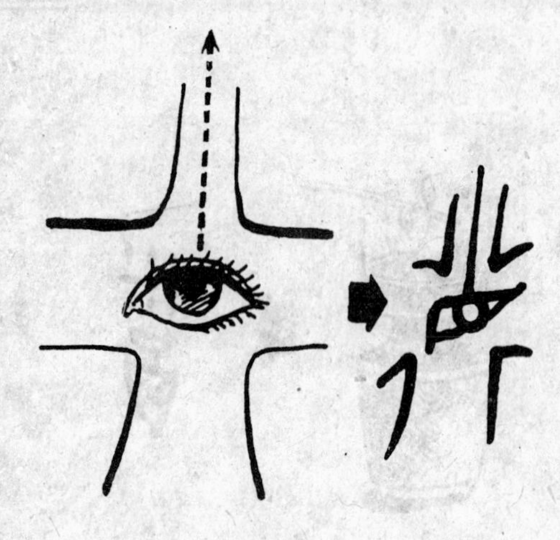

In oracle bone inscriptions, the 彳 or 行 of this character indicated the path and the direction, the eye staring straight ahead indicated integrity. 心, heart, was added to it in bronze inscriptions. To do and to think according to the upright principles is "moral." Hence, its original meaning was "moral."

得 dé

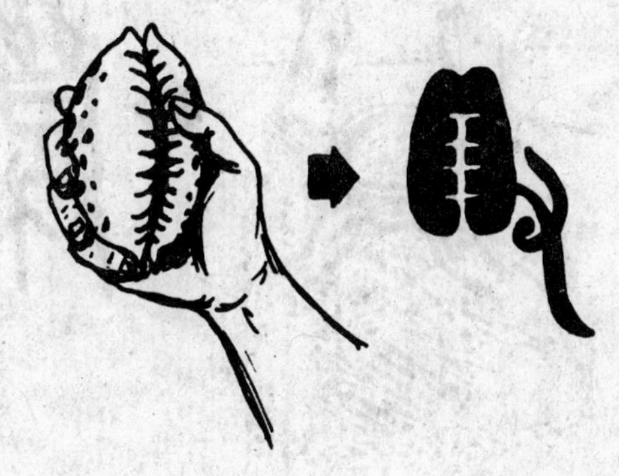

Graphically, it looks like a hand holding a 贝, shell, which was a form of currency in ancient times and symbolized valuable or precious items (see Case 贝). Therefore, it means "to get" or "to acquire." It also means 贪得, "to acquire insatiably."

登 dēng

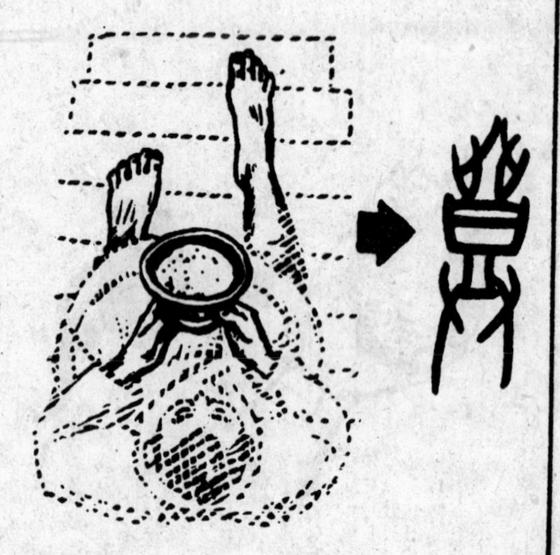

As an earthenware sacrificial utensil, 登, looks like 豆, dòu (see Case 豆). Graphically, it is composed of a pair of feet on the upper part and two hands attached to the lower part, symbolizing mounting the sacrificial altar with a sacrificial utensil in hand. Hence, its meaning is "to mount or ascend."

帝　dì

〔附〕 禘

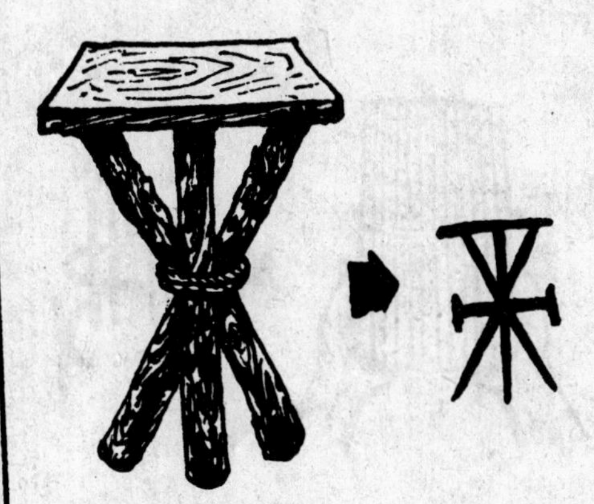

It is the original form of 禘, dì, a grand sacrificial ceremony to Heaven or ancestors. Graphically, it looks like several sticks of wood supporting an altar. Later, it was loaned to mean 帝 of 帝王, dì wáng, emperor and king.

典 diǎn

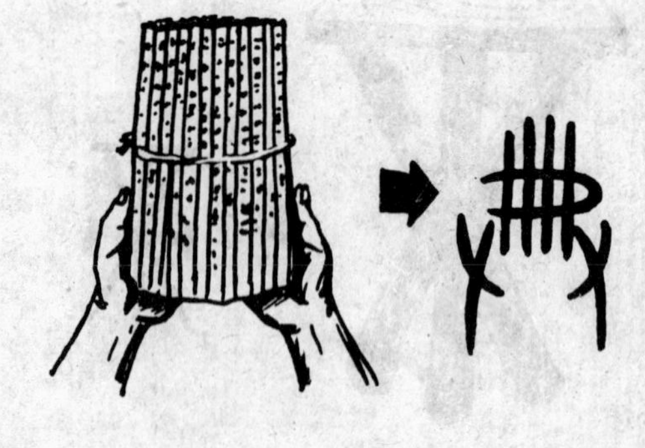

In oracle bone inscriptions, its form was two hands holding a 册 (book, see Case 册), meaning important literature or book. It extends to mean "standards," "rule," "law," etc.

奠 diàn

〔附〕郑

Its original meaning was a jar of wine laid on a platform (in oracle bone inscriptions) or on a table (in bronze inscriptions) being offered to the dead. It also means "to lay," "to set up" and "to settle," e.g. 奠定, set up, and 奠基, to lay a foundation. It was interchangeable with 郑 in ancient books.

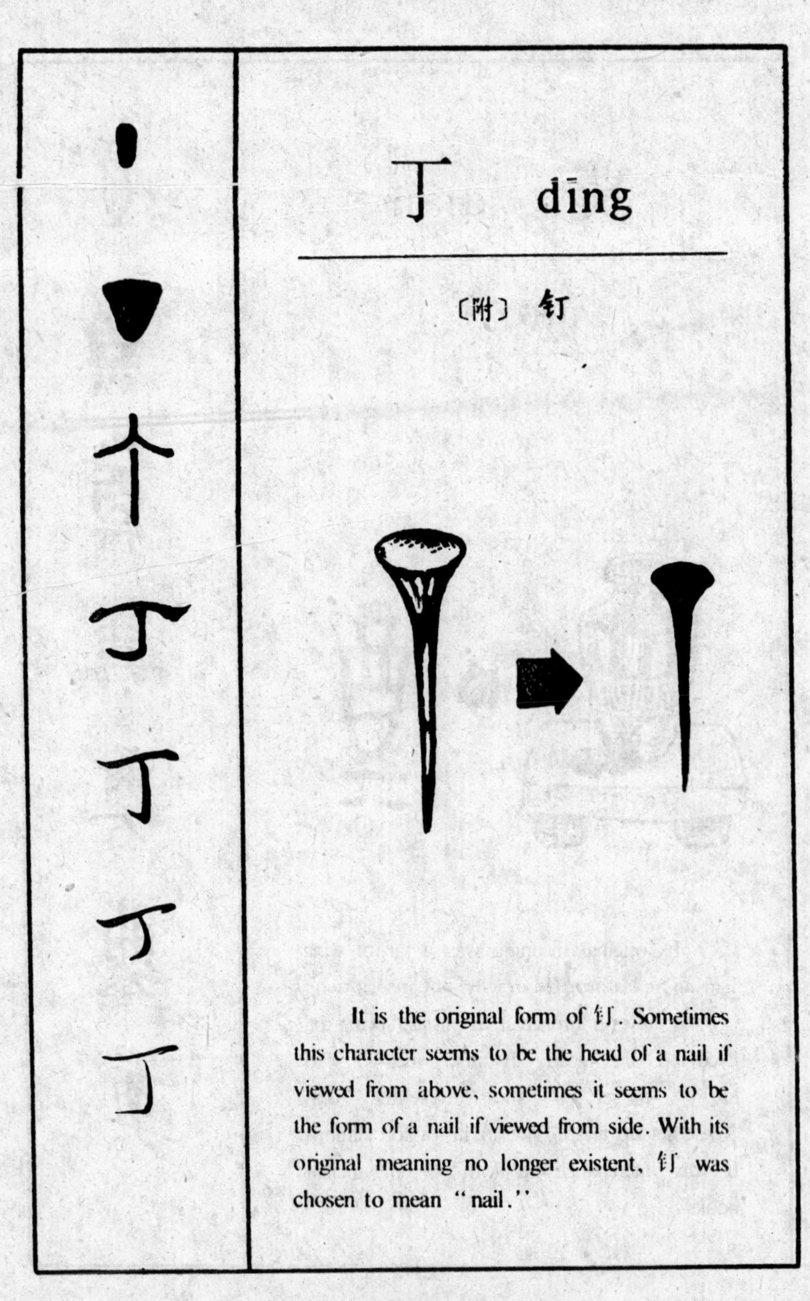

丁 dīng

〔附〕钉

It is the original form of 钉. Sometimes this character seems to be the head of a nail if viewed from above, sometimes it seems to be the form of a nail if viewed from side. With its original meaning no longer existent, 钉 was chosen to mean "nail."

鼎 dǐng

With three legs and two ears, a "tripod" was a utensil in which to cook food in ancient times. Later, it was regarded as a valuable utensil and a symbol to inherit the crown of the state. In oracle bone and bronze inscriptions, this character was a vivid hieroglyphic.

东(東)dōng

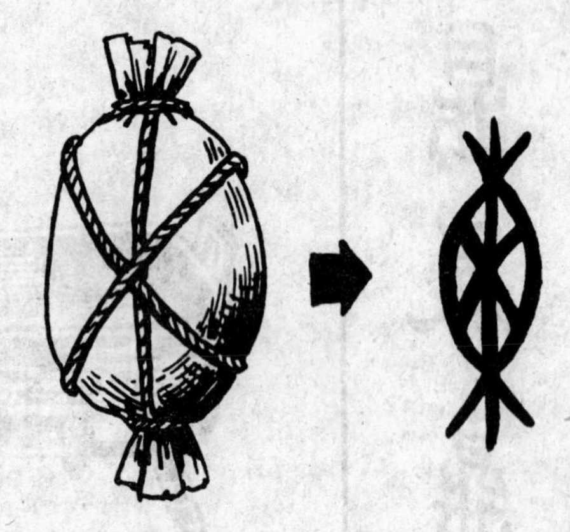

Originally, it indicated 橐, tuó, a kind of sack. Without bottom, when filled, this sack is fastened at the two ends. Later, it came to mean "east."

冬 dōng

〔附〕 终

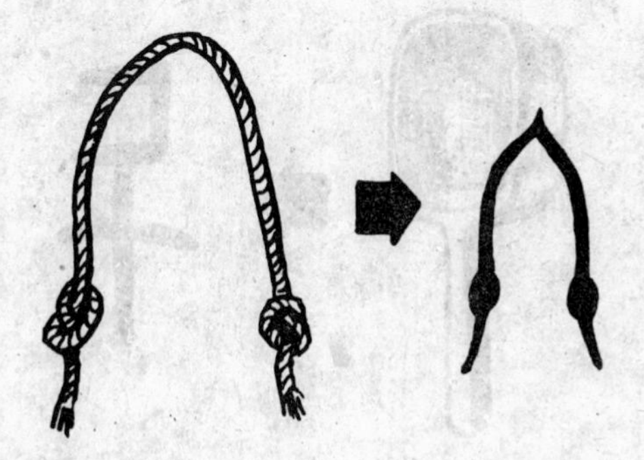

Its earliest form was like a rope knotted at the two ends, meaning "end." Later, it was loaned to mean the last season of the year, winter, and the character 终, end was then invented.

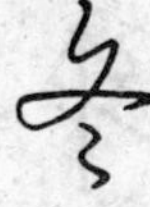

斗 dǒu

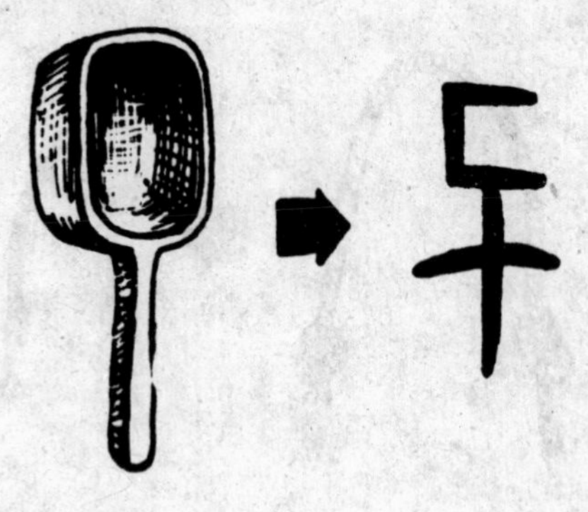

It was a wine vessel in ancient times as well as a unit of dry measure for grain equaling a decaliter. A 斗 is ten 升, ten liters. In oracle bone and bronze inscriptions, it was like a big spoon with a handle. In simplified versions 鬥 is simplified to 斗.

豆 dòu

With a high stand, in ancient times it was a container of food used in sacrificial ceremonies. The difference between 豆 and 登 is that the former is made up of wood and the latter is made up of clay. As for 豆, bean, it was called 菽, shū, in ancient times, and it was called dòu only after the Han Dynasty.

对(對)duì

A hand holding a stand upon which candles burn means "towards" and extends to mean "answer."

队(隊)duì

〔附〕坠　隧

It is the original form of 坠, to fall. In oracle bone inscriptions, it was a child falling from a mountain. In bronze inscriptions, the form of child changed to that of an animal. In ancient books, sometimes it was loaned for use in 隧, tunnel.

兑 duì

〔附〕悦 锐

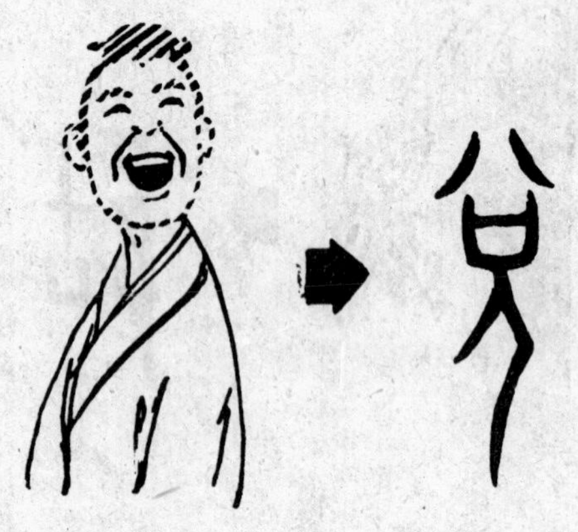

It is the original form of 悦, yuè (happy). In this character, the lower part is a man and the upper part is an open mouth whose raised lines indicate smiling or laughing. It is interchangeable with 锐.

盾　dùn

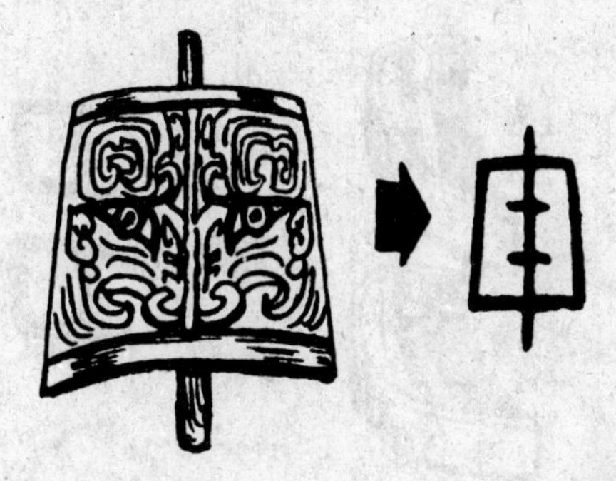

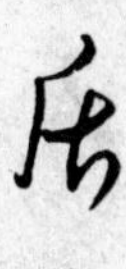

It was a shield used for protection in fighting in ancient times. In oracle bone and bronze inscriptions, it was a square-shaped or ladder-shaped shield, with a handle in the middle of it.

多　duō

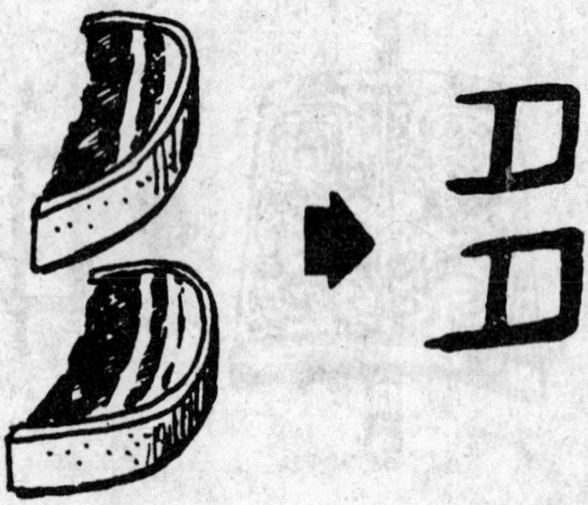

Originally, it was composed of two pieces of meat juxtaposed. The composition of this character falls into the category of using two or three same things to symbolize multitude, which can be seen in 品, products, 林, woods and 森 forest.

儿(兒)ér

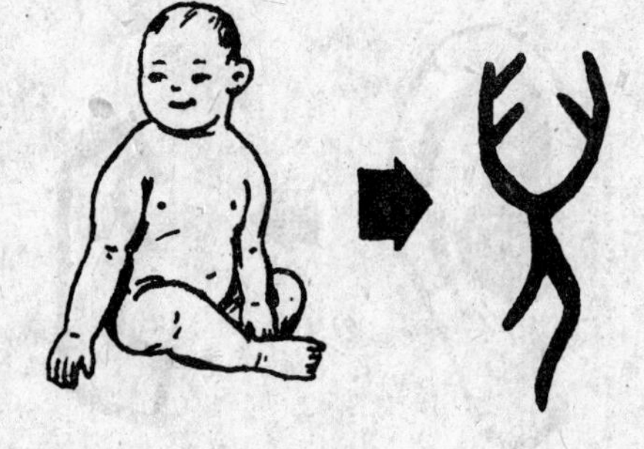

Graphically, it was like a baby with the upper part as the head, of which the fontanel is not yet closed as it is the case with newly-born babies.

耳 ěr

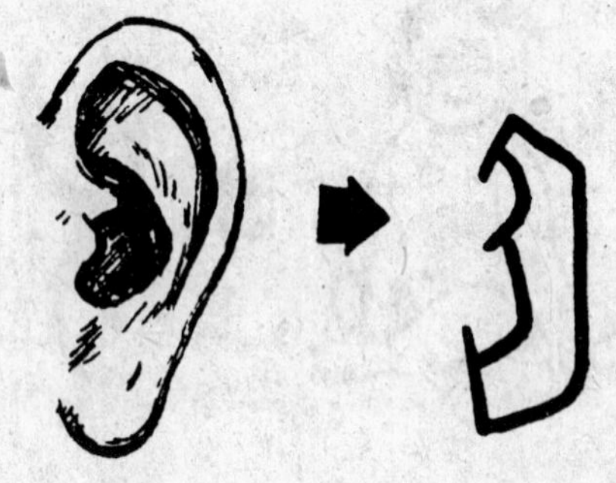

In oracle bone inscriptions, the character was a vivid picture of an ear. But since the time of small seal characters on, it was no longer pictographically symbolic.

尔(爾)ěr

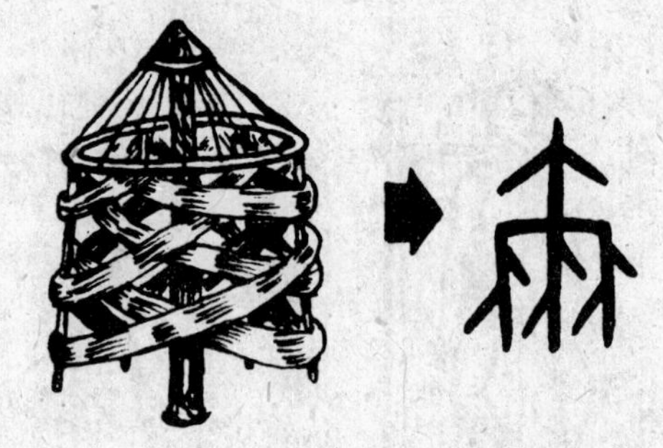

Originally, it represented a silk rack. Later, it was used as a pronoun or an auxiliary word. Its original form was 檷, nǐ. The simplified form of 爾 is 尔, ěr, which has been in use since Warring States Period (475 B.C.-221 B.C.).

伐 fá

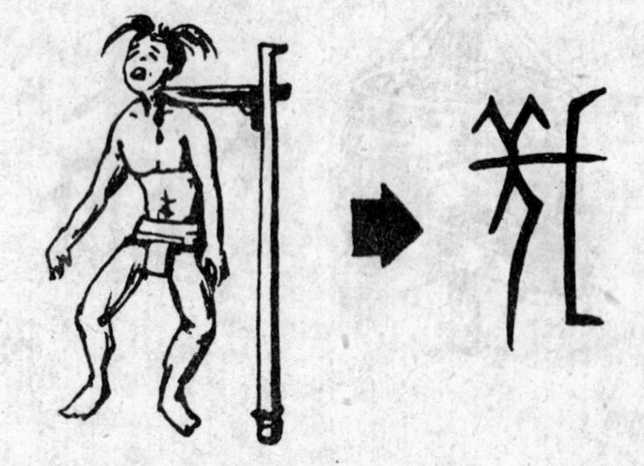

Its original meaning was "to behead" (e.g. 伐 + 羌 in oracle bone inscriptions meant "to behead ten people of the jiāng," a nationality in primitive times). Later, it extended to mean "to chop off" and "to go on a punitive expedition." Graphically, it is a 戈, a weapon in ancient times, cutting the head of a man.

凡 fán

Like a plate, it is the earliest form of 盘 (see Case 般). Its original meaning of plate disappeared later. Today, it means "generally" and "in summary." It also extends to mean "ordinary" and "common."

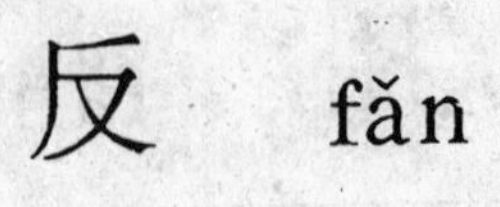

〔附〕攀 返

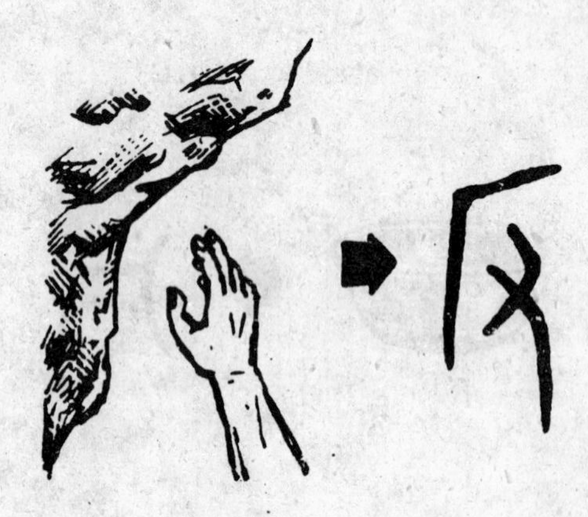

A hand climbing towards the rocks was its original form. Later, with the original meaning no longer existent, it was loaned to mean "on the contrary," "to rebel," etc. It extends to mean "to return" and in such cases it is written as 返.

方 fāng

〔附〕 枋

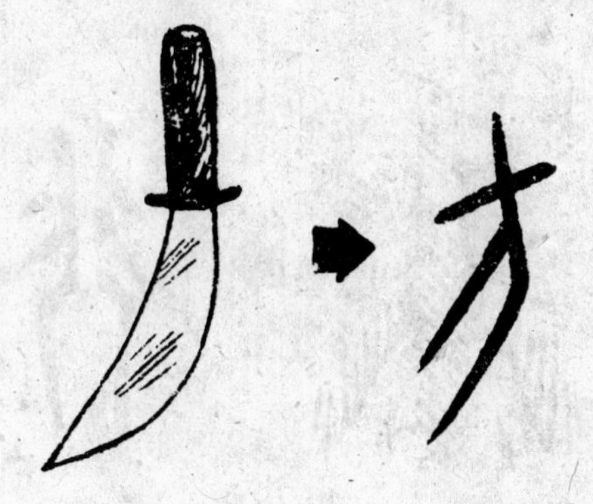

It is the original form of 枋, meaning "handle of a knife." In oracle bone and bronze inscriptions, it was knife-shaped, and on the blade of the knife a short horizontal plane was added to be the self-explanatory symbol. Later, it was used to mean "square" e.g. 方圆, square and round.

非　fēi

〔附〕飞　诽

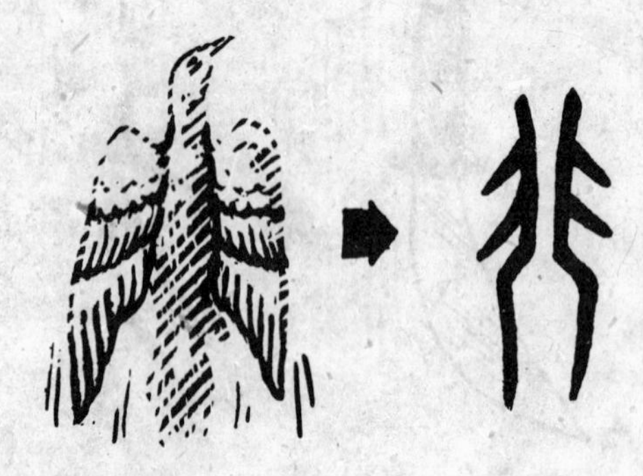

Like a bird soaring to great heights with two wings spreading, this character is the original form of 飞, to fly. Later, it was loaned to indicate 非, no. It is interchangeable with 诽.

分 fēn

A knife cutting a thing into two halves, "to split or divide" was its original meaning, which is still in use today.

丰(丯,豐)fēng

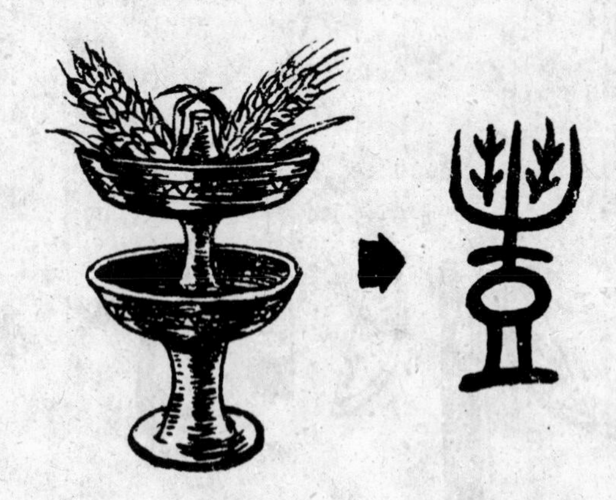

Originally, it indicated two characters: 豊, a container of sacrificial offerings in ancient times, extending to mean "abundant," and 丯, like a tree growing with lush leaves, initially meaning "luxuriant." The two characters are interchangeable and are combined and simplified to 丰.

凤(鳳)fèng

〔附〕 风

In oracle bone and bronze inscriptions, it was like a phoenix, and the phoenix feathers are very obviously carved. A 凡 is added on the upper right corner to indicate its sound. It is also loaned for use in the character 风, wind.

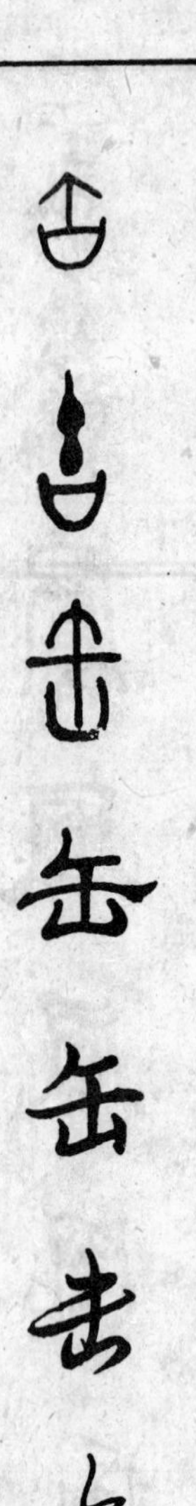

缶 fǒu

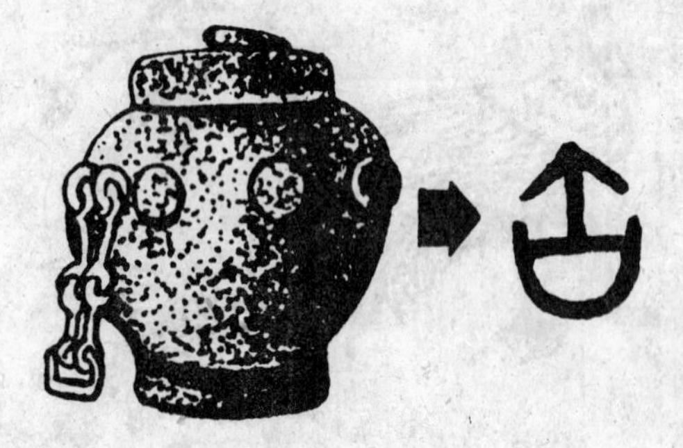

Graphically, this character is a jar with the upper part as its lid and the lower part as the body. Characters with 缶 as their radical usually have something to do with earthenware, e.g. 缸, vat, 罐, jar, and 陶, pottery.

夫 fū

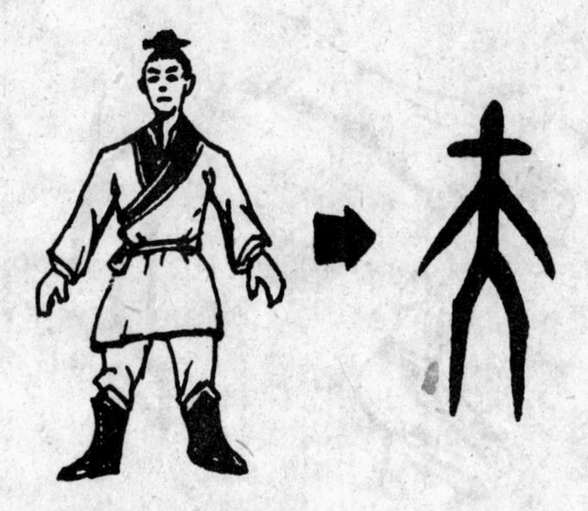

This is a standing person, with a short horizontal plane added on his head to indicate his hair is bound with a hairpin and symbolizes that he is an adult. Its original meaning was "adult male," and its extended meaning is "married man."

服 fú

Graphically, a huge hand captures a man and makes him surrender. This is its original meaning, which still can be found in 降服, yield, and 使服从, make one obey. Later, the phonetic symbol 凡 was added. In bronze inscriptions, 凡 changed to 舟, boat, while in lì shù (official script) it changed to 月, moon.

弗　fú

〔附〕拂　弼

It is the original form of 拂, which is pronounced as bì when it means "to correct." Graphically, it looks like ropes binding two wood sticks and making them straight. Later, it was used as a form of negation.

孚　fú

〔附〕俘　孵　稃

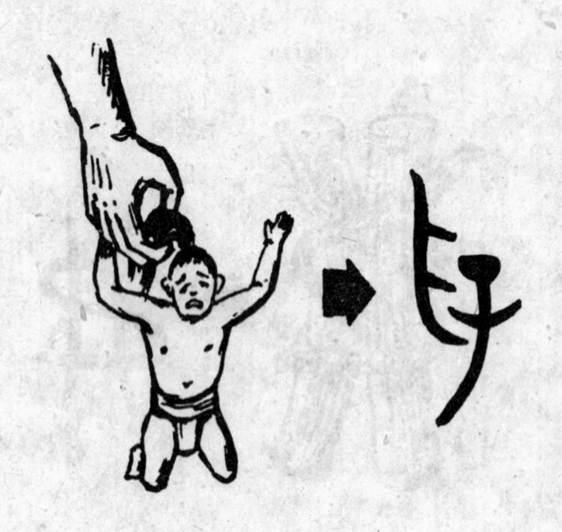

It is the original form of 俘, to capture. Graphically, it is a huge hand (爪, zhǎo, claw, hand) capturing a small person (子, zǐ, son). Its original meaning was "what the soldier captures." In ancient books it was interchangeable with 孵 and 稃.

福　fú

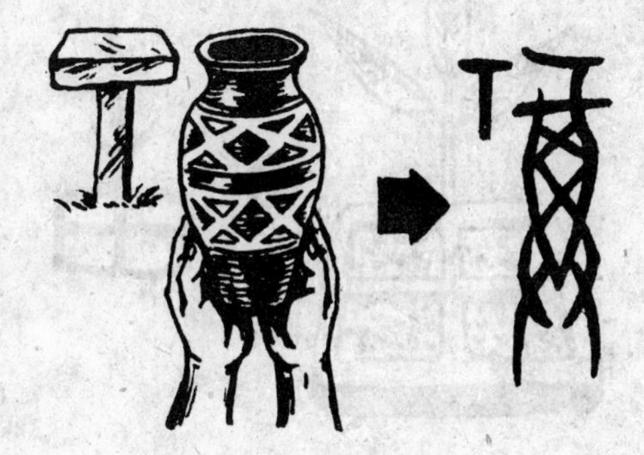

In oracle bone inscriptions, it was two hands raising a big wine vessel to pray to the gods in front of the altar. Later, the two hands were omitted, and it gradually evolved into its present form.

甫 fǔ

〔附〕 圃

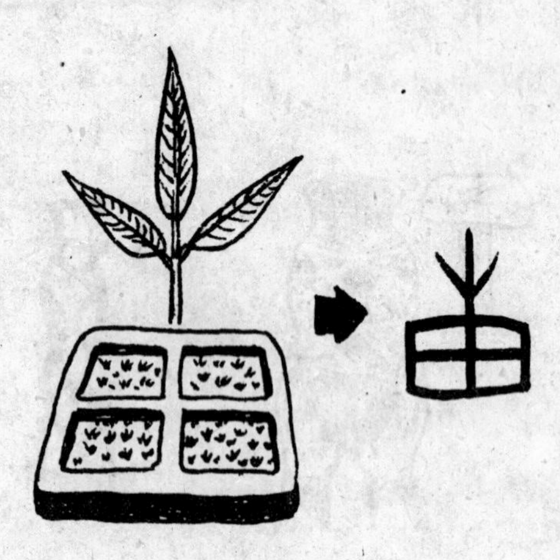

A seedling growing in a 田, field, is its form in oracle bone inscriptions, and it is the original form of 圃, garden. Since bronze inscriptions, it evolved into two characters: 圃, pǔ, with 囗 added, and 甫, fǔ, just (only), with 用 changed from 田.

父 fù

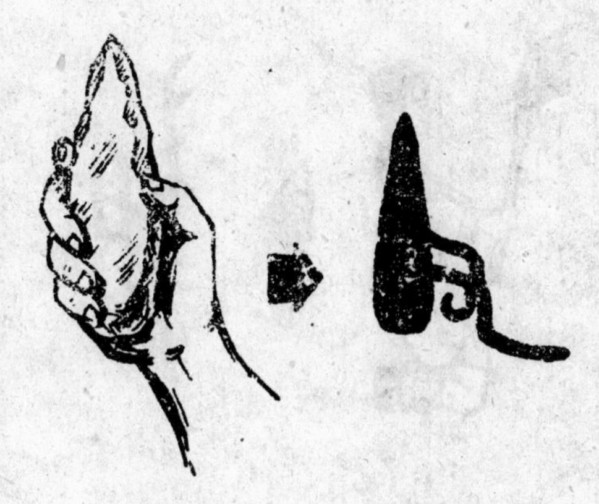

Originally, it was a hand holding a stone ax, symbolizing a laboring man, e.g. 田父 means "farmer." Later, it began to indicate "father." It is also the general address for elder members of the family, e.g. 祖父, grandfather, 伯父, and 叔父, uncles.

妇(婦)fù

With a broom in her hands, a woman is doing cleaning, which is part of the everyday work for a housewife. Therefore, it indicates "a married woman." In oracle bone inscriptions, 帚, broom, sometimes is interchangeable with 妇, woman.

复(復,複)fù

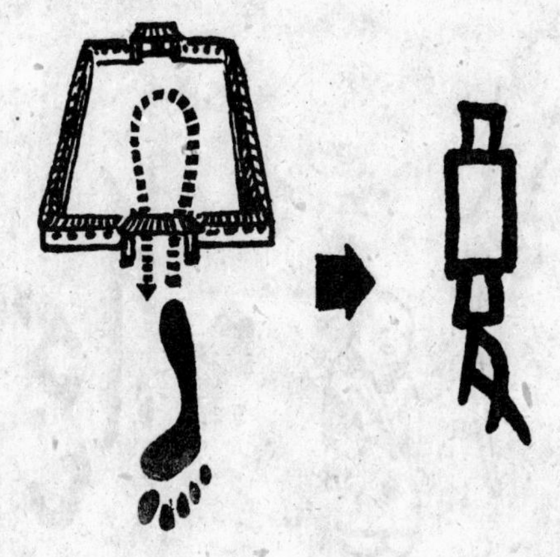

Its original meaning was "to take the old way." In oracle bone inscriptions, the upper part of this character was a village and the lower part was a foot symbolizing coming to this place once again. Later, it was written as 復. Then it was simplified to its original form 复, and it is also the simplified version of 複.

改 gǎi

Graphically, a child is kneeling down, and a hand beside him is holding a stick and beating him. This child is taught to correct mistakes. Hence, its original meaning was "to change" and "to correct."

干 gān

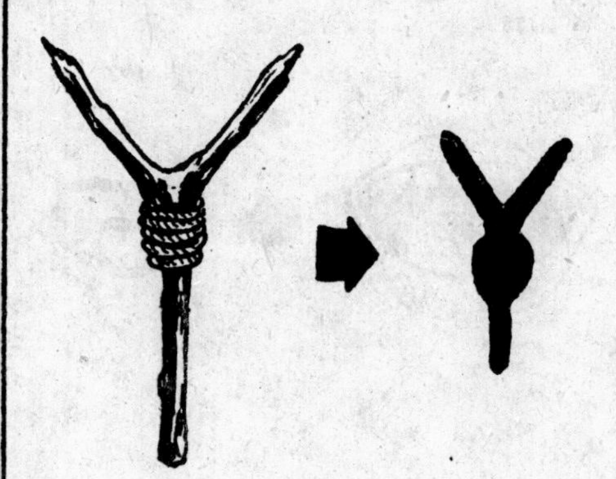

It originally indicated a primeval weapon made up of a fork of tree branch, which can spear a wild animal or an enemy. In ancient books, it also indicated a shield, e.g. the idiom 大动干戈, massive use of weapons. It is also the simplified version of 幹 and 乾.

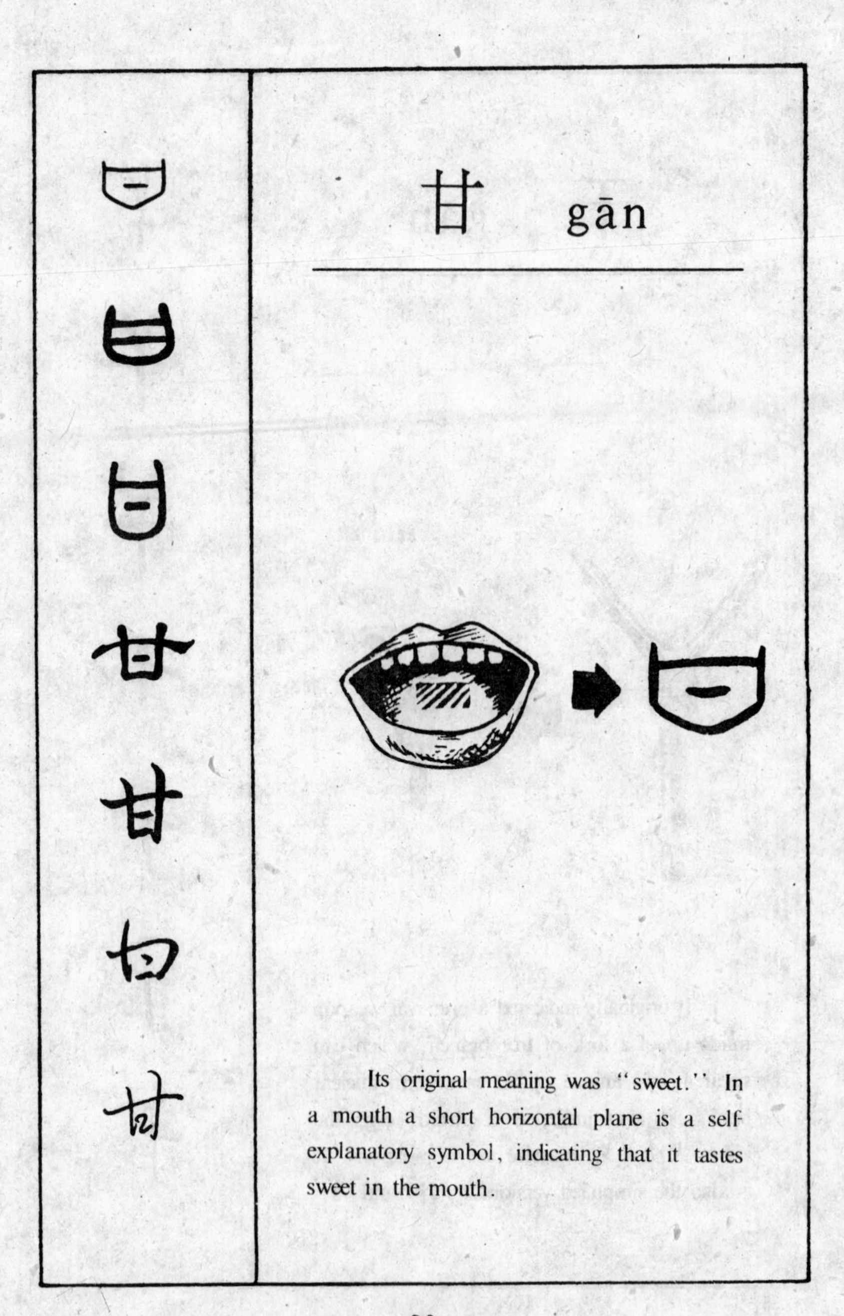

甘 gān

Its original meaning was "sweet." In a mouth a short horizontal plane is a self-explanatory symbol, indicating that it tastes sweet in the mouth.

高 gāo

Graphically, it is a high building with the upper part as the pointed roof, the middle part as a wall and tower and the lower part as a gate in the foundation. Originally, the high building is used to indicate "high" or "tall."

羔　gāo

The upper part of this character is a "sheep" and the lower part is "fire." It indicates a sheep being roasted. The most delicious mutton is that of a lamb, hence it means "lamb."

告 gào

〔附〕 牿

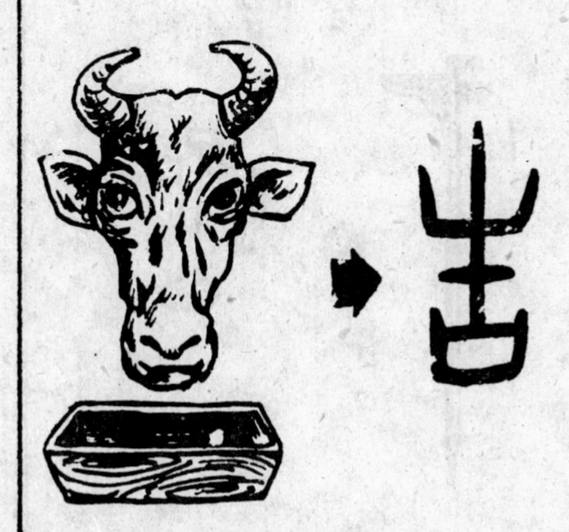

It is the original form of 牿, gù, a stable. Composed of an ox head with a trough under it, it signifies a stable or a place where livestock are fed.

戈 gē

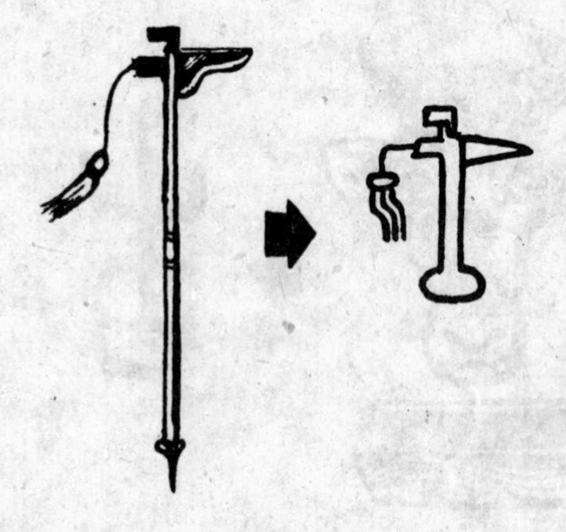

It is a dagger-ax, an ancient weapon. With a long shaft and a dagger fixed on one end, it was used to hit and hook especially in Shang Dynasty (1600-1100 B.C.) and Warring States Period (475-221 B.C.). Today, the idiom 大动干戈, massive use of weapons, is still used.

 gè

〔附〕格

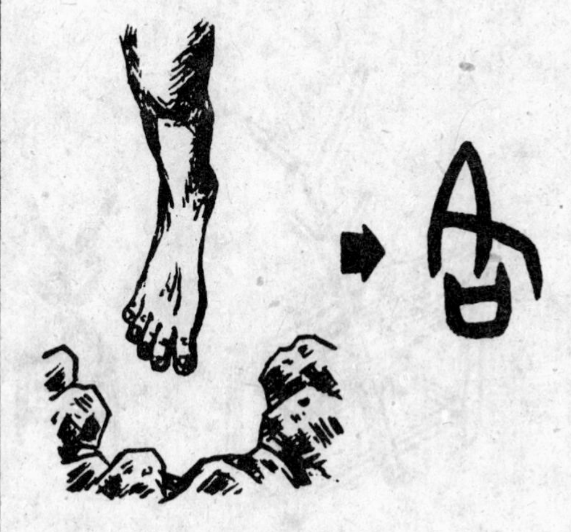

A foot is approaching the cave's door (looks like a 口, mouth). Hence, its original meaning was "to approach" and "to come." Later, it was written as 格 with such a meaning.

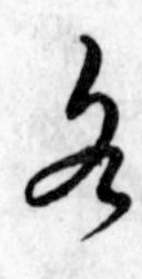

庚 gēng

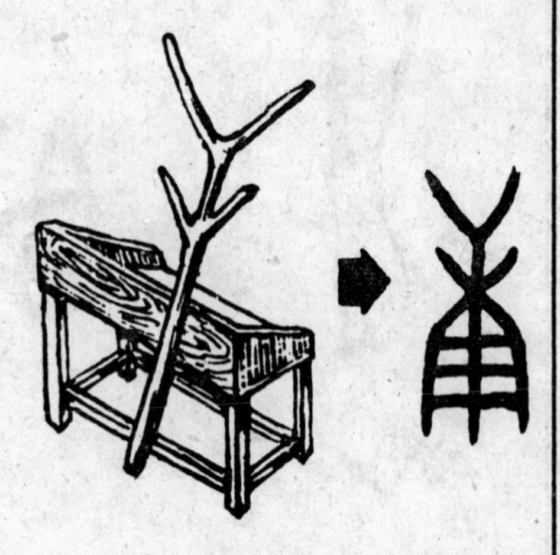

Its original meaning was "a thresher." The form of this character is a rack with a forked thresher in the middle of it. Reference can be found in Case 康. Later, it was used to be the seventh of the Ten Heavenly Stems.

更 gēng

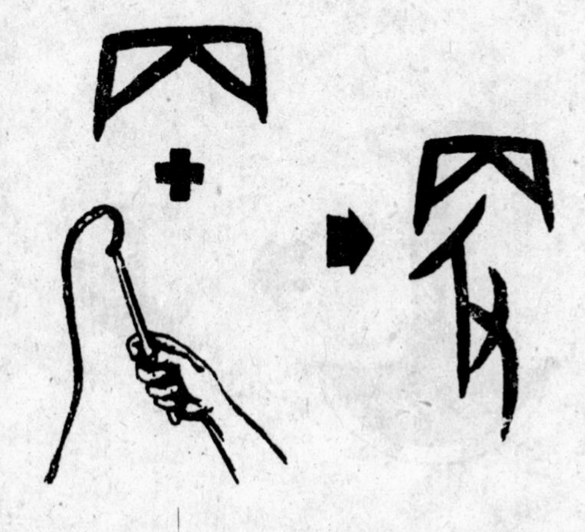

The lower part of this character is a hand with a whip, indicating its meaning; the upper part is 丙, bǐng, indicating its sound. Hence, its meaning is "to force a person to change with a whip." It also means "to replace," "to continue," etc.

工 gōng

In early bronze inscriptions, it looked like a cutting tool with a curved blade. Its original meaning was "tool." It extends to mean "worker," and even "clever" and "careful."

弓 gōng

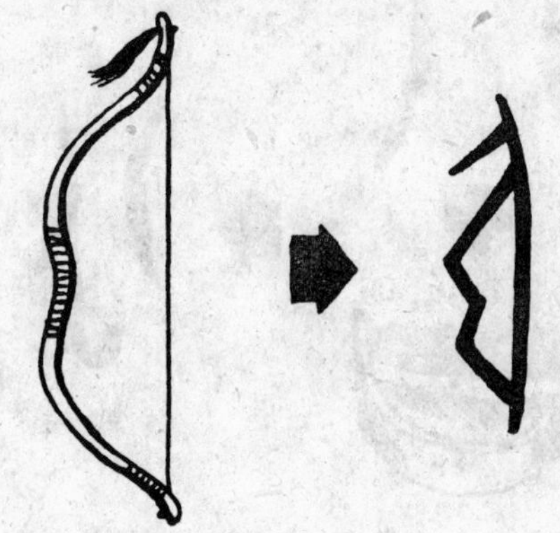

In oracle bone inscriptions, it was the likeness of a bow. In bronze inscriptions, the string was omitted, and it gradually evolved into its present form, in which the shape of bow cannot be easily traced.

公 gōng

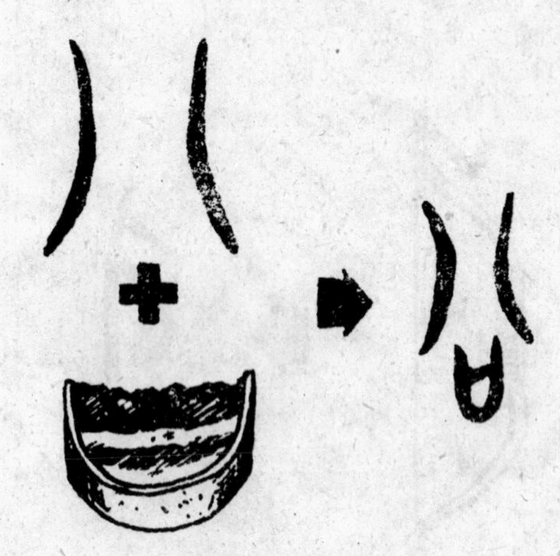

The upper part of this character 八 means "to divide" (see Case 八). The lower part 口, mouth, signifies the goods to be shared out (see Case 品). Hence, its meanings are "public" and "fair."

宫 gōng

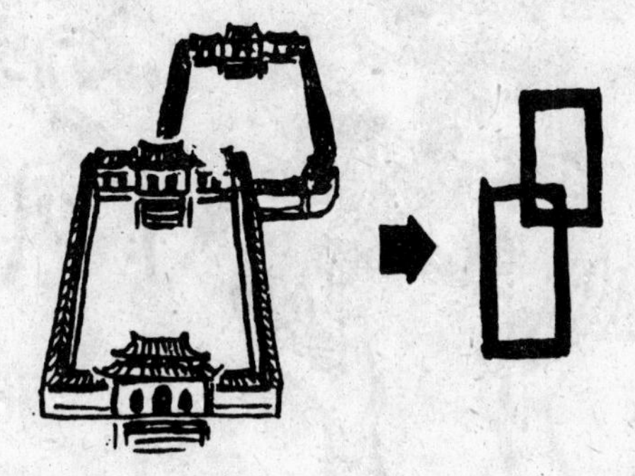

In early oracle bone inscriptions, this character was composed of two squares connected, signifying the buildings of the palace. Later, "宀", the symbol of house, was added.

龚(龔)gōng

〔附〕 恭

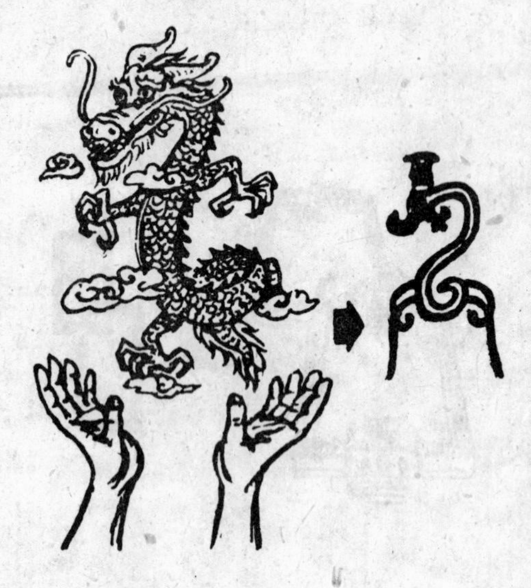

It is the original form of 恭 (gōng), respectful. Graphically, two hands raising towards a dragon, signifying "reverent" and "respectful." In small seal characters, 恭 came into use.

共 gòng

〔附〕 供

In oracle bone inscriptions, this character was graphically two hands raising a square-shaped item (in bronze inscriptions, two pillar-shaped items), signifying "to devote" and "common." In ancient times, it was interchangeable with 供.

苟　gǒu

〔附〕敬

It is the original character of 儆 and 警. Graphically, it is a dog half sitting on the ground with two ears on alert. Hence, its original meaning was "vigilance." In bronze inscriptions, it was loaned for use in 敬, meaning "solemn respect."

遘 gòu

〔附〕逅 覯 构

Its original form was 冓, and original meaning was "to meet." Graphically, it is two fish meeting head to head. Later, it evolved into 遘、逅 or 覯. It is interchangeable with 構（构）.

谷 gǔ

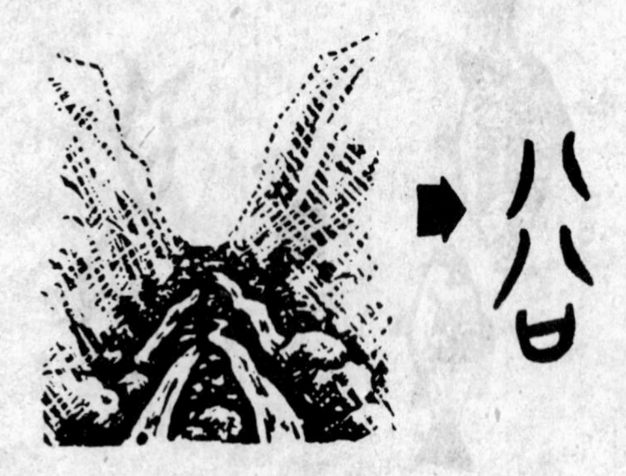

The inclined lines at the top of this character signify flowing water. The 凵 at the bottom signifies a mountain pass. Its original meaning was "the long and narrow strip of land between mountains or the place where water is flowing." Though 谷 and 穀 are different characters, now they are combined and represented by the former.

鼓 gǔ

As a pictograph, it is vividly delineated: a hand holding a drumstick and beating a drum, of which in the middle is the round drum face, at the top is decoration and at the bottom is the stand.

盥 guàn

A hand is washing in a basin, and drops of water are around the hand. Hence, its original meaning was "to wash hands." Now, 盥洗室 is still used for bathroom or lavatory.

光 guāng

Graphically, a man kneeling down is shone by the light of fire above his head. Hence, its meaning is "bright." It also means "to enlighten."

龟(龜)guī

As a typical pictograph, this character is the graphic representation of a tortoise, except that some forms of its variants are front viewed and some are side viewed.

鬼 guǐ

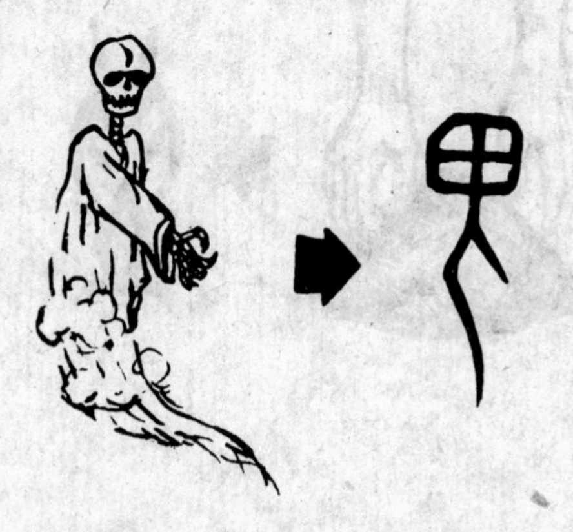

Primitive people believed that after death a man will become a frightening ghost. So the lower part of this character is a shape of man while the upper part is his monstrous head.

贵(貴)guì

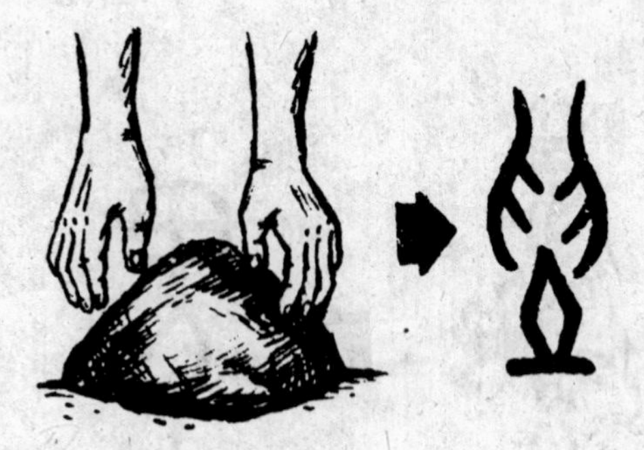

Able to produce everything, land was perceived as the most valuable possession. So in oracle bone inscriptions, it was two hands raising the earth. In its seal form, the radical 贝, cowrie, was added, which in ancient times was currency, symbolizing wealth.

国(國)guó

〔附〕 或 域

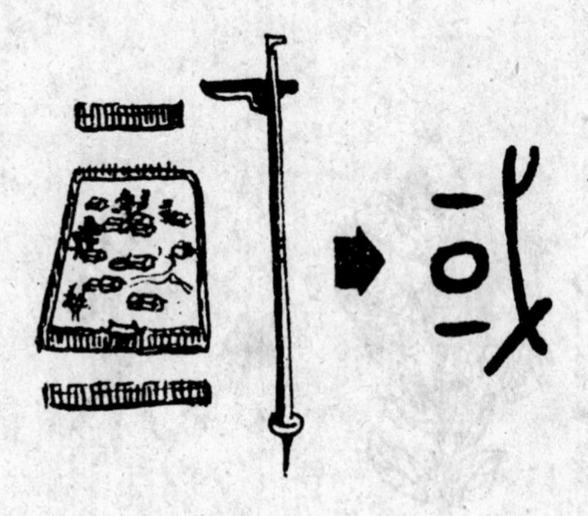

Its original form was 或. Graphically, it is 戈, a weapon, defending 口, a town. Later, a box frame was added symbolizing boundary. Hence, 国, signifies "country," "state" and "nation." In bronze inscriptions, 或 was adopted to be 域.

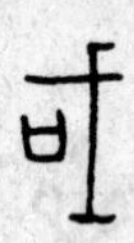
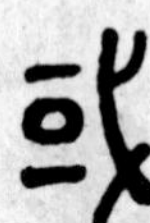

果 guǒ

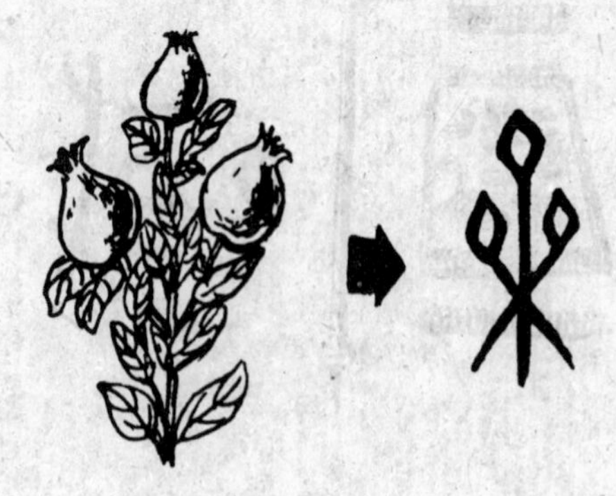

Its form is a tree bearing fruit. In oracle bone inscriptions, there is much fruit, in bronze inscriptions, the fruit is bigger, while in small seal characters the fruit at the upper part is altered to 田 making its original meaning difficult to trace.

亥 hài

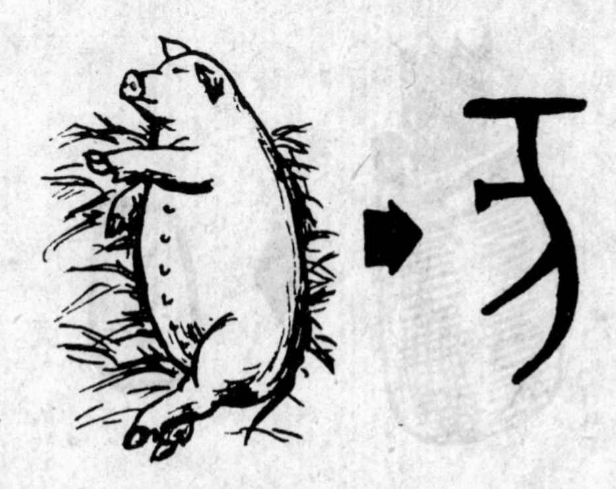

Its original meaning was 猪, zhīu, pig. Its form is a pig with the upper short line symbolizing the head and the lower part symbolizing the spinal column, limbs and tail. Later, the original meaning disappeared, but 亥 continues to serve as one of the twelve animals representing the Twelve Earthly Branches, symbolizing the year of the pig.

函 hán

Its original meaning was "arrow bag." In oracle bone and bronze inscriptions, it was like a box-shaped or oval-shaped bag with a small hoop added on one side to be hung on the waist belt. Later, it extended to mean "envelope," "letter," etc.

好 hǎo, hào

A woman is holding a newly-born baby in her arms, which naturally symbolizes goodness and happiness. Usually it is used as an adjective, and pronounced hǎo (third tone); if used as a verb, pronounced hào (fourth tone), it means "to like."

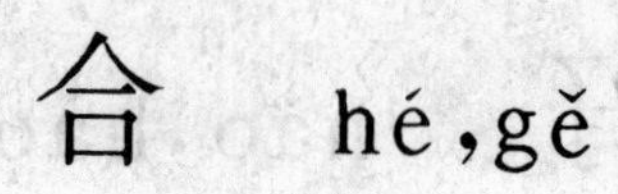

合 hé, gě

In ancient books, its upper part was a cone-shaped lid and its lower part was a round container. Hence, its original meaning was 闭合, "to close" and "to shut." It extends to mean "harmony" and "get together." It is also used to be a unit of measurement, a shēng, one liter, is ten 合, gě, deciliters.

何 hé

〔附〕 荷

It is the original form of 荷. Graphically, a man is walking forward with a hoe on his shoulder and his hands are holding the shaft of the hoe. This is the original meaning of this character — 荷 (hè), "to carry."

禾 hé

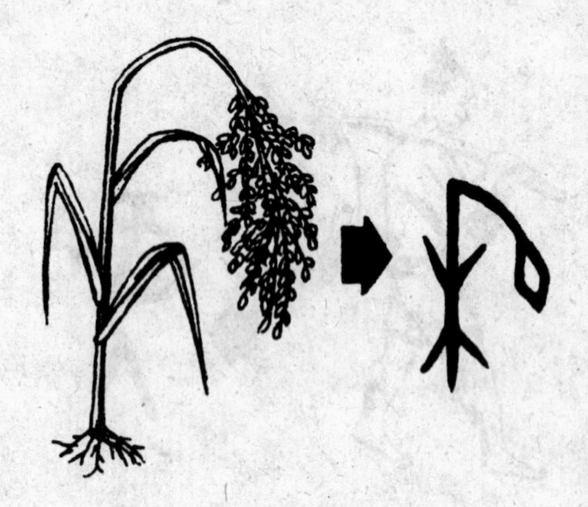

It is the graphic representation of ripe rice, the heavy paddy bending the stalk. Hence, its original meaning was "cereal." Later, it extended to mean other crops.

和 hé

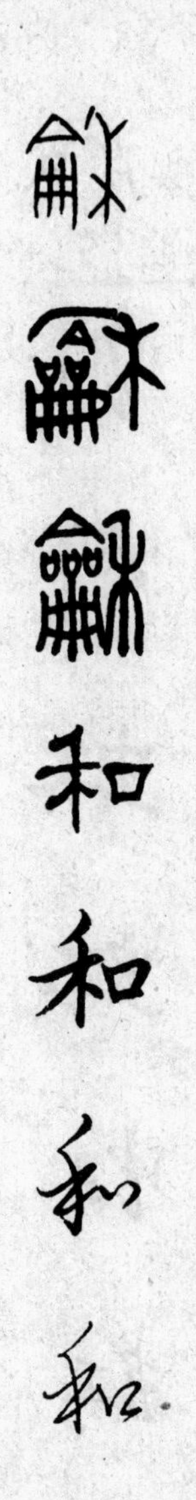

Initially, it was 龢, an ancient musical instrument. It was composed of 龠 (yuè, the name for an ancient musical instrument, indicating the meaning) and 禾 (indicating sound). Later it evolved into 和.

虹 hóng

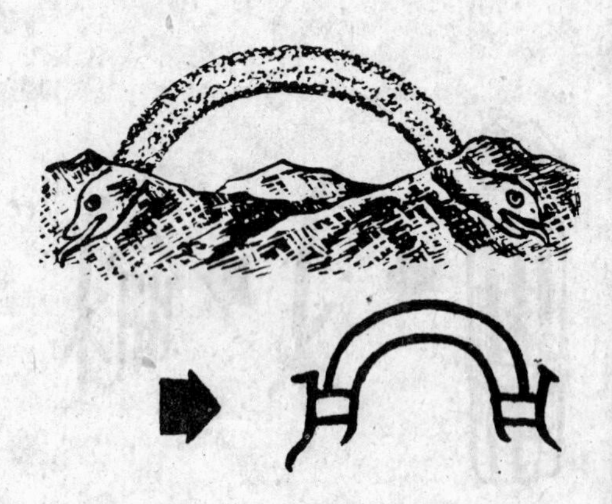

In oracle bone inscriptions, it was the form of a rainbow, and two snake heads were added because primitive people believed a rainbow is alive like a snake. Since the stone inscriptions, it has evolved into a pictophonetic character with the left figurative radical 虫, chōng, worm and the right phonetic radical 工, gōng.

侯 hóu

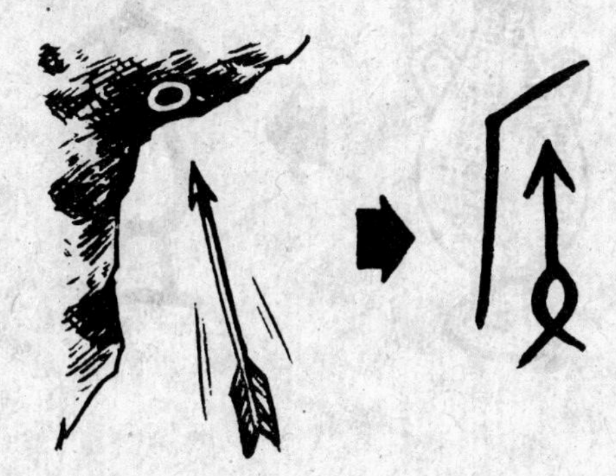

Its original meaning was an arrow target. Its original form was 矦, which is made up of 矢, shǐ, arrow, and 厂, cliffs, symbolizing the arrow head being shot at the target. In small seal characters, 人, man, was added.

壶(壺)hú

〔附〕 瓠

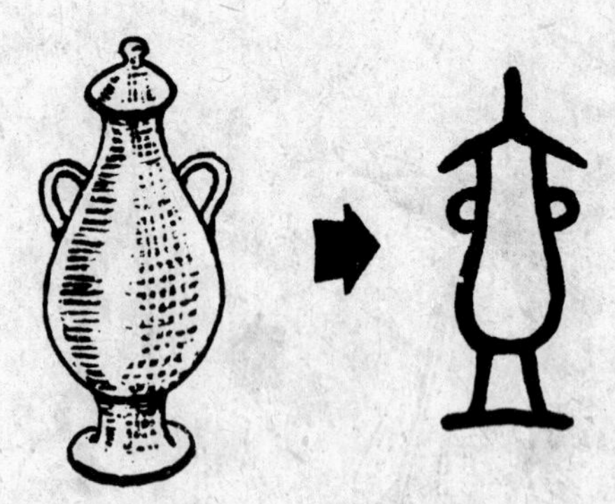

It is the vivid delineation of a flagon: the upper part is the lid, the middle part is the body and the lower part is the bottom. Two ears are added in some forms of this character. It is interchangeable with 瓠, hù, a vegetable.

虎　hǔ

It is graphically indicated by a leaping wild animal with an open mouth and sharp teeth and claws. Some forms of this character in oracle bone inscriptions have tiger stripes added, and the feature of the tiger is emphasized.

户 hù

In oracle bone inscriptions, it was the form of a door, which is its original meaning. After small seal characters and official script, it became more and more dissimilar. It extends to mean 住户, resident family.

画(畫)huà

〔附〕 划

In oracle bone inscriptions, its form was a hand holding a brush and drawing figures and lines. In bronze inscriptions, the lower part altered to 田, symbolizing marking the field boundary. Later, 劃(划, scratch) was derived from it.

化 huà

Graphically, two persons, one is standing on his feet, and the other one on his head just like acrobats or magicians do, signifying "to change." It extends to mean 造化, the nature that produces everything, 死亡, death, 融解, to dissolve, etc.

黄 huáng

〔附〕 璜

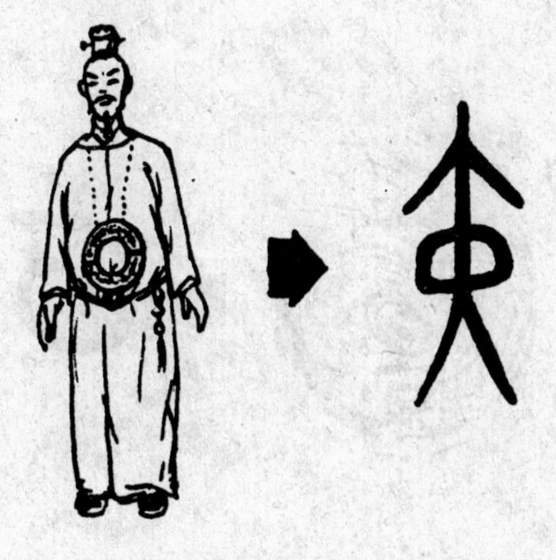

It is the original form of 璜: a man standing with a jade hanging on his bosom (originally it was a semicircled jade). Later, it was loaned to signify the color yellow. Since its original meaning fell into oblivion, a new word 璜 was coined to indicate its original meaning.

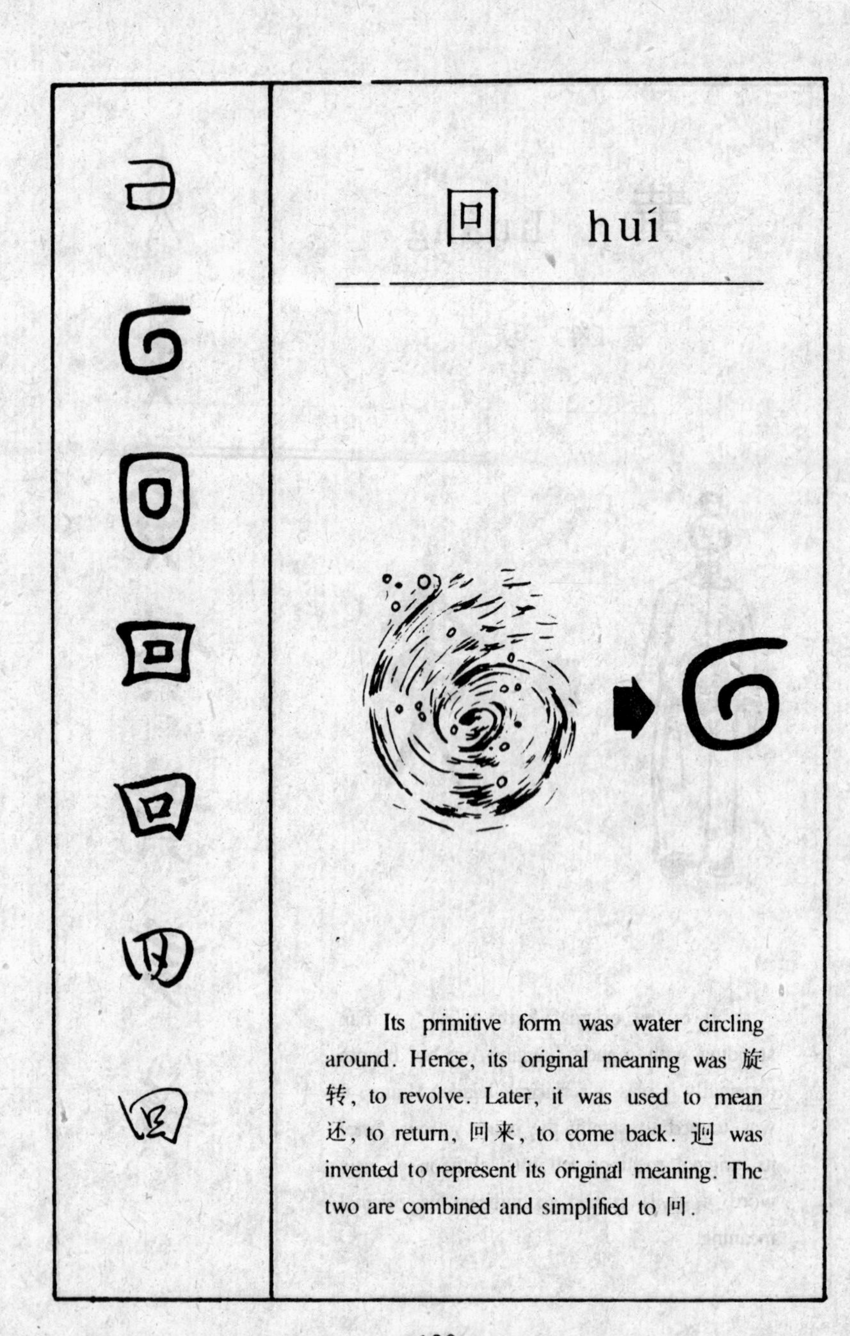

回 huí

Its primitive form was water circling around. Hence, its original meaning was 旋转, to revolve. Later, it was used to mean 还, to return, 回来, to come back. 迴 was invented to represent its original meaning. The two are combined and simplified to 回.

会(會)huì

〔附〕 脍

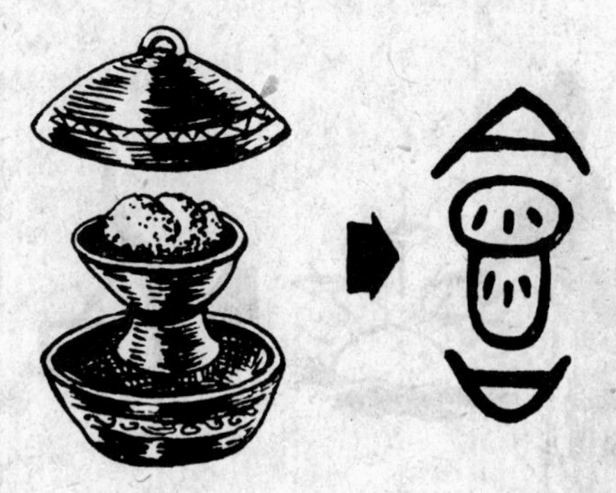

It is the original form of 脍 (kuài, minced meat or fish). The upper part is a cover, the lower part is a food container, and the middle part is the food itself. It also indicated the cover sometimes in ancient books.

昏 hūn

〔附〕 婚

In oracle bone inscriptions, its form was a sun setting to the height of one's arms, signifying the dusk time. This is its original meaning. It extends to mean 昏暗, dim, 胡涂, confused, etc. It is also the original form of 婚.

火 huǒ

〔附〕 伙

In oracle bone inscriptions, it was the delineation of a fire. It was not pictographic in bronze inscriptions. It is also an army unit, ten soldiers formed a 火. Sometimes it is written as 伙.

霍 huò

When heavy rain suddenly comes pouring down, three birds (indicating the multitude of birds) fly upward from the ground with quick sounds. Its original meaning is bird cry. Later, the three birds evolved into two birds, and eventually to only one.

获(獲,穫)huò

〔附〕 隻(只)

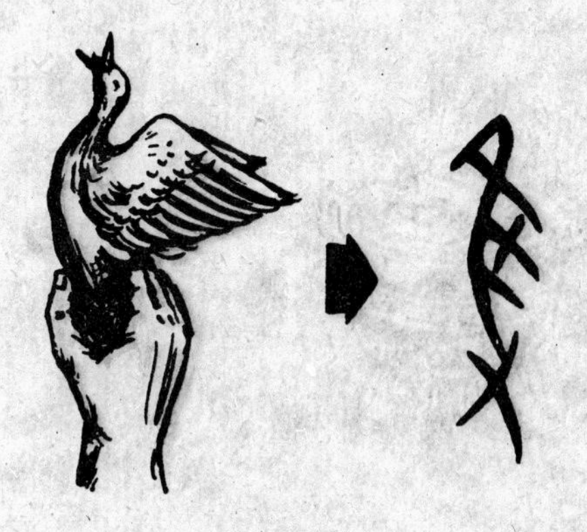

Its original form was 隻 . Graphically, it is a hand grasping a bird. Hence, its original meaning was "to capture." In small seal characters, the radicai 犬 was added to signify "to capture animals as well as birds." Later, the radical 禾 was added to indicate the harvest. In simplified versions, the two words are combined and simplified to 获.

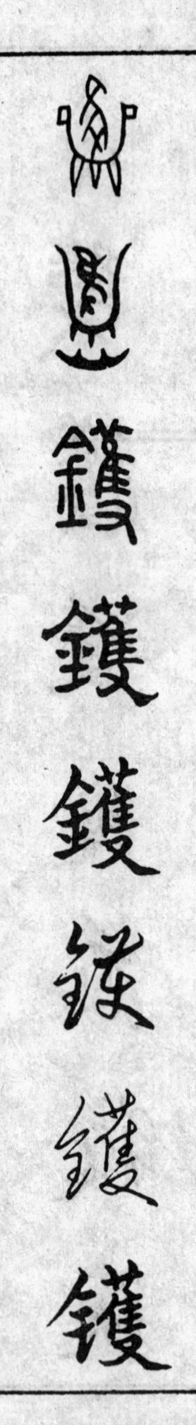

镬(鑊)huò

In oracle bone inscriptions, its form was a bird (indicating poultry) boiled in a 鬲 (lì, an ancient cooker, see Case 鬲) sometimes with the symbol for water. Since bronze inscriptions, the radical 金 has been added. Now in some dialects, 锅, pot, is still called 镬.

鸡（鷄）jī

In the early oracle bone and bronze inscriptions, 鸡 was a pictographic character. It was the form of a rooster. Later, it evolved into a pictophonetic character with the graphic symbol 隹 or 鸟 and the phonetic symbol 奚.

及 jí

Graphically, its lower part is a hand, catching the man in the upper part. Hence, its original meaning was 追上, 追赶, to catch up with. It still exists in combinations such as 及时, 及早, 来得及 and others.

集 jí

A bird perching on a tree was the original meaning of 集. Later, it extended to mean 聚集, to get together, and 集合, to assemble.

疾 jí

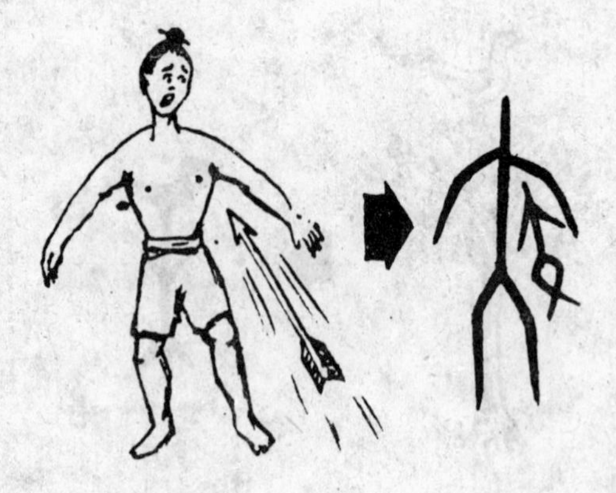

A sharp arrow is being shot into the chest of a man and naturally he is wounded or killed. Hence, its original meaning is 伤, wound, and 病, illness. Its extended meanings are 厌恶, to dislike, and 憎恨, to hate. In addition, the arrow is shot very fast, hence another meaning 迅速, fast.

吉　jí

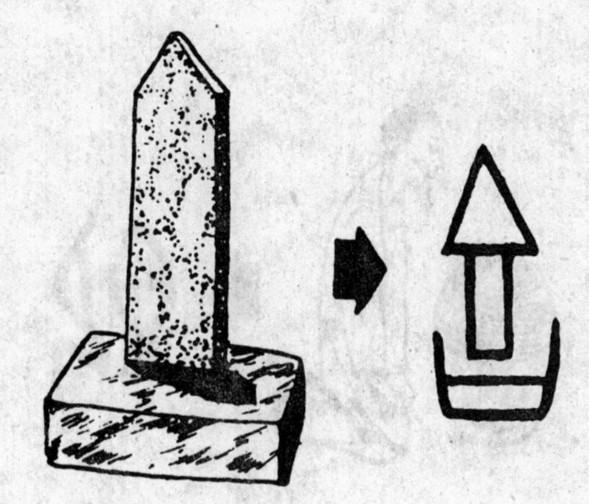

On a ceremonial occasion, 圭, an elongated pointed tablet of jade is stood on a sacred shrine signifying auspiciousness. Later, 圭 evolved into 士, from which it is then hard to trace its original meaning.

即 jí

As a typical ideograph, it has the left part as a food container and the right part as a man kneeling beside the food. Hence, its original meaning was 就食, to take the food. Its extended meaning is 接近 and 靠近 signifying "to approach."

既 jì

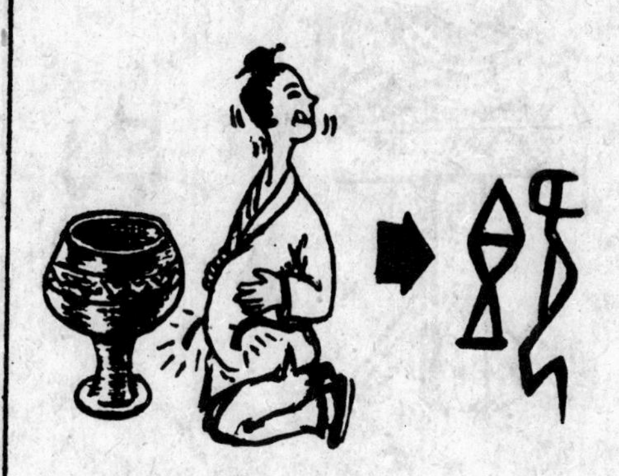

Contrary to 即, as the man kneels down beside the food container he turns his head back, signifying he is full. Its extended meaning is 完，尽，已经, etc. (see Case 即).

祭 jì

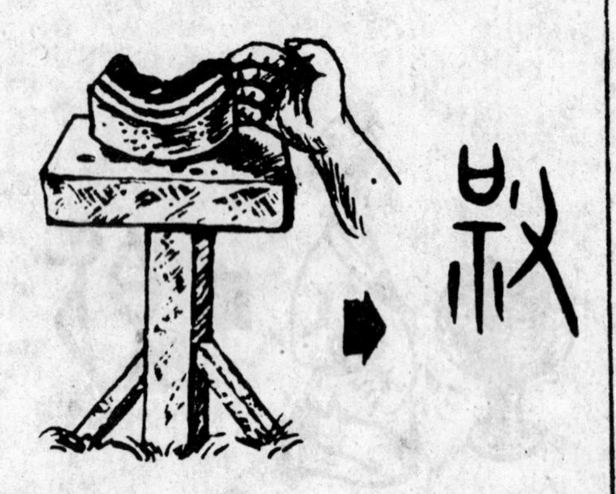

Its original meaning was "to kill domesticated animals as a sacrifice to gods and spirits." Its form is a hand putting a piece of meat on the altar. In oracle bone inscriptions, some versions of this character did not have 示, (symbolizing the meat held in the hand dripping with blood), but they share the same meaning.

家 jiā

In ancient times, when kings and aristocrats died, a temple was set up in which sacrifices were offered to them. When the common person died, it was impossible for him to have temple set up. Thus, under the roof of his family's house, a pig was set out to be offered to him, hence the form of 家. Later, it extended to mean "residence." among other meanings.

夹(夾)jiā

Its original meaning was 辅佐, to assist. Graphically, it is two small persons supporting a big man with two hands. Later, with the original meaning fading out, it extended to mean "clamp at the two flanks."

甲 jiǎ

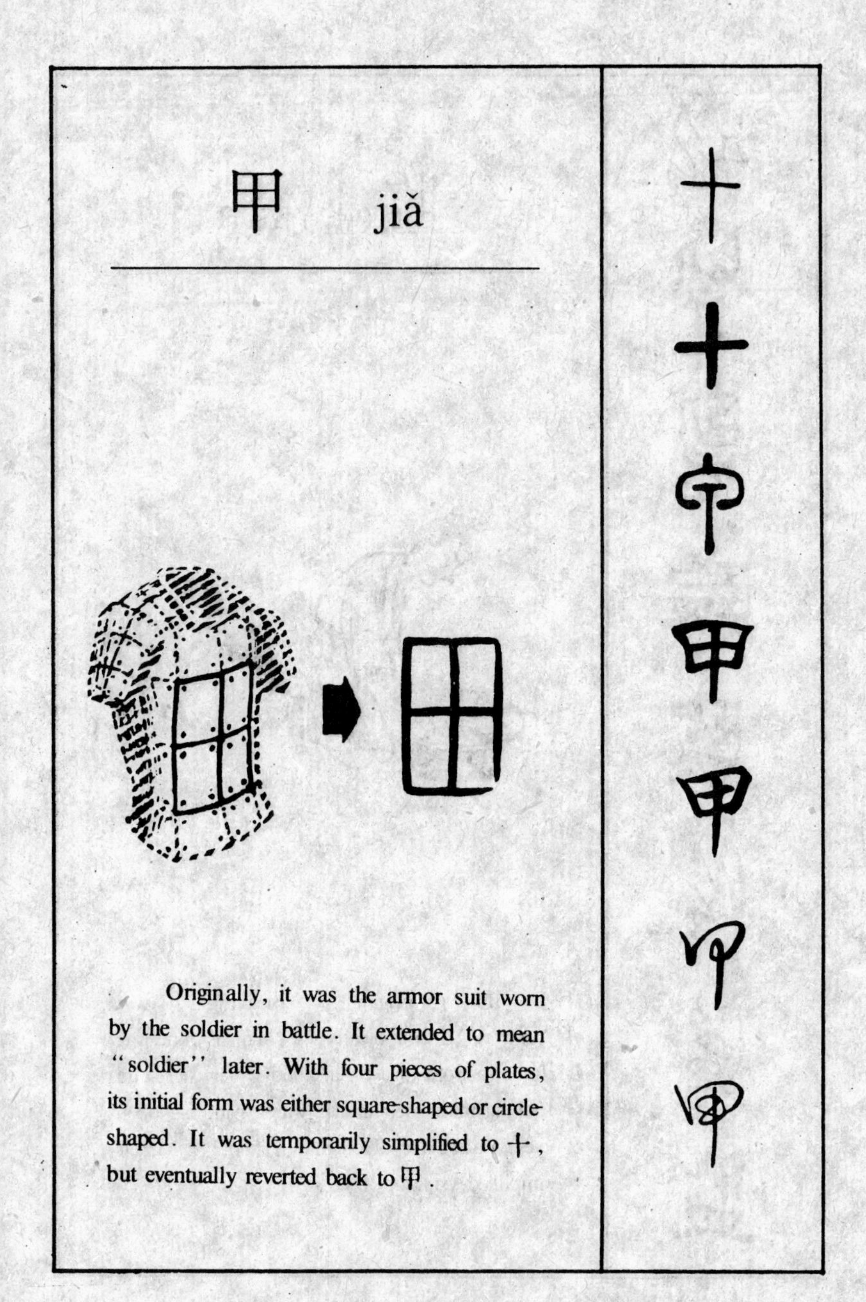

Originally, it was the armor suit worn by the soldier in battle. It extended to mean "soldier" later. With four pieces of plates, its initial form was either square-shaped or circle-shaped. It was temporarily simplified to 十, but eventually reverted back to 甲.

监(監)jiàn

〔附〕 鉴

Its original meaning was "mirror." Graphically, a man is kneeling down in front of a basin filled with water, and looking at himself in the water with his open eyes. Later, it evolved into 鑑 or 鑒 (their simplified version, 鉴).

见(見)jiàn

〔附〕 现

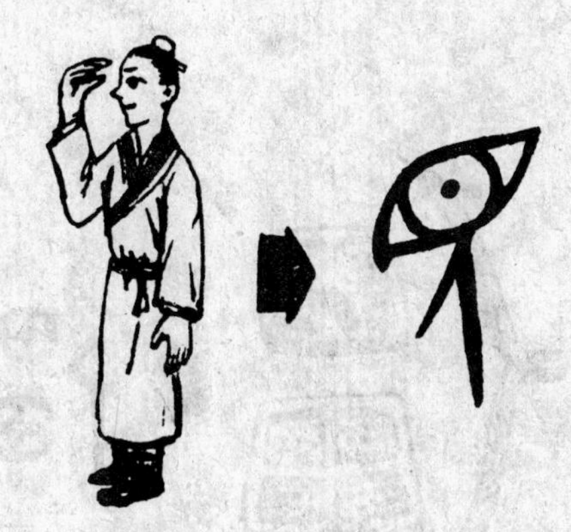

A man is looking forward with his big open eyes, hence, the idea 看见, to see. It extends to mean 见解 . opinion, 见识 , experience, etc. It is also used as a helping verb, indicating the passive tense. In addition, it is the original form of 现, appear.

疆　jiāng

〔附〕 强

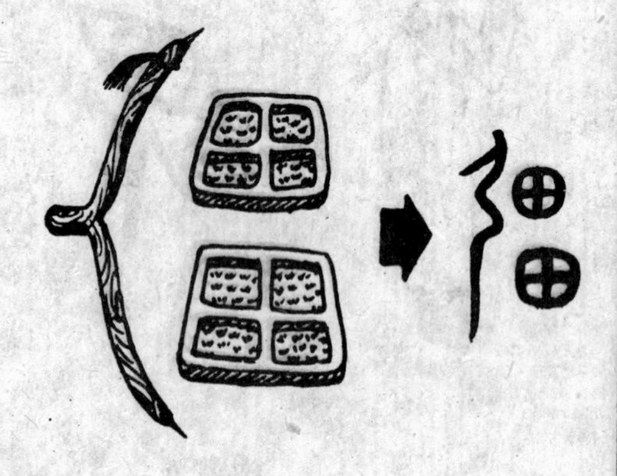

Originally, it was 畺. The left part of this character is a bow used to measure the land, the right part is two fields. Hence, its initial meaning was 划分疆界, to delineate and mark the boundary of lands. Later, it became interchangeable with 强, strong. And 土, earth, was added to indicate its original meaning.

降 jiàng, xiáng

Its left part is 阜, an earthly mountain; its right part is two feet going down the mountain. Hence, its meaning is "to go down," and it is pronounced jiàng (fourth tone). Later, it extended to mean 投降, to surrender, and 降服, to yield. In these cases, however, it is pronounced xiáng (second tone).

交 jiāo

〔附〕 蛟

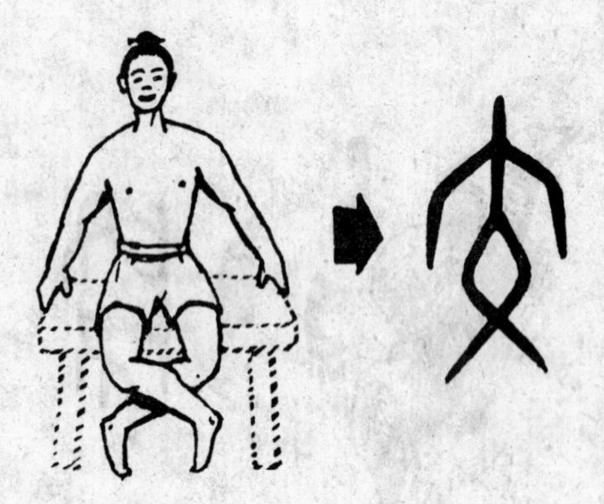

Graphically, it is a man with two legs folded. Hence, its original meaning was 交叉 or 交错, to crisscross, and from which comes other similar meanings. It is interchangeable with 蛟, a cruel dragon in ancient myths.

角 jiǎo

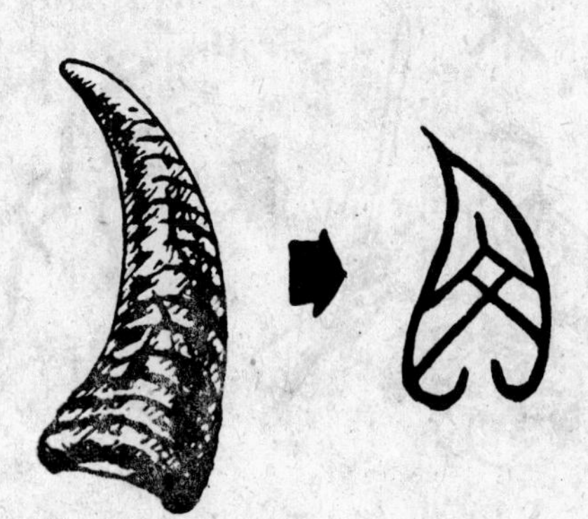

As a pictographic character, its form is a wild animal's horn. 角 is also the name for a type of wine vessel and a musical instrument in ancient times.

教 jiào

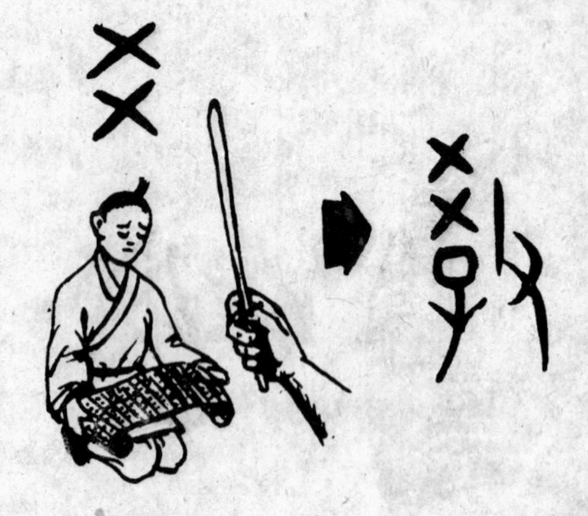

A hand of a teacher is holding a teaching pointer and urging a child to study. The upper part of this character 爻, yáo, is a phonetic symbol.

解 jiě

〔附〕 懈

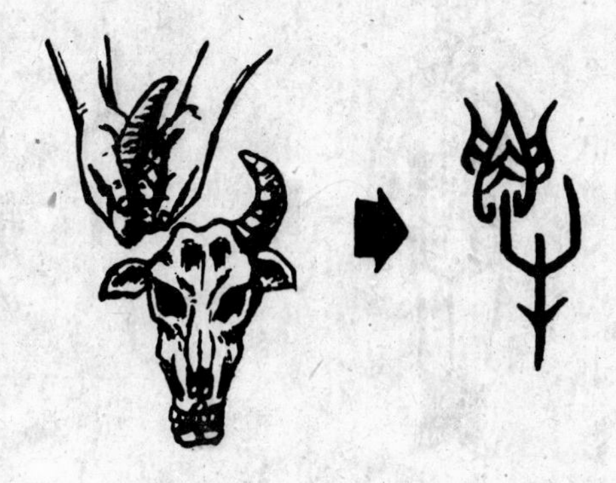

In oracle bone and bronze inscriptions, it was composed of an ox, 牛, a horn, 角, and two hands, signifying "removing the horn with two hands." In small seal characters, two hands were replaced by two knives. It was interchangeable with 懈 in ancient books.

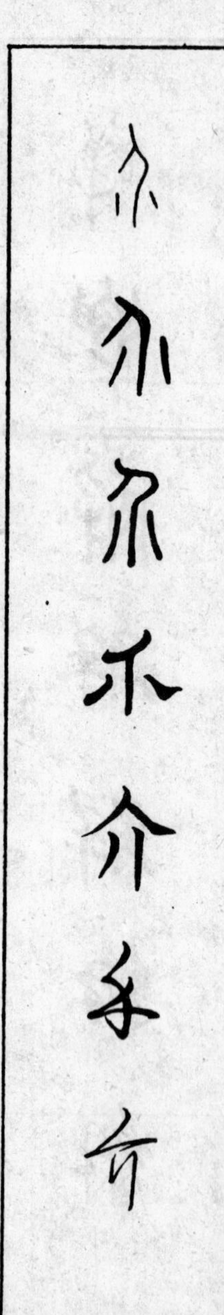

介 jiè

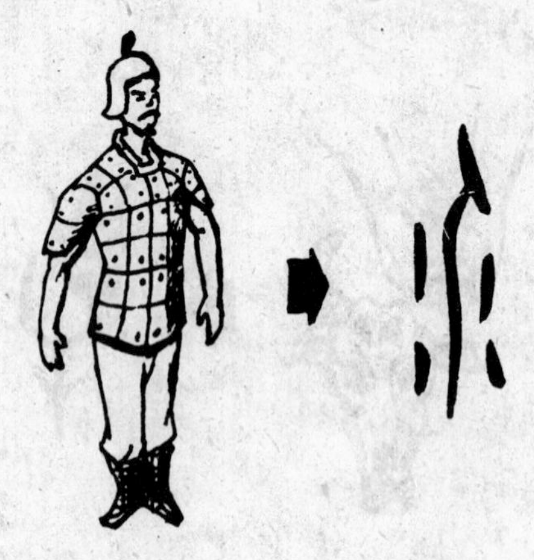

Its original meaning was armor. Graphically, it is a man with armor suit. Since official script, it is not easy to trace the original meaning.

戒 jiè

〔附〕 诫

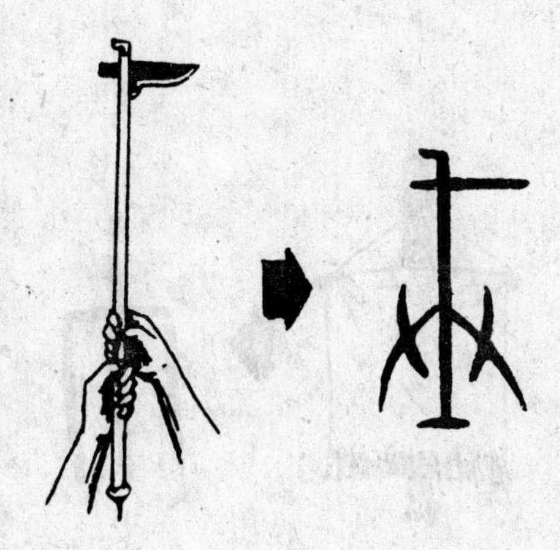

Two hands holding 戈, a weapon, closely, signifies the original meaning of this character: 防备, to guard against, and 警戒, to be on the alert against. It has another meaning 警告, to warn, and it is written as 诫 when with such meaning.

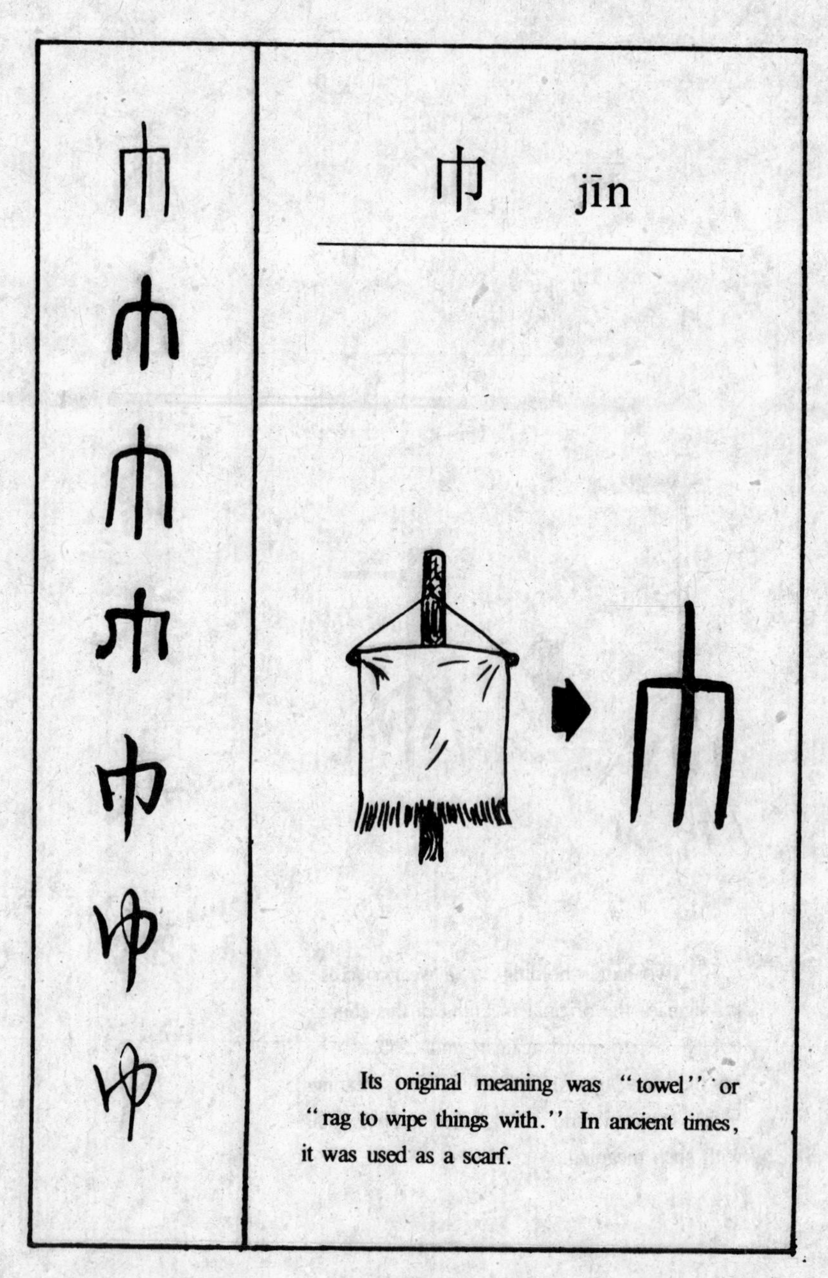

巾 jīn

Its original meaning was "towel" or "rag to wipe things with." In ancient times, it was used as a scarf.

斤 jīn

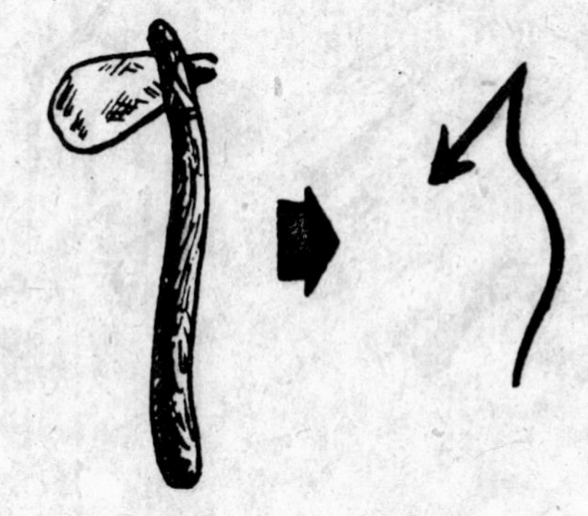

Originally, it was a stone ax. Later, it came to be used as a unit of weight. 斤斤 means 聪明鉴察, circumspect, at first, then it extends to mean 过分计较, and 斤斤计较, to bother about trifling matters.

进(進)jìn

In oracle bone inscriptions, its form was a bird, 隹, and a foot, 止, signifying "to go forward." In bronze inscriptions, 彳, chì, to walk, was added. In small seal characters 彳 and 止 were combined to 辵, chuò, which in official script became 辶.

晋（晉）jìn

〔附〕 搢

It is the original form of 搢, jìn, meaning 插, to insert. In oracle bone and bronze inscriptions, its form was two arrows inserted in a box-shaped or oval-shaped container. Later, it was commonly used to indicate 进, progress.

京 jīng

Its original meaning was 高冈, ridge. Since capitals were usually built on high lands, it acquired the extended meaning "national capital." Its form is a high city with the pointed tower and city wall. It also means "big."

晶 jīng

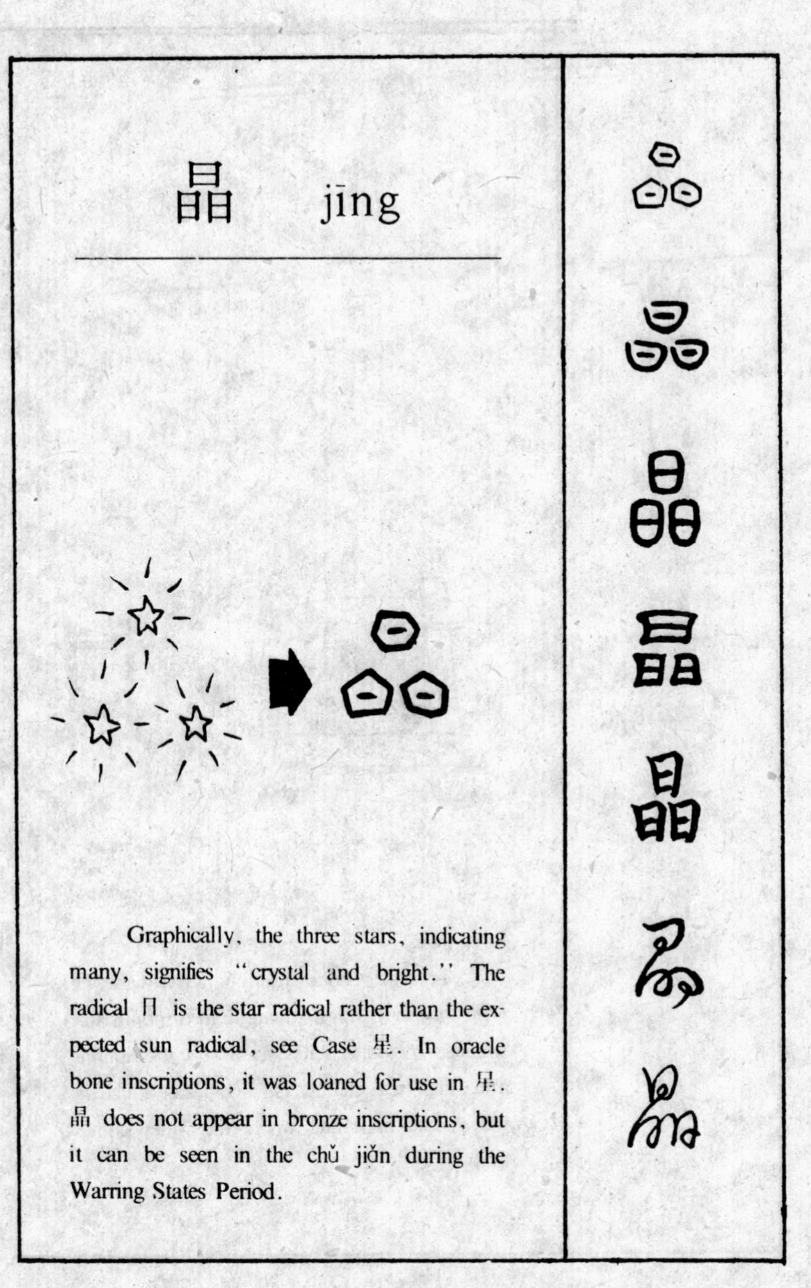

Graphically, the three stars, indicating many, signifies "crystal and bright." The radical 日 is the star radical rather than the expected sun radical, see Case 星. In oracle bone inscriptions, it was loaned for use in 星. 晶 does not appear in bronze inscriptions, but it can be seen in the chǔ jiǎn during the Warring States Period.

井 jǐng

In oracle bone inscriptions, it was the form of a well with a square-shaped mouth surrounded by stone plates. In bronze inscriptions and small seal characters, a dot was added in the middle indicating where the water comes from.

竞(競)jìng

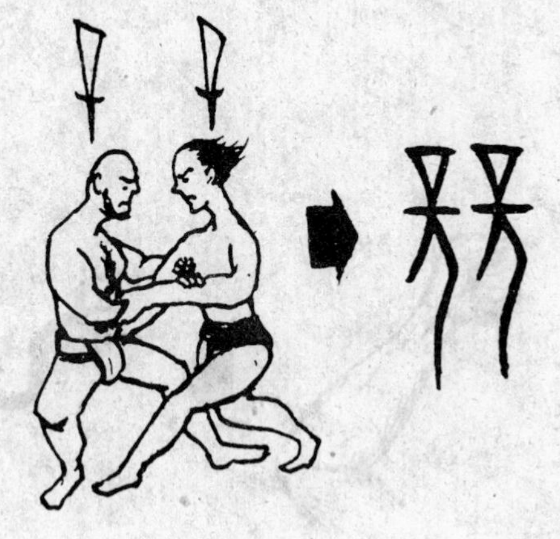

Its original meaning was 争逐, to contend. The ancient aristocrats enjoyed themselves by forcing slaves to wrestle. In oracle bone inscriptions, its form was two wrestling slaves with knife-shaped torture instruments above their heads.

九 jiǔ

〔附〕 肘

Its original meaning was "elbow." Graphically, it looks like the elbow of a man with the fingers balled into a fist. Later, it was loaned to be the number "nine" with its original meaning fading out. And 肘 was invented to signify its original meaning.

酒 jiǔ

In oracle bone inscriptions, its form was a wine jar with drops of wine on its two sides. In bronze inscriptions, it was replaced by 酉, i.e. the two characters are interchangeable. They became two different characters after the appearance of small seal characters.

旧(舊)jiù

〔附〕 鸺

Its original meaning was 鸺, xīu, an owl. In oracle bone inscriptions, it seems to be a cruel bird perching on its nest with round open eyes and standing crest. Later, it was loaned for use in 旧, old, losing its original meaning.

具 jù

〔附〕 俱

In oracle bone inscriptions, it was two hands raising 鼎, a food containing tripod. In bronze inscriptions, it was altered to 贝, and later to 目. Its original meaning was "to prepare," and its extended meanings are 供置, to set, and 完备, perfect,etc. It is also used as an adverb, interchangeable with 俱.

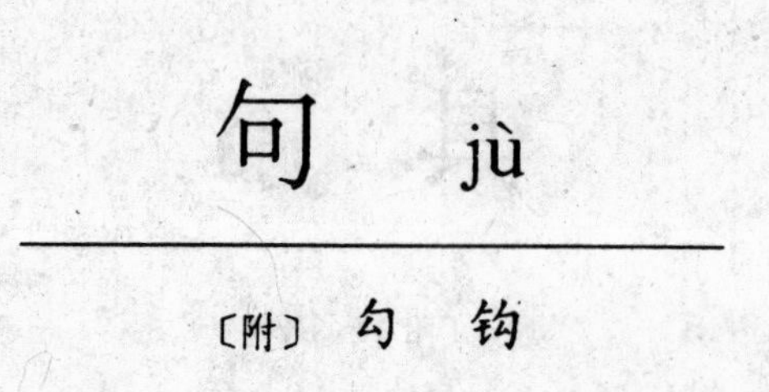

句 jù

〔附〕勾 钩

Its original meaning was "to bend or curve." It is interchangeable with 勾 and 钩. It is composed of 口, initially a square nail and 丩 (the original form of 纠), two entangled ropes.

爵 jué

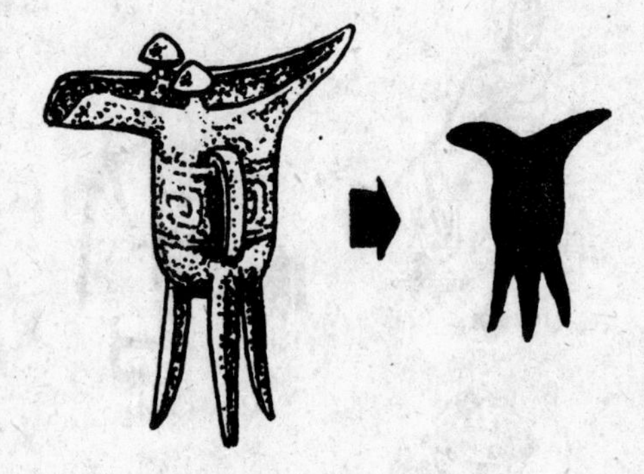

As an ancient vessel of wine, originally it was a graphically drawn pictograph. It later acquired the meaning of 爵位, the rank or title of nobility.

君 jūn

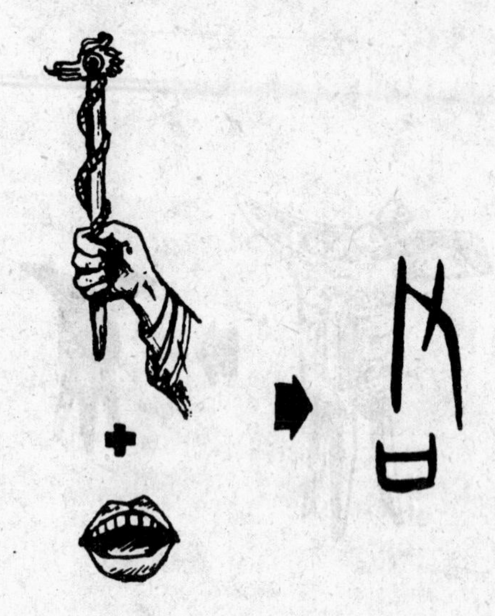

Its original meaning was "king." It is composed of 尹, his scepter, (see Case 尹) and 口 indicating his mouth with which he gives orders.

康 kāng

〔附〕 糠

It is the original form of 糠 (also 穅). In oracle bone inscriptions, it emphasized the chaff that is left below the thresher and cereal container.

考 kǎo

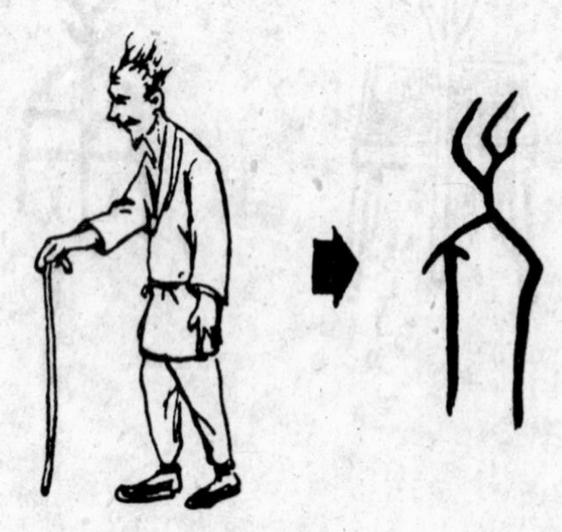

Its original meaning was "old." Its form is an old man with sparse hair and a bent back and the phonetic symbol 丂 is then added. Later, it was usually used in 考察, to investigate, and 考核, to examine.

克 kè

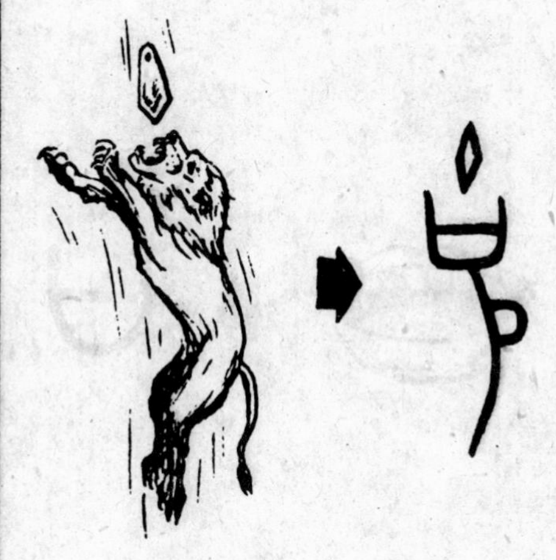

A stone ax is smashing a wild animal with an open mouth, signifying "to conquer." In modern Chinese, this meaning is retained in 克服, to overcome, and 攻克, to capture.

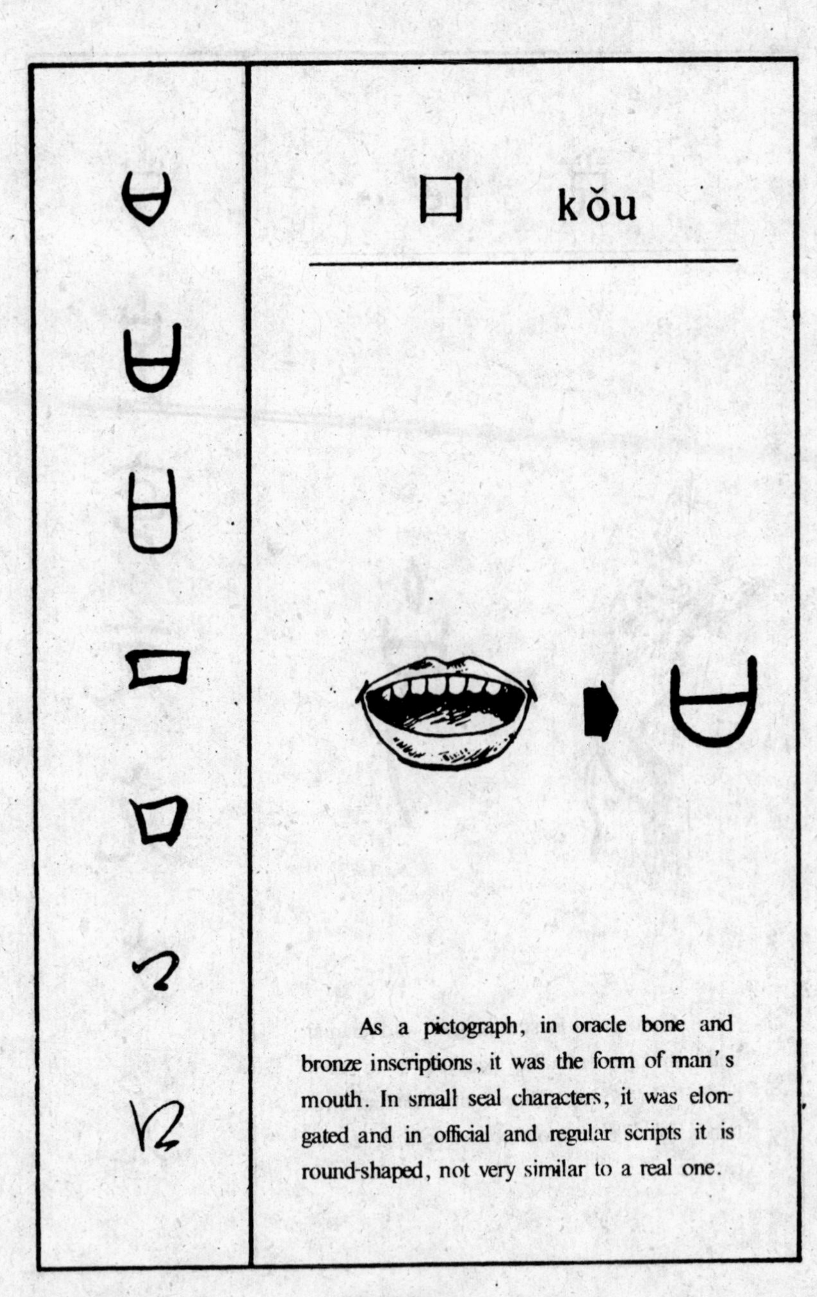

口 kǒu

As a pictograph, in oracle bone and bronze inscriptions, it was the form of man's mouth. In small seal characters, it was elongated and in official and regular scripts it is round-shaped, not very similar to a real one.

来(來)lái

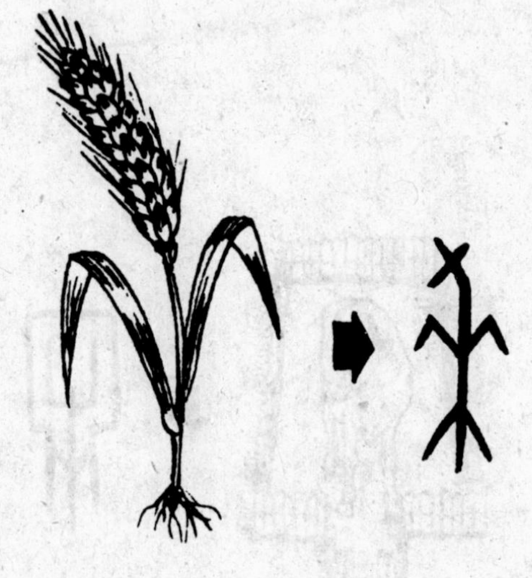

Its original meaning was "wheat." Later, it was loaned for use in 来, come. Then 𪎩 was invented to signify the original meaning. One saying goes that 来 is wheat, while 麦 is barley.

牢 láo

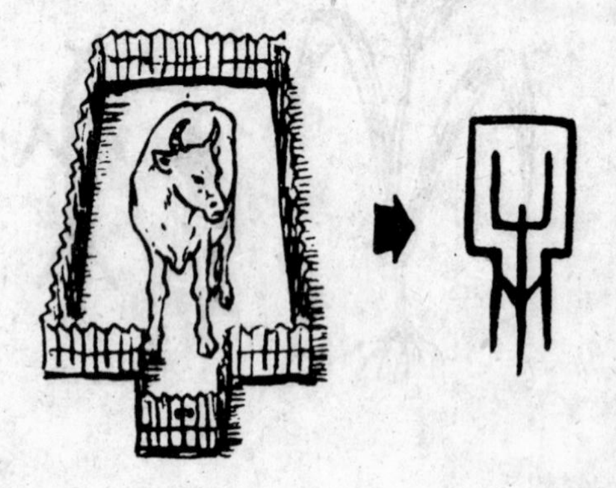

Its original meaning was a stable. Its form is an ox encircled by a fence. Its extended meanings are "prison" and "firm" or "secure."

老 lǎo

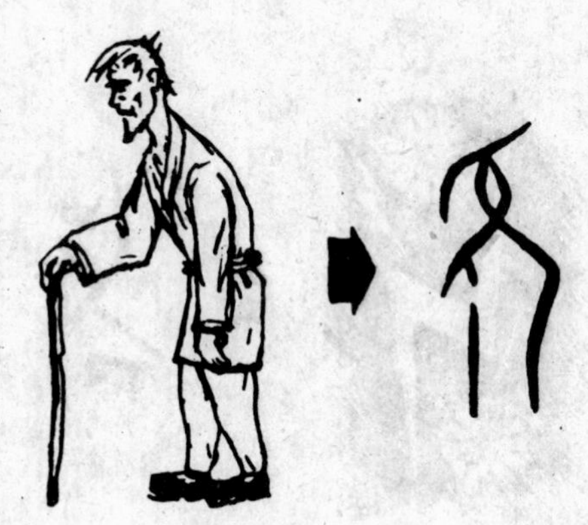

A hunchbacked man with sparse hair is walking with the help of a cane. This is what an old man looks like. Its original meaning was "aged." Its extended meanings are "lasting," "out of date," etc.

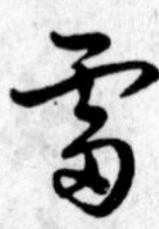

雷 léi

In oracle bone inscriptions, the curves in this character are the flashes accompanying the thunder indicated by the rings. In bronze inscriptions, the ring alters to wheel-shaped carvings and the sound is emphasized. Also, the "rain" is added to hint that the thunder claps mostly on raining days.

力 lì

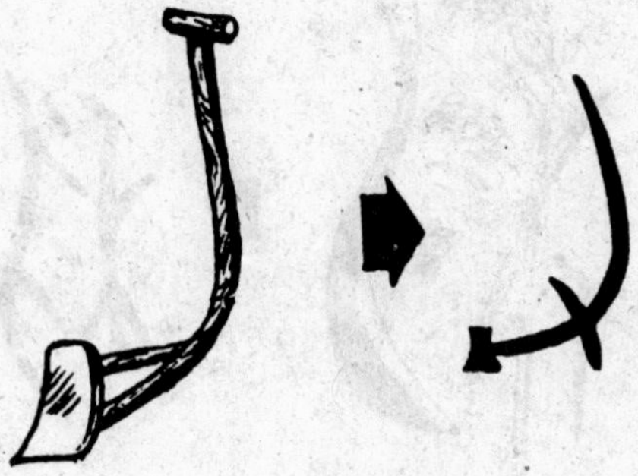

In early bronze inscriptions, it is explicit that 力 is an ancient ploughing instrument, i.e. 耒, lěi, whose original form is 来. It takes strength to plough, hence 力 is loaned to mean "strength."

力

力

利 lì

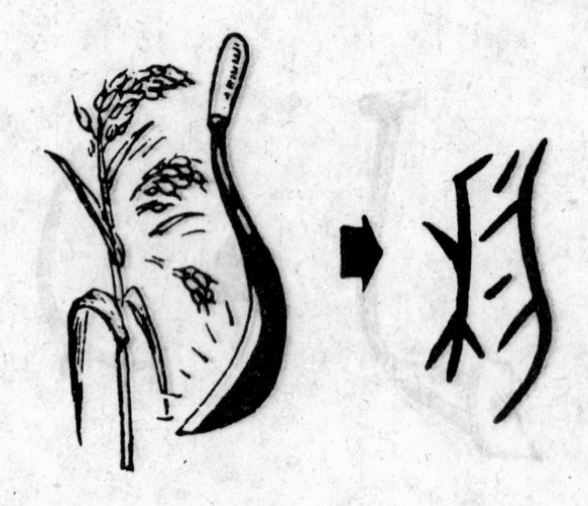

Its original meaning was 锐利 and 锋利, sharp. Its form is a sickle cutting rice and the paddy falling down. Later, it extended to mean 利益, 利润, interests, as well as others.

丽(麗)lì

〔附〕 俪 骊

Graphically, it is a deer with a pair of good-looking antlers. Hence, its original meaning was "a pair" or "a couple." Later, it became written as 俪. It also means 华丽, magnificent, and 美丽, beautiful. It is interchangeable with 骊.

丽

栗 lì

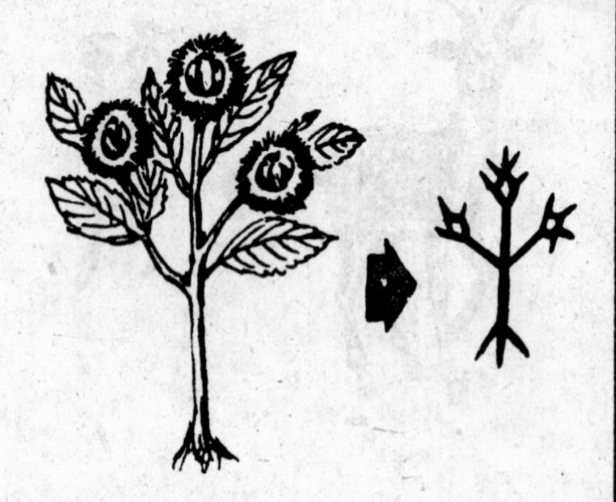

A tree with many thorny fruits is the 栗, chestnut tree. Later, it was loaned to mean "to shiver (because of terror or cold)" and it evolved into 慄. Now, 栗 has resumed from 慄.

鬲 lì

〔附〕 隔 膈

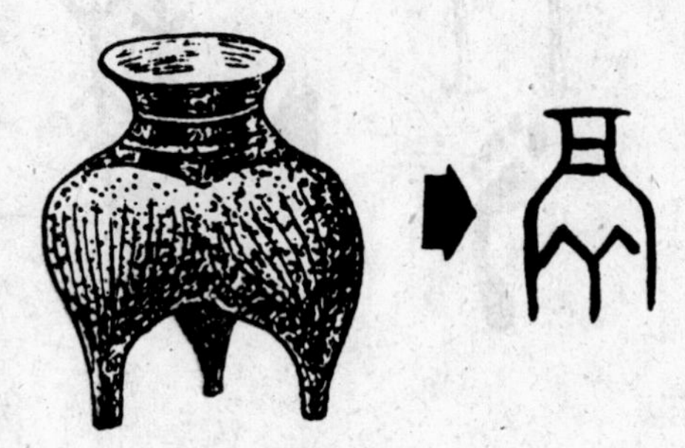

It is a tripod cooker, fire can be put under it. It is interchangeable with 隔 and 膈.

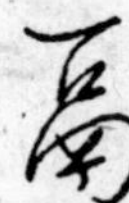

历(歷，曆)lì

Its original meaning was "to pass through." In oracle bone inscriptions, its form was a foot passing through the woods. In bronze inscriptions, the two 木 transformed into two 禾 and 厂 was added signifying cliffs. Later. 曆 was derived. Now, 曆 and 歷 are combined and simplified to 历.

〔附〕 位

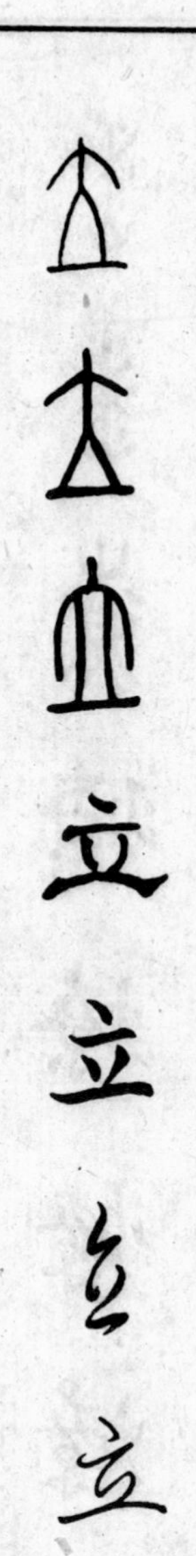

Graphically, a man is standing straight with two feet separated. Hence, its original meaning was "to stand." It was interchangeable with 位 in ancient books.

燎 liáo

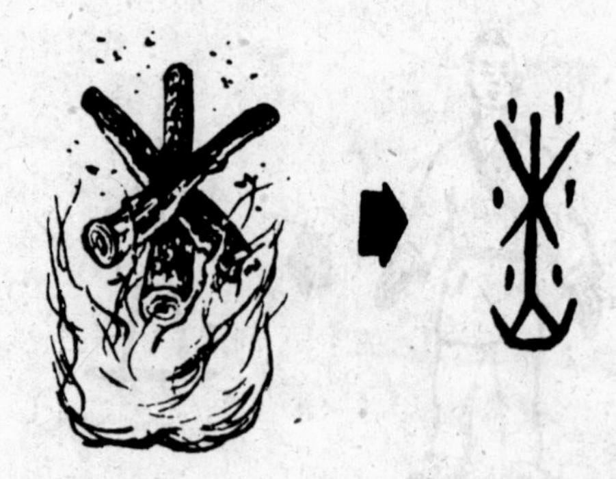

Its original form was 尞 . Graphically, its upper part is crisscrossed firewood, the lower part is fire, and the dots are the sparks bursting from the burning wood.

林 lín

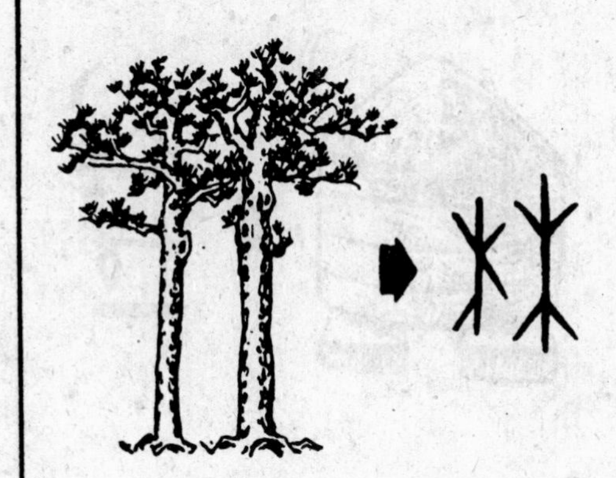

Graphically, two trees are standing side by side, signifying a multitude of trees, i.e. forest. Such composition can be referred to Case 多, 品, 晶, and 星.

廩

廩

廩

廩

廩 lǐn

Its original meaning was a granary. Its early form was wood laid on stones to build a storehouse. The upper part is the crescent moon indicating the crops and grain are stored at night.

令 lìng

Graphically, a man kneeling down is giving orders to people under a huge roof. 令 and 命 are synonyms, but the former also means 使, shǐ, to make, to let, e.g. 臣能令君胜, I can make you succeed.

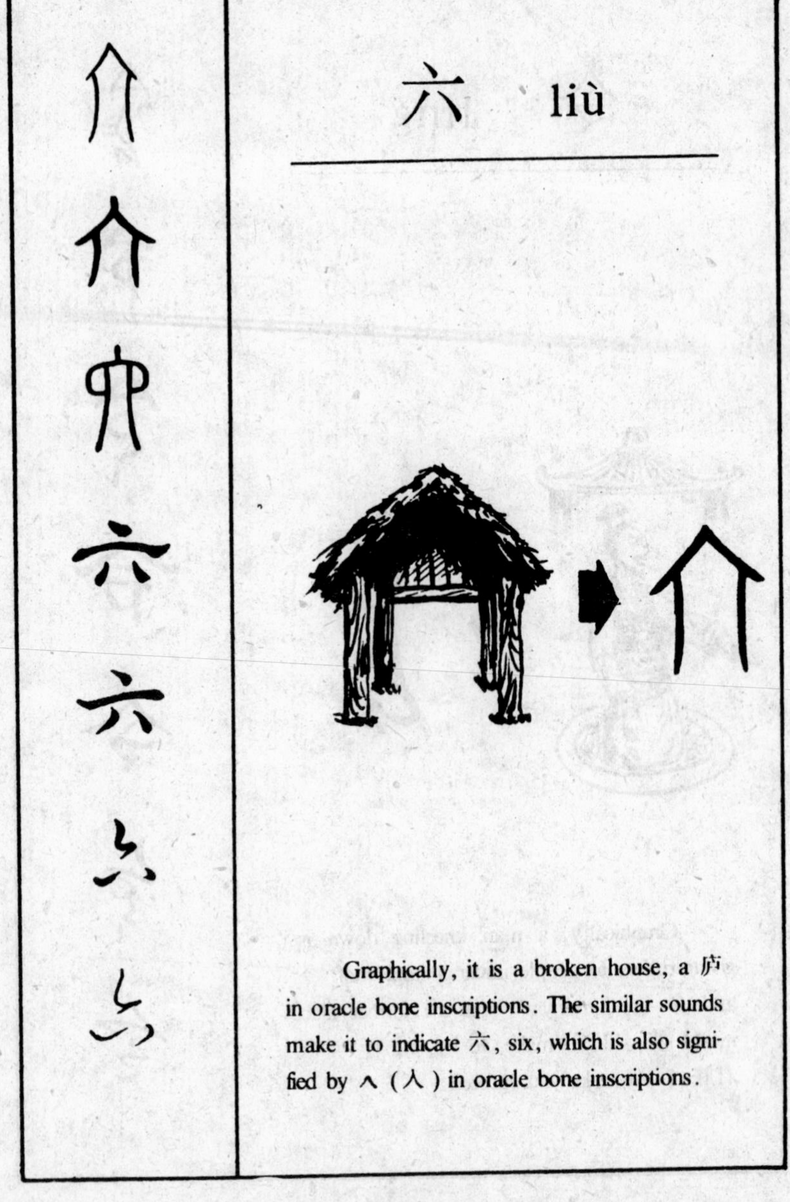

六 liù

Graphically, it is a broken house, a 庐 in oracle bone inscriptions. The similar sounds make it to indicate 六, six, which is also signified by ∧ (入) in oracle bone inscriptions.

龙(龍)lóng

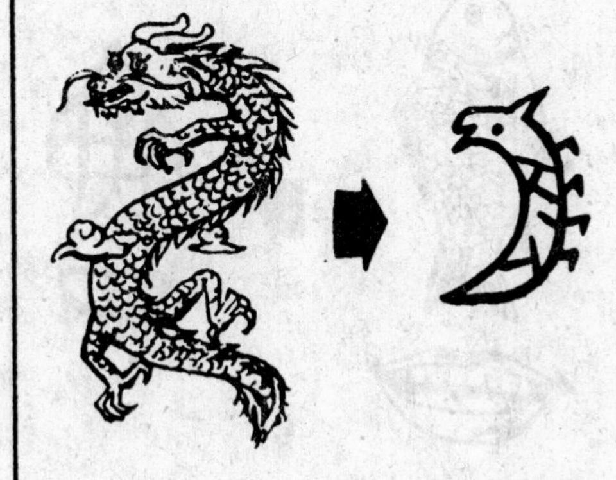

The dragon is a special animal in ancient Chinese mythology with horns on its head, scales on its body and a long tail as well. Since small seal characters, it was very hard to trace its original form.

鲁(魯)lǔ

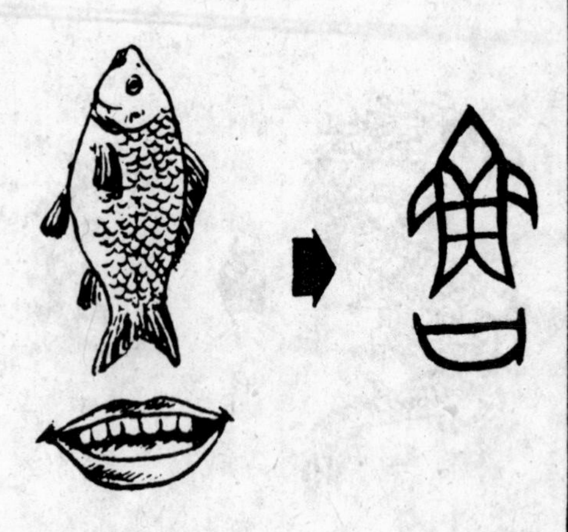

Its original meaning was "beautiful." With the upper part as a fish and the lower part as a mouth, it signifies that the delicacies have been eaten. Later, it began to mean "stupid."

鹿 lù

As a pictograph, it is the masterpiece of ancient artists in both oracle bone and bronze inscriptions. With forked horns, big eyes, a pointed mouth, a light figure and leaping hooves, it perfectly depicts the features of a deer.

麓 lù

Its original meaning was "the foot of mountain." Composed of 林 and 鹿, it indicates the land where the deer lives in. 鹿 is its phonetic symbol. 录 is also the phonetic symbol in some forms of this character.

禄(祿)lù

〔附〕 录 渌

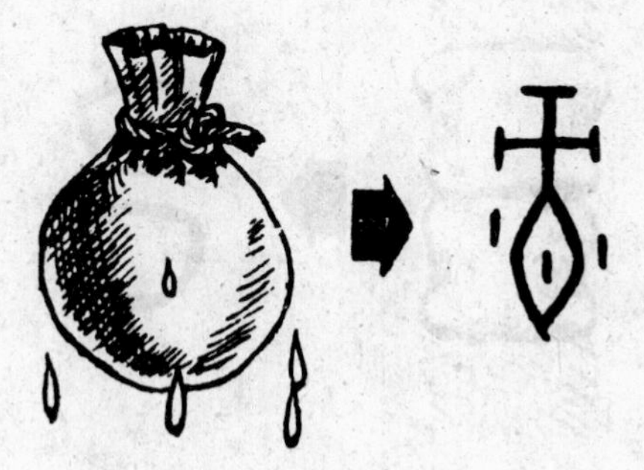

Graphically, it is a cotton bag with the upper horizontal plane indicating the opening of the sack and H as the tie. The fillings are wet, hence the drops of water are dripping out. This is 渌, the original form of 录, the two were interchangeable in both oracle bone and bronze inscriptions.

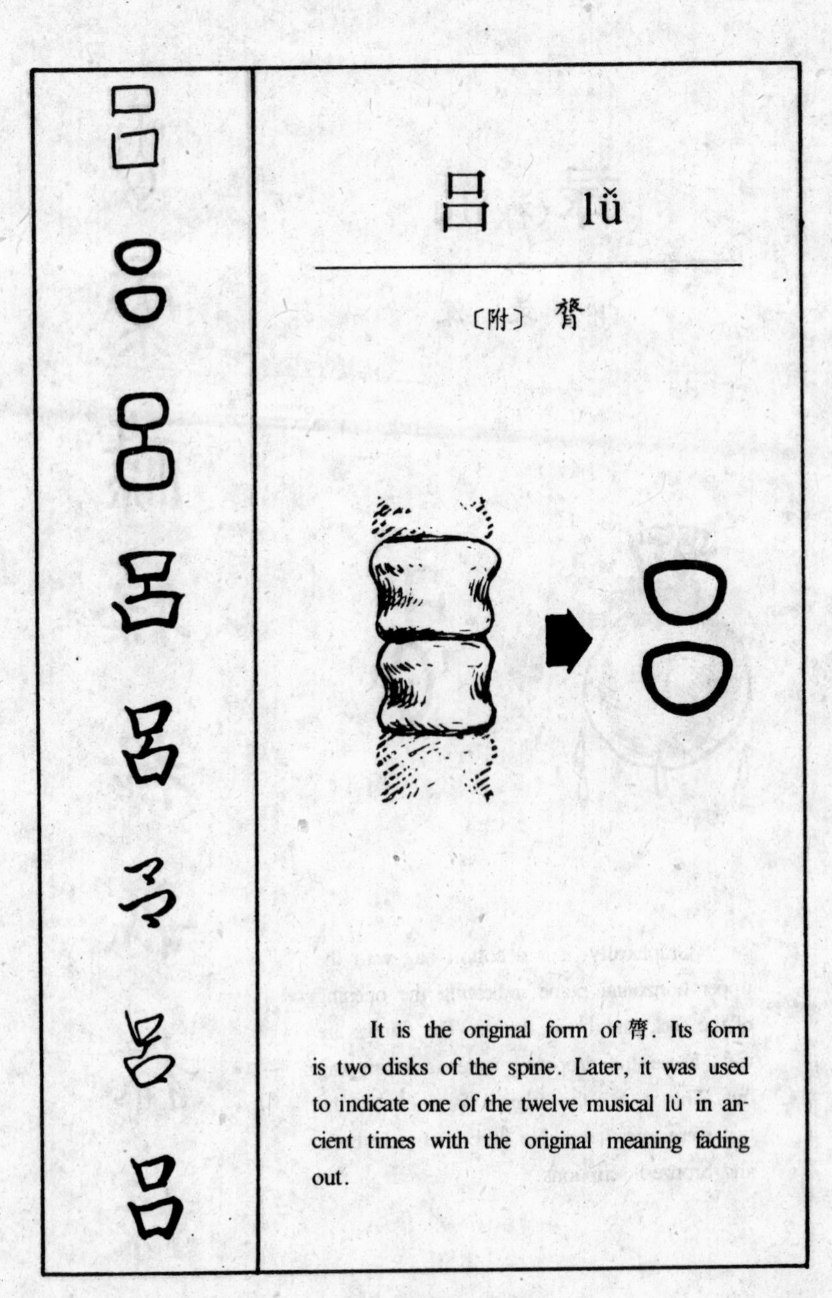

吕 lǚ

〔附〕 膂

It is the original form of 膂. Its form is two disks of the spine. Later, it was used to indicate one of the twelve musical lǜ in ancient times with the original meaning fading out.

旅 lǚ

Two soldiers (indicating the multitude of the army) get together near the flagpost with a waving flag. Hence, its original meaning was 军旅, army. In ancient times, 500 soldiers constituted a 旅. Later, it extended to mean "to travel" and "tourist."

罗(羅)luó

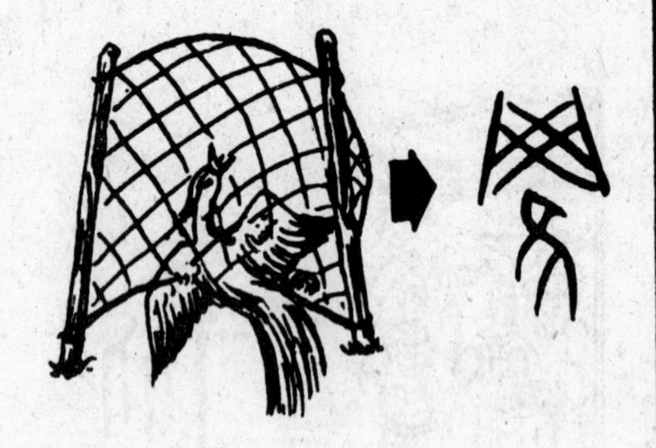

Its original meaning was "bird net." Now, it is used in 罗网 and other phrases. In oracle bone inscriptions, its form was a net catching a 隹, bird. Later, 糸 was added to indicate silk-woven net. Its extended meaning is "soft silk knit goods."

马(馬)mǎ

As a pictograph, it is the vivid depiction of a horse. The long face and the horse's mane are clearly delineated. Since the characters from the Warring States Period and small seal characters, it no longer resembles a horse.

买(買)mǎi

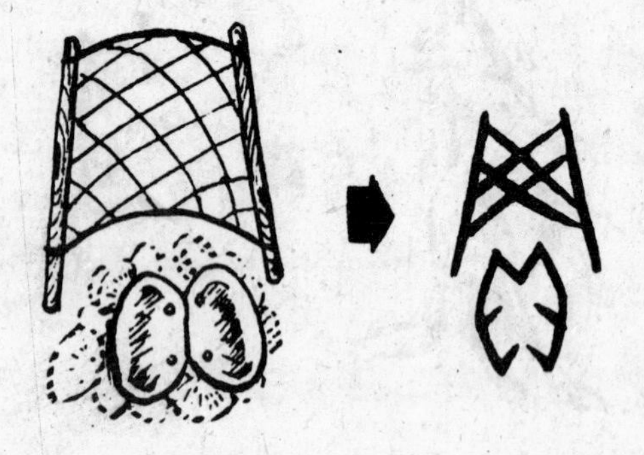

Getting goods in market is 买, to buy. The upper part of this character is 网, net; the lower part is 贝, the ancient currency, using which goods can be obtained through purchases.

麦(麥)mài

Its form is wheat. The root 夂 depicted at the bottom has altered to the foot of man since oracle bone inscriptions. Hence its ambiguous meanings.

眉 méi

As a pictograph, it is the form of an eye and brow. In bronze inscriptions, it has other forms. In ancient books, 眉寿 meant "longevity."

美 měi

Its original meaning was "beautiful." Its form is a man with sheep horns and such ornaments as feathers. Adorned in such ornaments, the man is regarded to be beautiful. Its extended meanings are 甘美, delicious, 赞美, praise, etc.

每　měi

〔附〕晦　敏

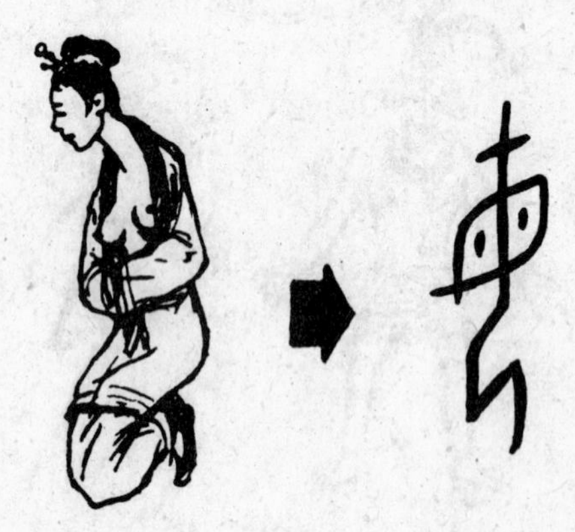

It is the variant form of 母, which graphically is a kneeling woman with ornaments on her head and her two breasts exposed. In bronze inscriptions, it was interchangeable with 晦 and 敏.

门(門)mén

In oracle bone and bronze inscriptions, its form was two shutters, and the door frame was added in some forms of this character. The simplified version 门 comes from the regularization of its cursive form.

麋 mí

麋, the David's deer, was a pictograph in oracle bone inscriptions. In stone inscriptions, the phonetic symbol 米 was added.

米 mǐ

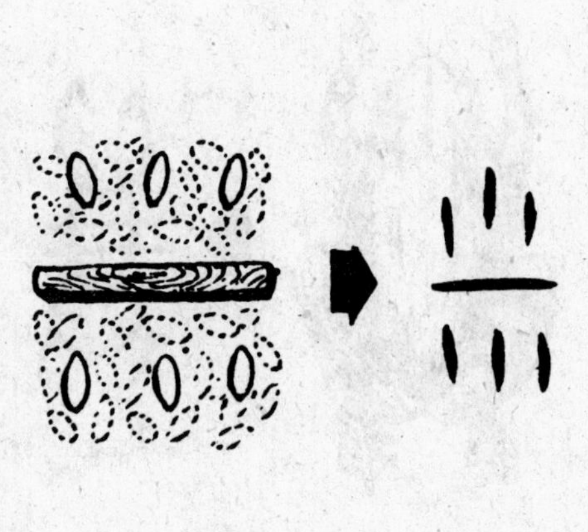

Its form in oracle bone inscriptions was like a scattered paddy. The horizontal plane in the middle is the separation of the racks where the rice is spread and dried. Since Warring States Period characters and small seal characters, the horizontal plane has changed to 十.

黾(黽)mǐn，měng，miǎn

〔附〕渑

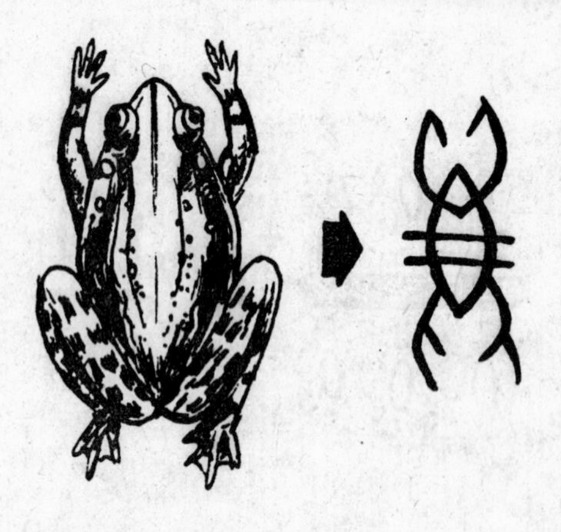

When it indicates a frog, it is pronounced měng, which is in very limited use. In modern Chinese, 黾勉, mǐn miǎn, to make efforts, is a written phrase. It is interchangeable with 渑 when it indicates place names.

皿 mǐn

Like a drawing section of a container, it was a pictograph in oracle bone and bronze inscriptions. Characters such as 盆, 盘 and 盂 with 皿 as the radical are always close to "container" in meaning.

明 míng

Seen from the earth, 日, the sun, and 月, the moon, are the brightest planets, which constitute 明. Hence, its original meaning was "bright." The radical 日 can be seen written as 囧, jiǒng, sometimes, indicating seeing the moon through the windows. Both share the same meaning.

名 míng

It is composed of 夕, night, and 口, mouth. At night a person in the distance can only be distinguished if he answers to the calling of his name.

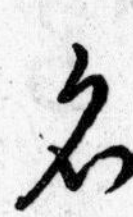
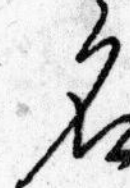

鸣

鸣(鳴)míng

Composed of 口, mouth, and 鸟, bird, its original meaning was "a bird singing." It also generally indicates "the sound of a horse, tiger, deer, etc." It extends to mean "let it make noise," e.g. 鸣玉, 鸣玲, 鸣炮, etc.

命　mìng

In oracle bone inscriptions, 命 and 令 are in the same form (see Case 令). Since bronze inscriptions, 口 has been added on 令 forming 命. Hence, its original meanings were 命令, order, and 差使, errand. It also means 生命, life, 命运, destiny.

莫 mò

〔附〕 暮

As an ideograph, its original meaning was "the time the sun sets." Graphically, it is the sun setting down in the grass at dusk. Later, it was loaned to mean "do not," and 暮 was invented with the radical 日 to indicate its original meaning.

母　mǔ

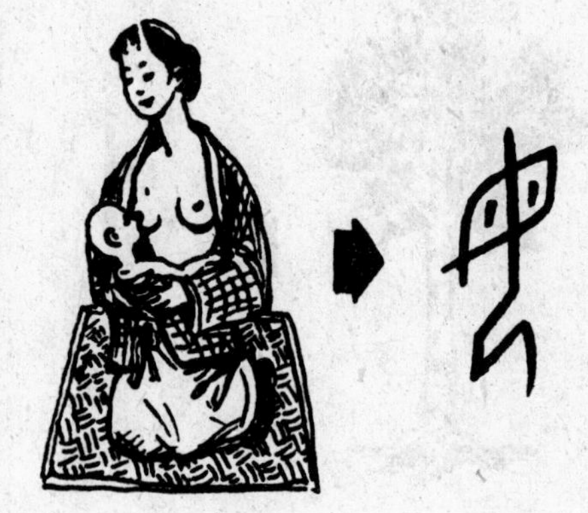

A woman is kneeling down with her breasts exposed, forming the symbol of a mother. It also indicates the elder female generation (e.g. 祖母, grandmother, 伯母, aunt, etc.) or simply female.

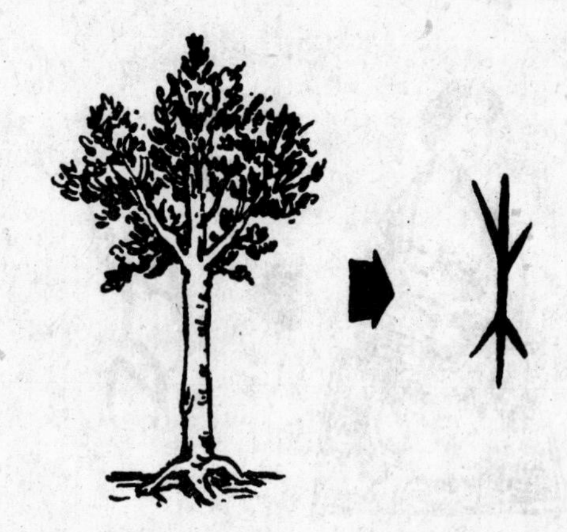

As a pictograph, its form resembles a tree. The slanting planes in the upper part are branches, and in the lower part roots. Hence, its original meaning was "tree." Its extended meanings are "lumber" and "wood."

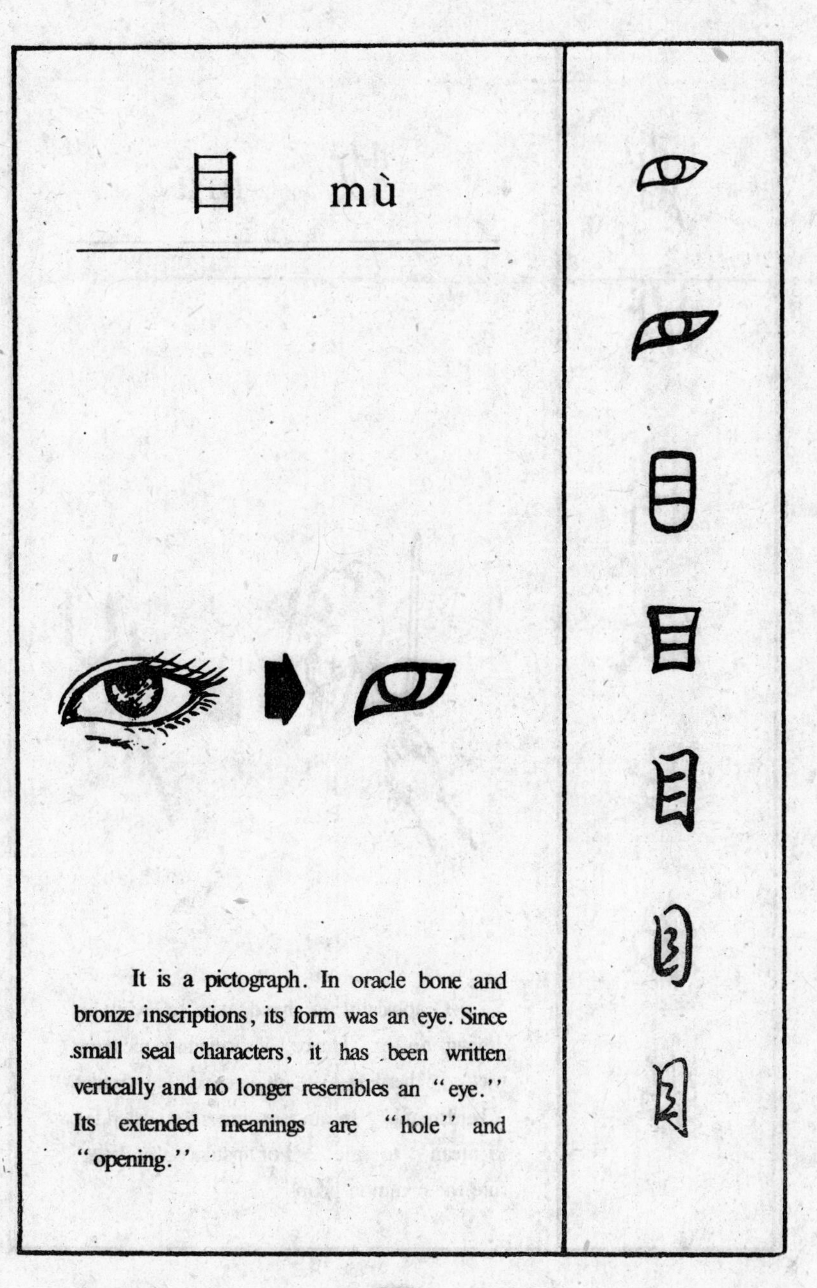

目 mù

It is a pictograph. In oracle bone and bronze inscriptions, its form was an eye. Since small seal characters, it has been written vertically and no longer resembles an "eye." Its extended meanings are "hole" and "opening."

牧　mù

Graphically, a hand with a whip is driving an ox. Hence, its original meaning was "herding." It also indicates "herdsman." In ancient times, it extended to mean "to rule." For instance, 牧万民, rule the common people.

穆 mù

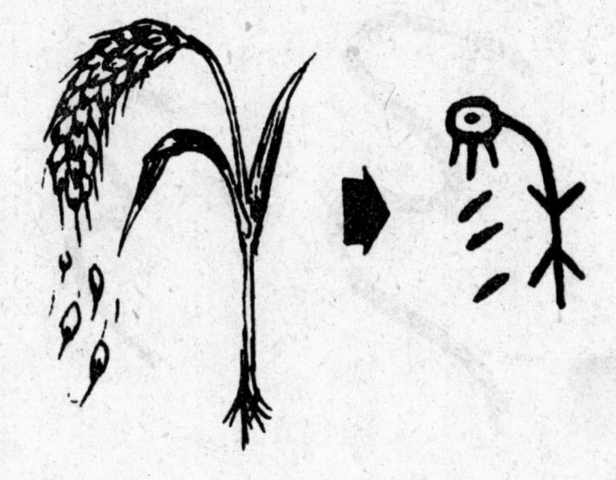

Graphically, it is clearly indicated by the delineation of a crop bending with the ripe paddy. With its original meaning inexistent, now it usually is used to mean 和畅, gentle and pleasant, 壮美, magnificent, 和睦, harmony, etc.

乃 nǎi

In oracle bone and bronze inscriptions, it was the form of a rope. But since the oraclè bone inscriptions, it has been used to indicate the second person — "you." Another version of this character is 迺 (also 廼). Today, the two are combined and simplified to 乃.

南 nán

Originally, it was the name of an ancient musical instrument and a dance. Graphically, it is a ring-shaped musical instrument with a tie in the upper part to hang. Later, it was loaned to indicate "south."

男 nán

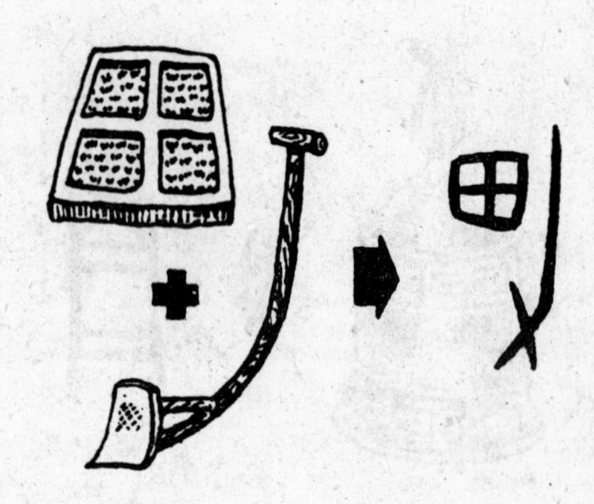

Composed of 田 and 力, it indicates the ancient plowing instrument 耒 (lěi, see Case 力). Plowing the fields was the main responsibility of man in ancient time. Hence the meaning "man."

内 nèi

〔附〕 纳

The upper part of this character is a framework of a house, the lower part is 人 (see Case 人). Entering the house means "to be inside" and refers to "the inside of the house." It extends to mean "to accept" and "to take in." Later, it changed to 纳.

逆 nì

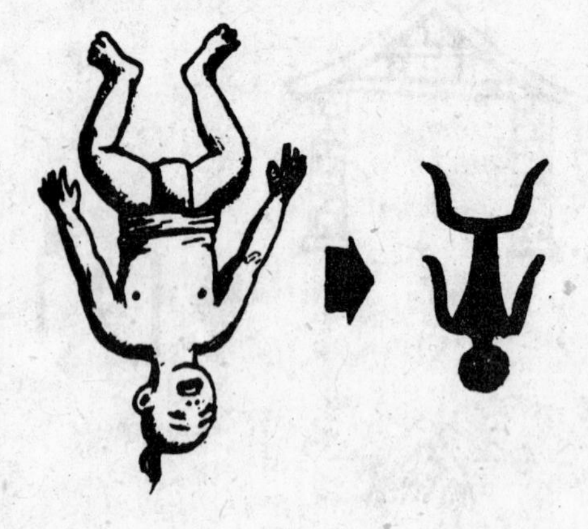

Its original form was 逆, a man with his head down and feet up. Later, the radicals 彳 and 止 or 辵, chuò, were added signifying "in motion." Hence. [illegible] original meaning was "unsmooth." I[illegible] extends to mean "against," "beforehan[illegible]" etc.

年 nián

Its original meaning was "harvest." Graphically, it is a man carrying the ripe crops to his home.

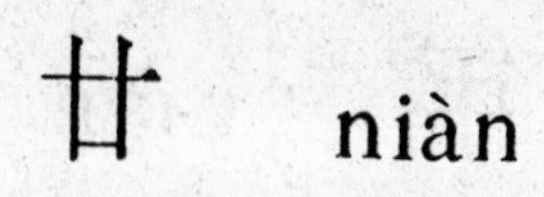

廿 niàn

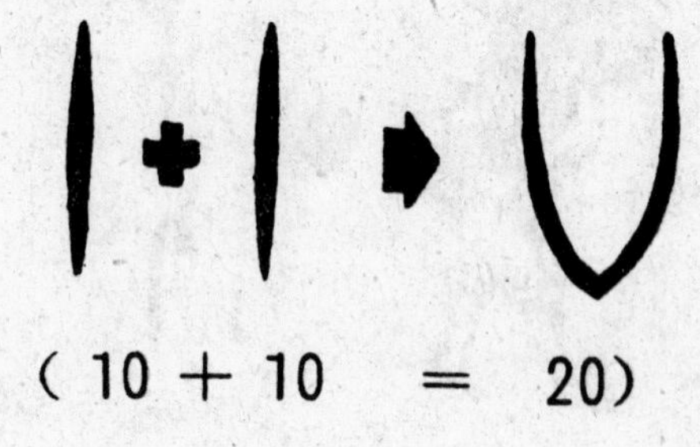

In oracle bone and bronze inscriptions, 十 was usually written in the form of a vertical structure | (see Case 十). Lint two 十 at the bottom, hence 二十, twenty, also 卄.

鸟(鳥)niǎo

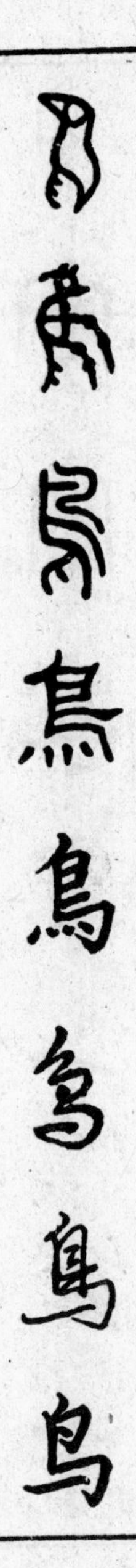

In oracle bone and bronze inscriptions, it was the vivid portrait of a bird whose beak and long claw are emphasized. Characters with the radical 鸟 are always some kind of bird.

宁(寧)níng

A table is stood in the house, and a container 皿 with food is laid upon the table, signifying ample food and clothing and a life of plenty. Later, the radical 心 was added to indicate 安心, at ease, and 安宁, tranquil.

牛 niú

As a pictograph, it is the form of the head of an ox. The long and curved horns are emphasized. It is very clearly delineated.

农(農)nóng

In oracle bone inscriptions, its form was composed of 林 (indicating the plowing land) and 辰 (a kind of hoe, see Case 辰) with a hand beside in some cases of this character. In bronze inscriptions, the radical 林 changed to 田, field, which later changed to 囟 and 曲 in small seal characters and official script respectively.

弄　nòng

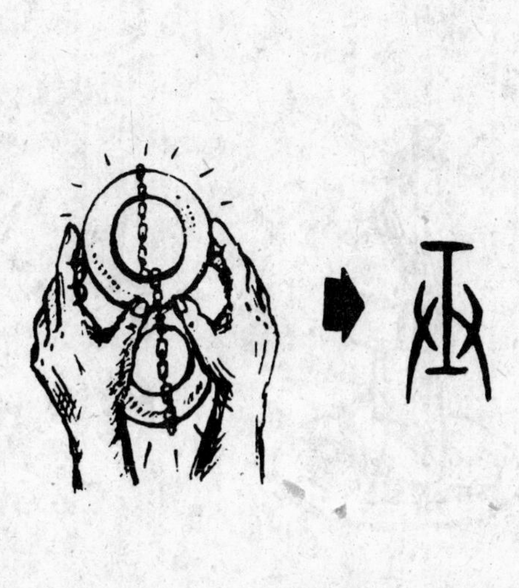

Its original meaning was "to feel and play with the hands." Graphically, it is two hands holding a piece of jade, feeling and judging it. Later, it extended to mean "to play with," "to bully," "to play a musical instrument," etc.

女 nǚ

〔附〕汝

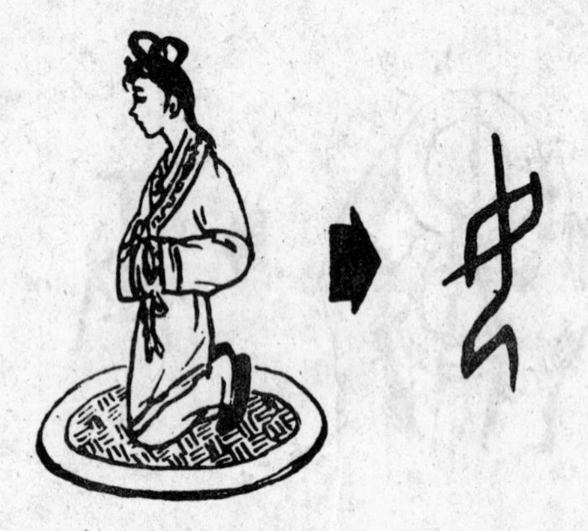

With two hands folded gently on her bosom, a woman is kneeling on a straw mat as the ancient people used to do. Hence, its original meaning was "woman." In ancient books, it was loaned to be 汝, rǔ, "you," which was coined later.

旁 páng

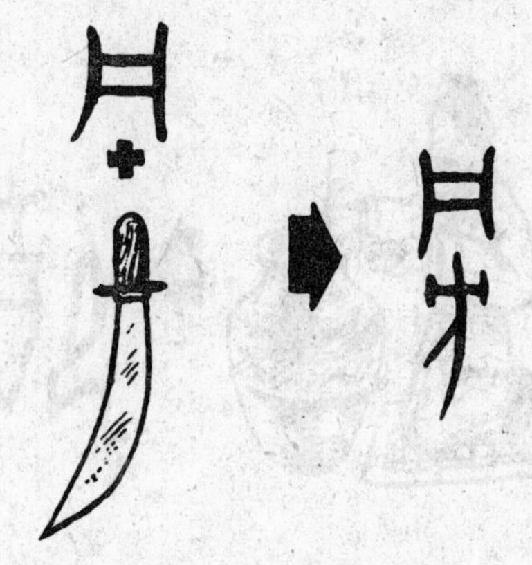

With the radical 方, "location," which is also its phonetic symbol, as the lower part and the initial 凡, "all," as its upper part, originally it meant "all directions."

配 pèi

A man is kneeling beside a jar and is blending and preparing the wine inside. Hence, its original meaning was "preparing wine." Later, it extended to mean 婚配, marriage, 配偶, consort, 分配, distribution, 相配, match, etc.

彭 péng

〔附〕澎

Originally, it was the onomatopoeia of the drum sound. The left part of this character is the shape of a drum (see Case 鼓) and the right part is three slanting lines indicating the drum sounds. It is interchangeable with 澎.

朋 péng

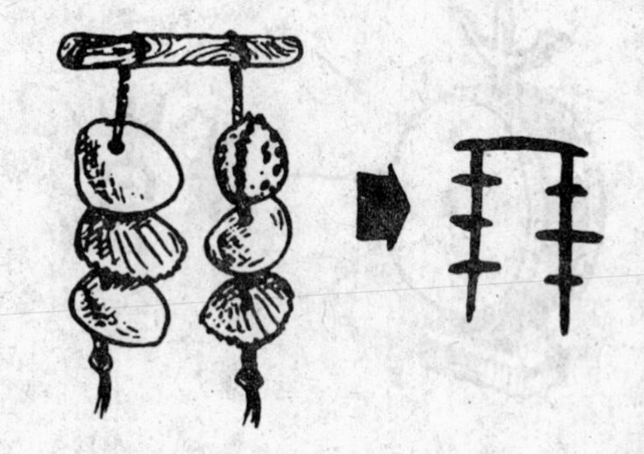

Its original meaning was the name for a unit of currency. Graphically, it is two clusters of cowries. Five cowries form one cluster and two clusters form one 朋. Later, it extended to mean 朋友, friends, 朋党, clique, etc.

品 pǐn

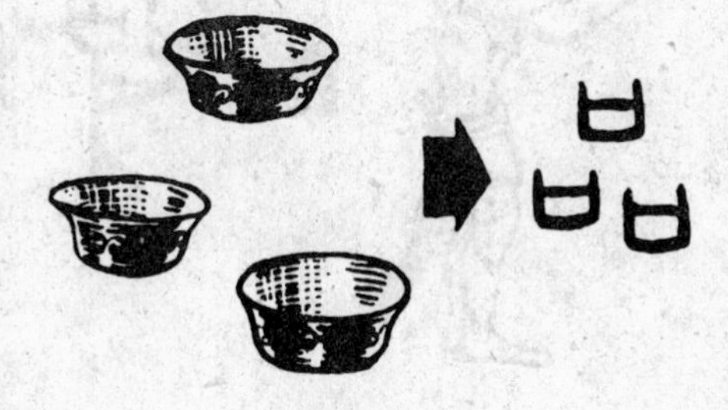

Its original meaning was "many." Graphically, it is composed of three containers (three 口) signifying numerous. Later, it extended to mean "kind," or "type," "personality," "to judge," etc.

仆(僕)pú

Its original meaning was "slave." In oracle bone inscriptions, it was a slave wearing tail-ornamented clothes holding a dust-pan with the symbol of the punishment knife (辛) over his head. In simplified versions 僕 and 仆 (pū, to take a prone position) are combined and simplified to 仆.

七 qī

〔附〕 切

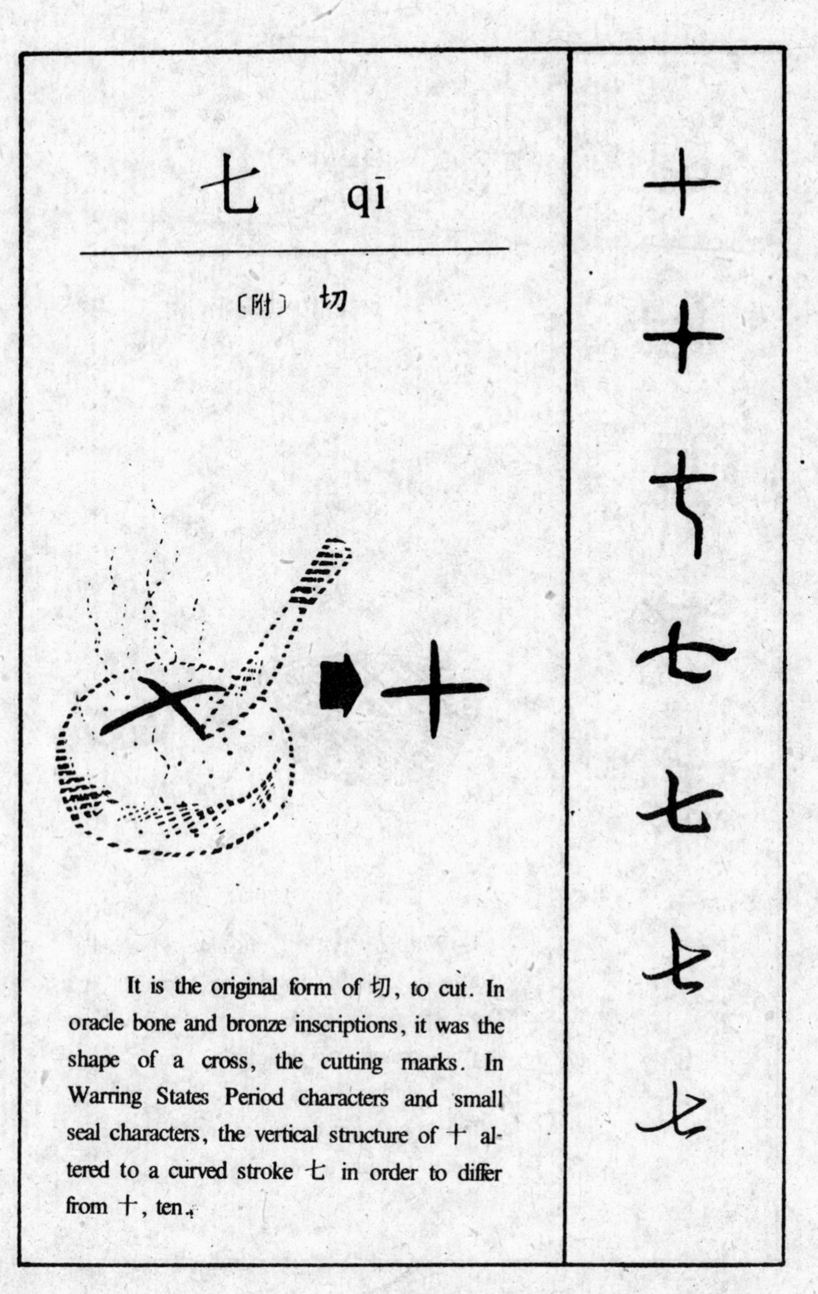

It is the original form of 切, to cut. In oracle bone and bronze inscriptions, it was the shape of a cross, the cutting marks. In Warring States Period characters and small seal characters, the vertical structure of 十 altered to a curved stroke 七 in order to differ from 十, ten.

其 qí

〔附〕 箕

With the original meaning "dustpan," it is the original form of 箕. The upper part is the front part of the dustpan and the crossed lines indicate the pan is made up of bamboo strips and wicker. 其 was loaned to be a function word, and 箕 was invented to indicate the original meaning.

齐(齊)qí

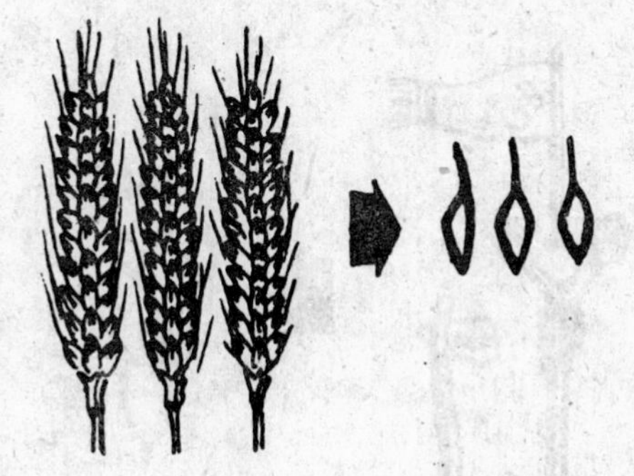

The wheat in the field was growing in the even order, therefore, the primitive people used three wheat heads to indicate 齐, order. Later, the three heads were not arranged in even order.

祈 qi

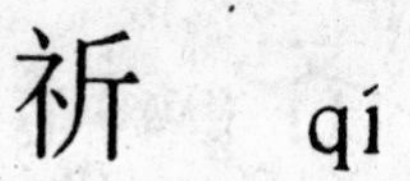

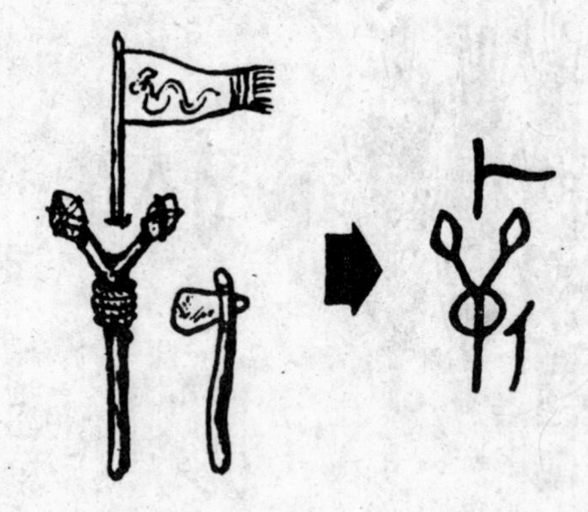

In oracle bone inscriptions and bronze inscriptions, it was usually written as 旂, the variant form of 旂. 㫃 is the form of a flag, 单 and 斤 are ancient weapons. Later, it was loaned to mean 祈求, to pray.

启(啟)qǐ

Graphically, a hand opening the shutter of the door, originally it meant "to open." Its extended meaning is "to straighten out." It also means "statement" in 陈述, announcement.

三 气 气 氣 氣 氣 氣 气

气(氣)qì

〔附〕 乞迄讫饩

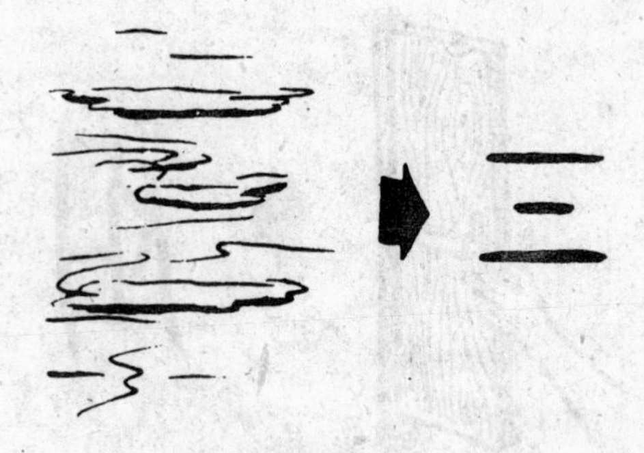

Its earliest form was three lines, signifying the airflow. Later, the two horizontal planes curved in order to be different with 三, three. In ancient books, it was loaned to be 乞, 迄 and 讫. The complex version actually is the original form of 餼 (饩, xì).

弃（棄）qì

Its original meaning was "to abandon." Its early form was two hands throwing away a dead baby (some are indicated by the inverted 子, son) with a dustpan (see Case 其).

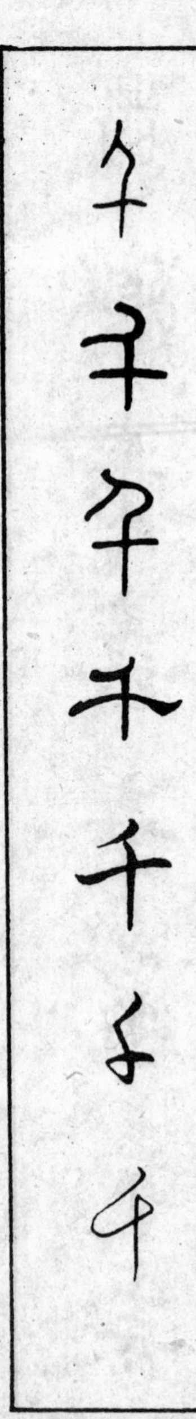

千 qiān

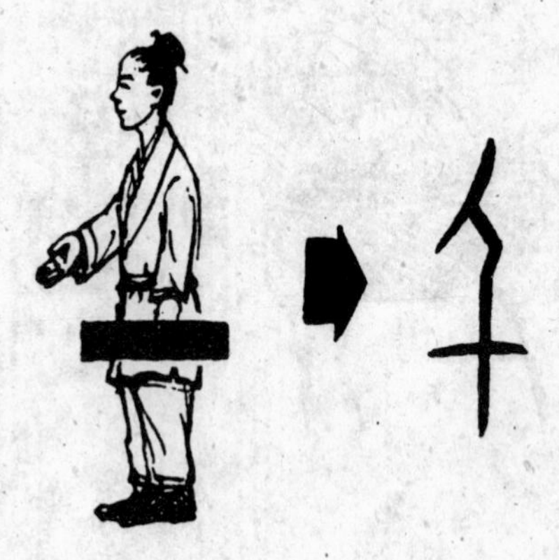

It is very hard to indicate the numeral for one thousand with a pictograph. Hence, a horizontal plane (indicating 一, one) is added on 人, man, with the similar sound to signify this numeral. One thousand through five thousand are indicated by [glyph], [glyph], [glyph], [glyph] and [glyph] respectively.

前　qián

〔附〕剪

Its original form was 歬. A foot (止) on a boat (舟) indicates the boat is advancing. Later, 舟 evolved into 月, 止 evolved into 䒑, and "knife" (刂) was added, forming 前, progress, the original form of 剪, which is coined with 刀 and 前.

欠 qiàn

Its original meaning was "to yawn." In oracle bone inscriptions, its form was a man kneeling down and yawning. Later, it extended to mean "deficit" and "to lack."

羌 qiāng

It is the name of the ancient Qiang nationality living in the west of China. Graphically, it is a man with the horn-shaped ornaments that are characteristic of the nationality.

且 qiě

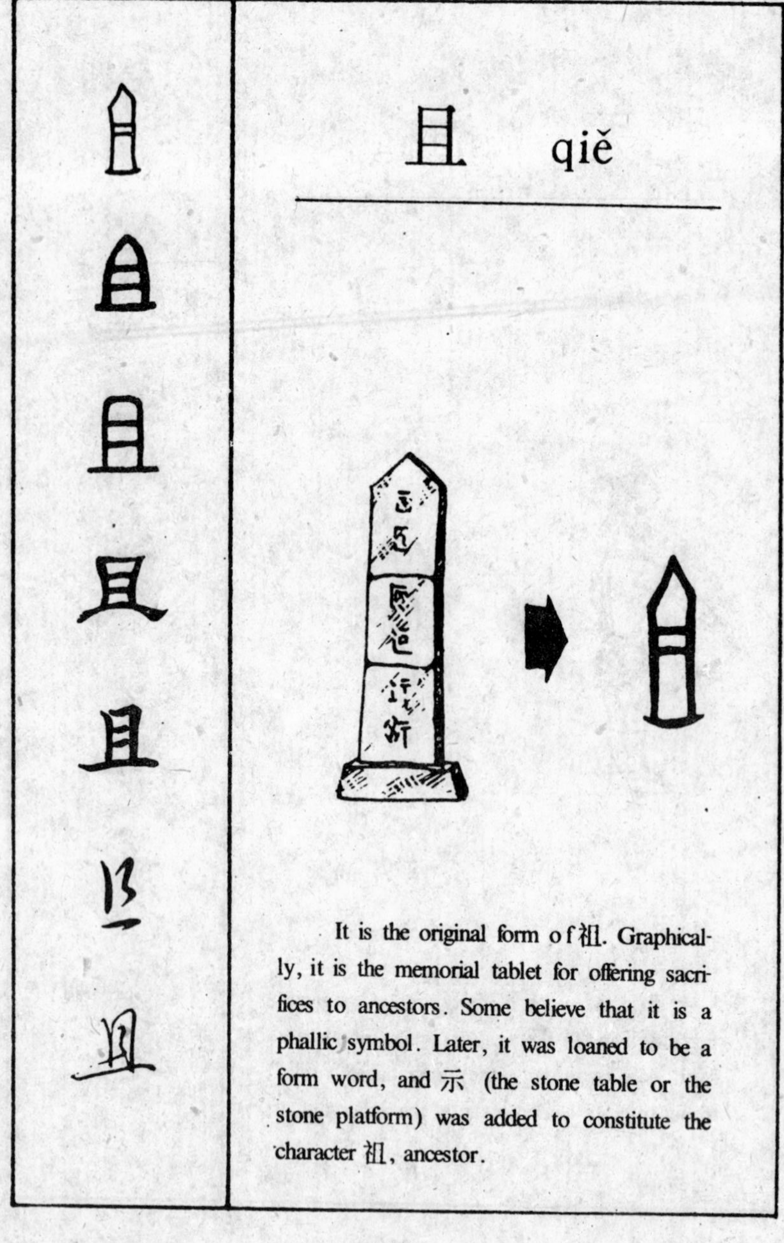

It is the original form of 祖. Graphically, it is the memorial tablet for offering sacrifices to ancestors. Some believe that it is a phallic symbol. Later, it was loaned to be a form word, and 示 (the stone table or the stone platform) was added to constitute the character 祖, ancestor.

妾 qiè

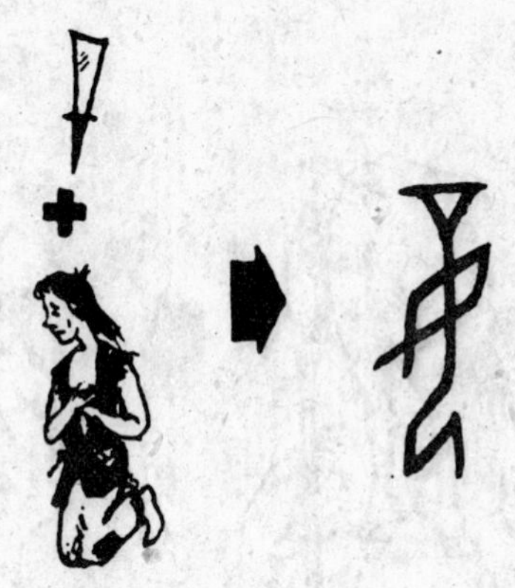

Its original meaning was "woman slave." In oracle bone inscriptions, its form was a kneeling woman with the symbol of punishment knife over her head, indicating she is a slave. Later, it came to mean a concubine.

侵 qīn

Its original meaning was "to advance gradually." In oracle bone inscriptions, its form was a hand with a broom sweeping off the dust on an ox, signifying "to clean gradually." In bronze inscriptions, it was a hand cleaning a man with a broom. Later, it extended to mean "to attack" and "to violate."

禽 qín

〔附〕 擒

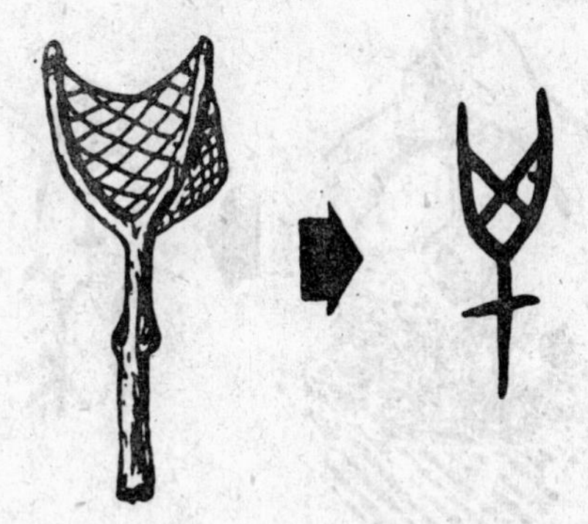

It is the original form of 擒. Its original meaning was "to capture." In oracle bone inscriptions, its form was a bird net with a shaft. The phonetic symbol 今 was added in bronze inscriptions. Later, it evolved into the general term for birds.

秦 qin

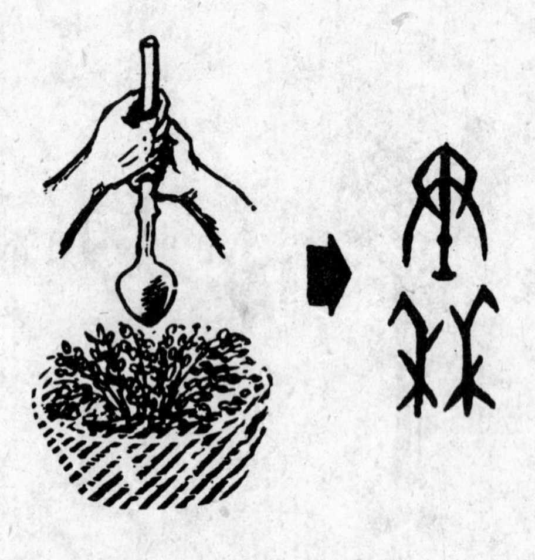

As an ideogrpah, originally it was a place name and an ancient kingdom, which is the center of today's Shaanxi Province. Since this region was rich in cereal production, this character is formed by two hands husking "rice" with a pestle. 夫 is the simplified version of 舂.

寝(寢)qǐn

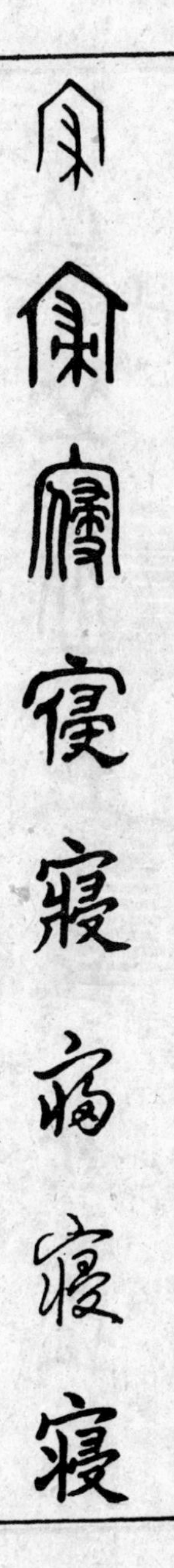

A broom is in a house, indicating the house is cleaned for people to take rest. Hence, its original meaning was "to lie down and take rest or sleep." It also means "bedroom." In ancient books, it was interchangeable with 寝.

丘 qiū

As a pictograph, its original meaning was "hill." In oracle bone inscriptions, its form was the vivid delineation of two hills. It changed gradually in bronze inscriptions and small seal characters. In official script, it did not resemble two hills.

求 qiú

〔附〕 裘

It is the original form of 裘. In oracle bone and bronze inscriptions, it was a pictograph symbolizing a fur coat. Later, it was loaned for use in 寻求, to seek, 乞求, to pray for, etc. The pictograph 裘 was invented to indicate its original meaning.

囚 qiú

Its form is a man cast into prison. Hence, its original meaning was "to take into custody." It also indicates the person sent to prison, the prisoner.

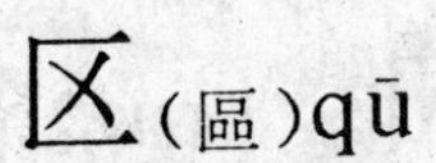

区(區)qū

〔附〕 瓯

As the original form of 瓯, a small ceramic food container, it is three small containers on a shelf. Later, it extended to mean 区别, difference,区域, region, etc., and 瓯 was then coined.

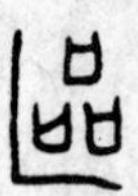

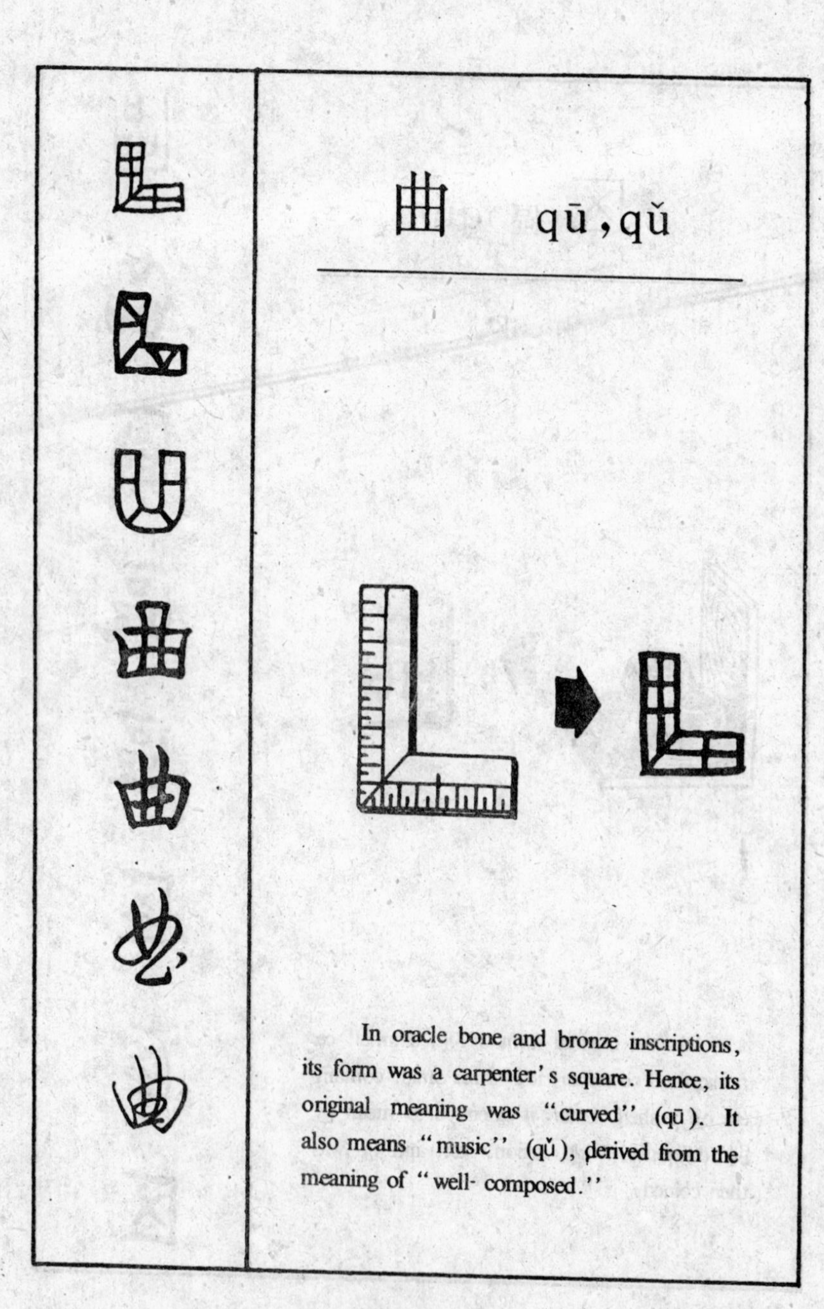

曲 qū，qǔ

In oracle bone and bronze inscriptions, its form was a carpenter's square. Hence, its original meaning was "curved" (qū). It also means "music" (qǔ), derived from the meaning of "well- composed."

取 qǔ

〔附〕娶

In ancient wars, the winners used to cut off the ears of dead enemies or prisoners. Its original meaning was "to overcome" and "to seize." It extends to mean "to take," "to marry a woman," etc. With the meaning "to marry a woman," it was later written as 娶.

去 qù

The upper part of this character is the form of a man and the lower part is the exit of the dwelling cave. Hence, its original meaning was "to go away."

泉 quán

Originally it indicated "water source" and "underground water." Its ancient form was a spring head among mountain rocks and from the head the spring is flowing. Since official script, graphically it is no longer a pictograph.

犬 quǎn

As a pictograph, its form is a dog with its tail bending upwards. It is the case especially in the early bronze inscriptions. In modern Chinese, it is usually used to form a compound rather than used singularly.

雀 què

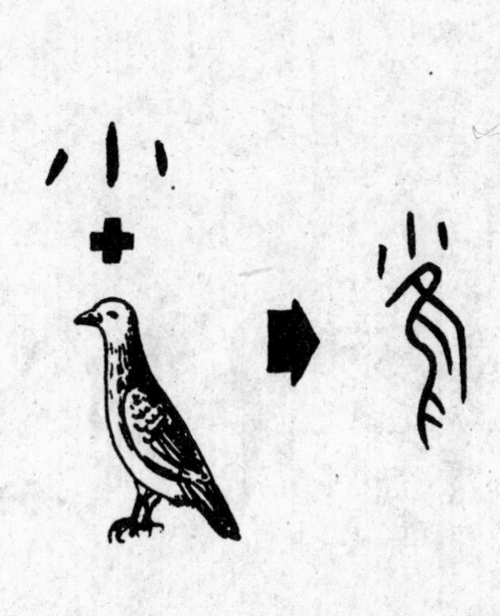

Its original meaning was "sparrow." It also serves as the general term for small birds for it is composed of 小, small, and 隹, zhuī, bird.

冉 rǎn

〔附〕 髯

It was the original form of 髯, rán, the whiskers. Graphically, it is the form of whiskers. It also means the beard. Later, it was mostly used to be 冉冉, to fall or rise softly or slowly. And the character 髯 was invented to convey the original meaning.

人 rén

As a pictograph, in oracle bone and bronze inscriptions, it is the side-viewed delineation of a man standing with one hand extending forward. Since official script, its form has changed a lot. The two strokes of this character became the two legs in regular script.

日 rì

It is a pictograph with the original meaning "sun." It extends to mean "the daytime" and "one day."

戎 róng

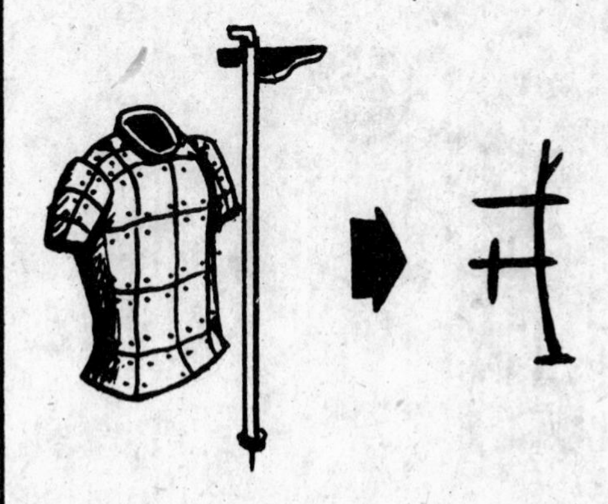

Composed of 戈, an ancient weapon, and 甲, armor, it is the general term for all weapons. It extends to mean "soldier," "war," etc.

如 rú

Its original meaning was "follower" and "to follow." It is composed of 口, order of the master and 女, obedient woman. Later, it was used as a conjunction.

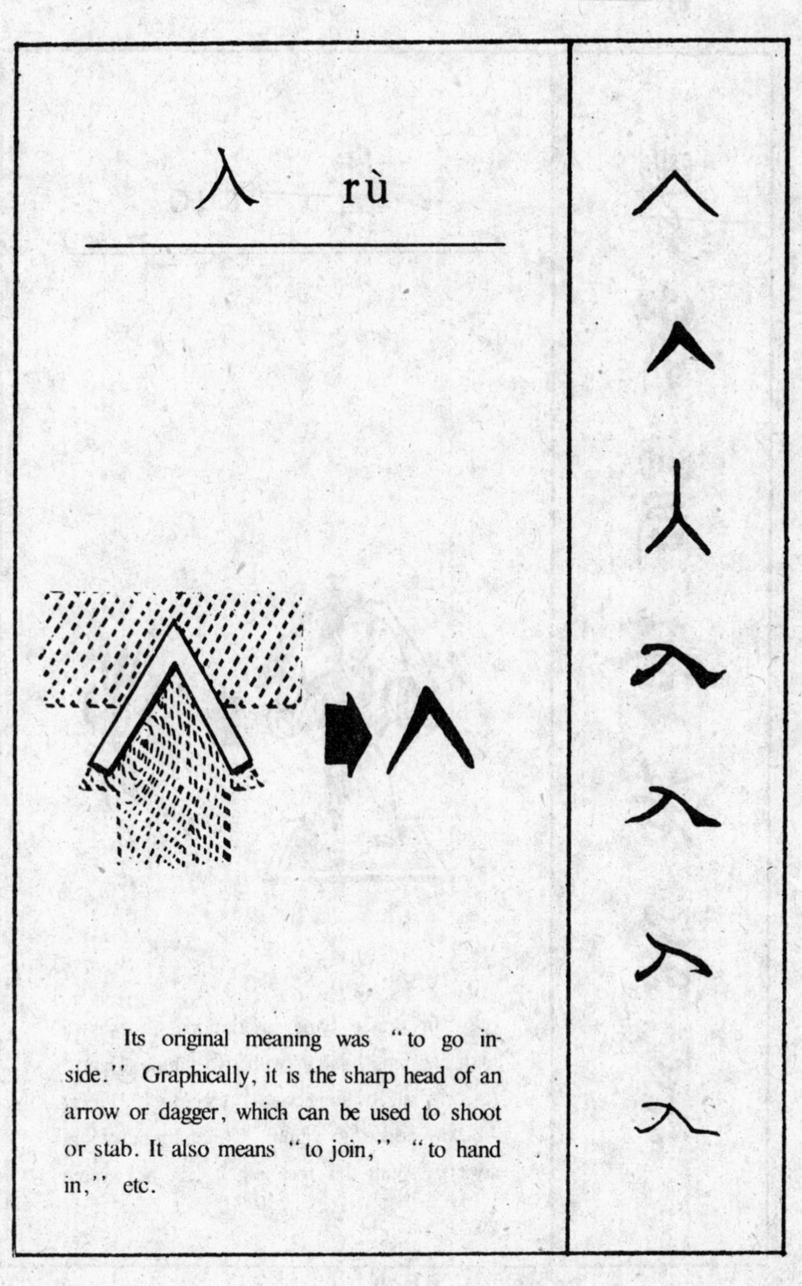

入 rù

Its original meaning was "to go inside." Graphically, it is the sharp head of an arrow or dagger, which can be used to shoot or stab. It also means "to join," "to hand in," etc.

若 ruò

〔附〕 诺

In oracle bone inscriptions, it was a man combing his hair with two hands. Hence, its original meaning was "smooth." Later, 口 was added to signify "an affirmative answer." With this meaning it can be written as 诺.

卅 sà

(10+10+10=30)

Its meaning is "thirty." In oracle bone and bronze inscriptions, 十 in most cases was represented by the vertical structure (see Case 十). Therefore, two 十 together are 廿 (see Case 廿); three 十 together are 卅.

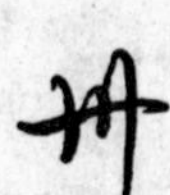

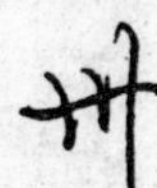

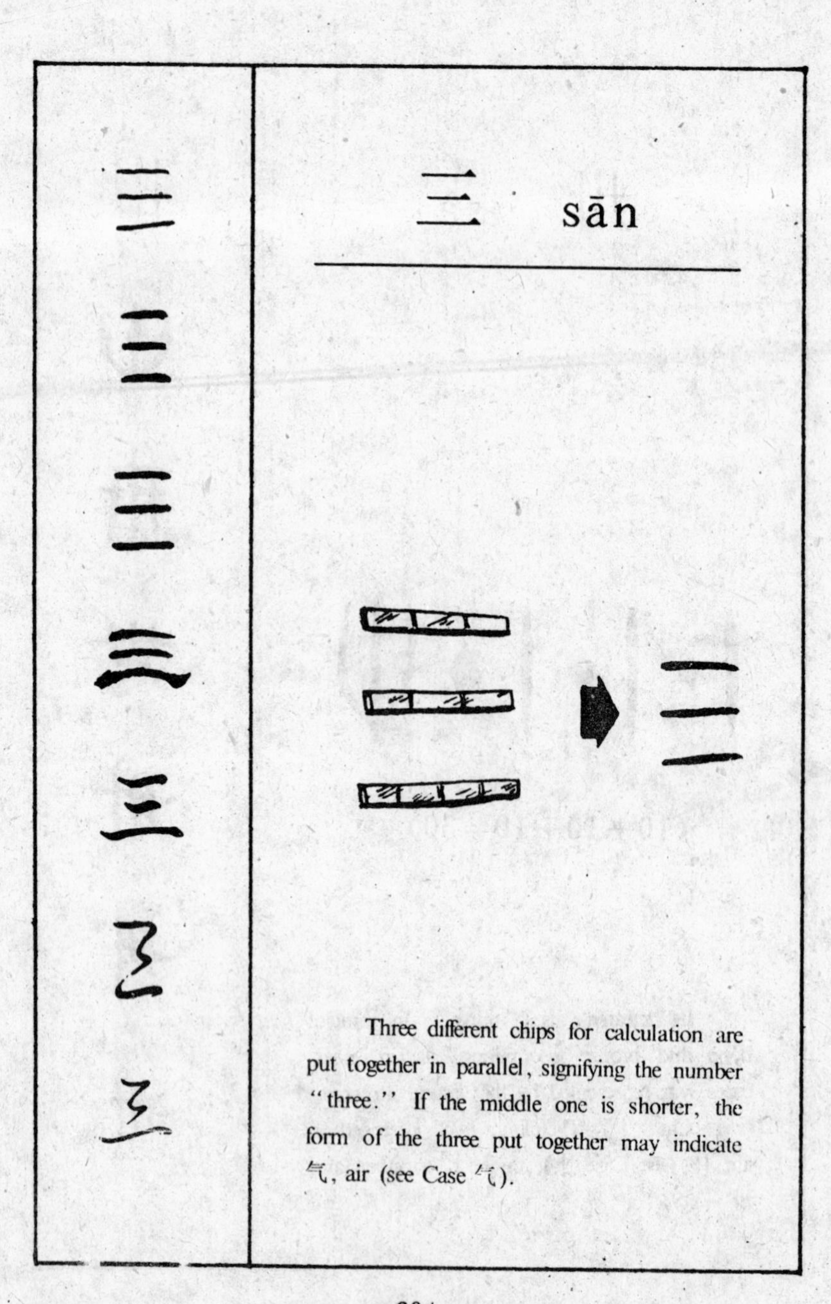

三 sān

Three different chips for calculation are put together in parallel, signifying the number "three." If the middle one is shorter, the form of the three put together may indicate 气, air (see Case 气).

丧(喪)sāng

〔附〕 桑

Graphically, it is a mulberry tree. In oracle bone inscriptions, 桑 and 丧 share the same form. In bronze inscriptions, the radical 亡 was added to indicate 丧亡, to die. In ancient times, 桑主, the tablet of the dead, was made up of mulberry wood, which may give some insight to the formation of this character.

啬(嗇)sè

〔附〕 穑

As the original form of 穑, it has the original meaning "to harvest the crops." Graphically, it is the ripe crops in the fields or the crops piled up on a stone for preparation.

山 shān

Its original meaning was "the part bulging from the surface." As a pictograph, it is the likeness of three peaks, which were of the same height in oracle bone inscriptions. In bronze inscriptions, the middle one was emphasized.

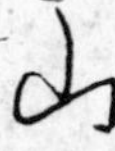

商 shāng

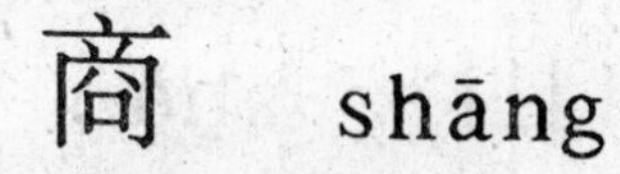

It was the original form of 赏. In oracle bone inscriptions, it was a vessel of wine put on a stand, signifying the thing to be awarded. In oracle bone and bronze inscriptions, 商 was replaced by 赏.

上 shàng

It is a self-explanatory character. Graphically, it is composed of two horizontal planes of which the lower, longer one is the horizon and the upper short one is the indicative symbol. In order to be distinguished from 二, two, with the two horizontal planes of the same length, its form gradually changed.

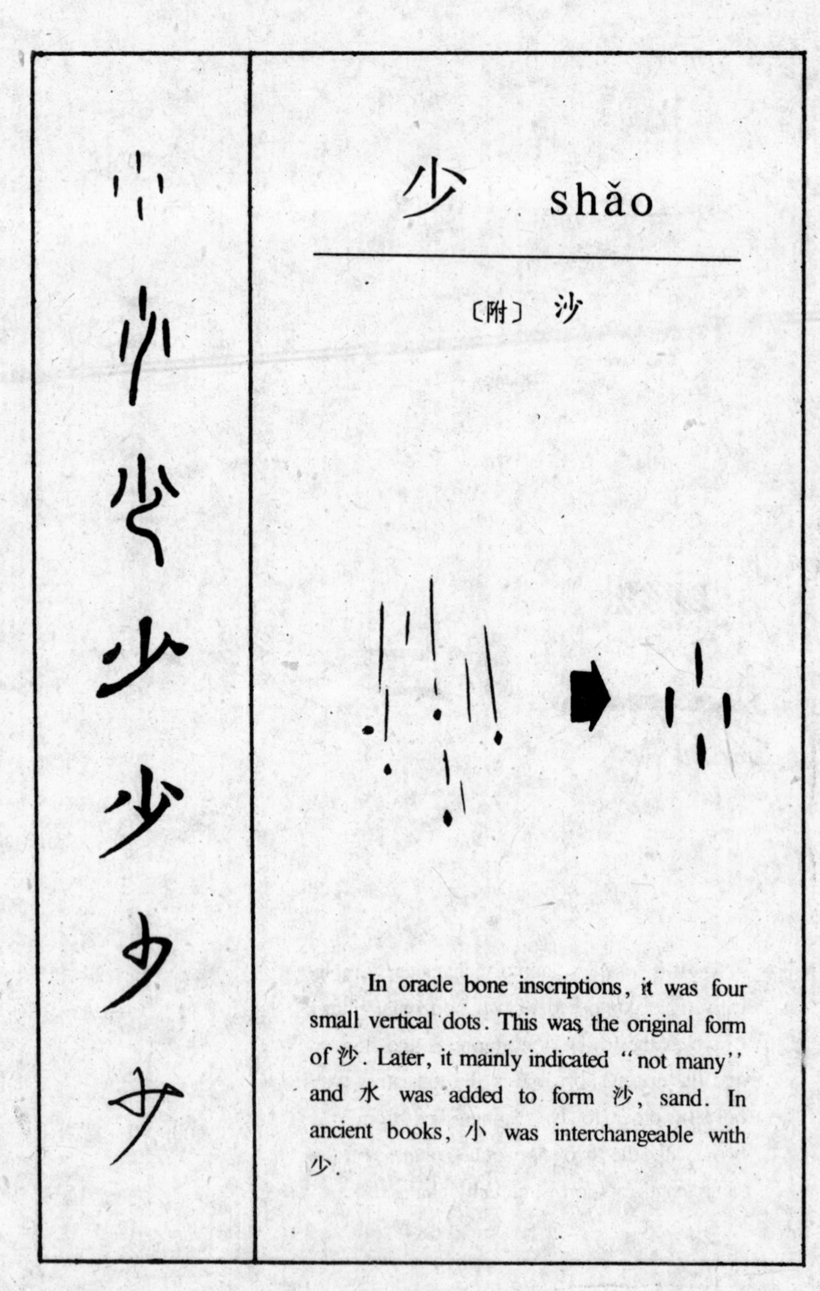

少 shǎo

〔附〕 沙

In oracle bone inscriptions, it was four small vertical dots. This was the original form of 沙. Later, it mainly indicated "not many" and 水 was added to form 沙, sand. In ancient books, 小 was interchangeable with 少.

舌 shé

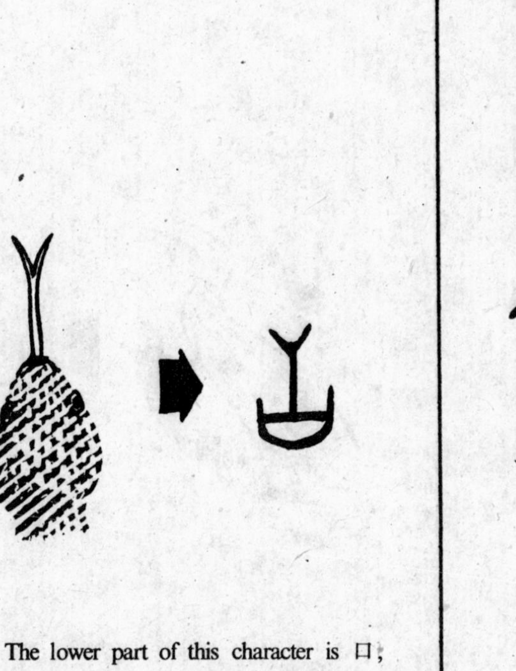

The lower part of this character is 口, mouth, and the upper part is the tongue extending out. Probably because the difference between the man's tongue and the animal's tongue is very slight, the snake's tongue is used to be the indicative symbol for the tongue in general.

涉　shè

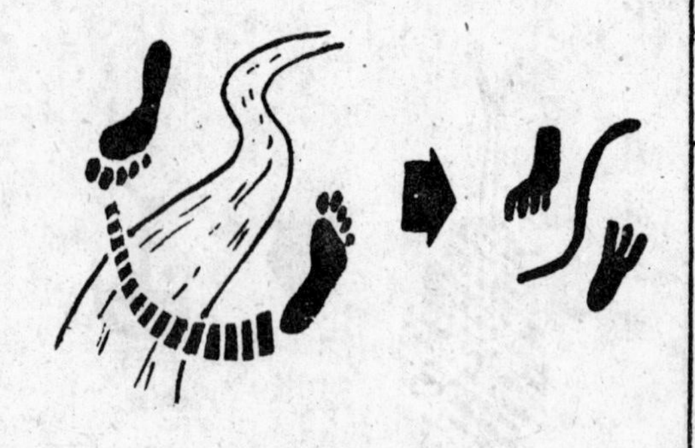

Its original meaning was "to wade across a stream." Graphically, it is a winding stream with one foot on each bank. It is an ideograph. Now, 跋山涉水, "to climb mountains and ford rivers" is still used.

射　shè

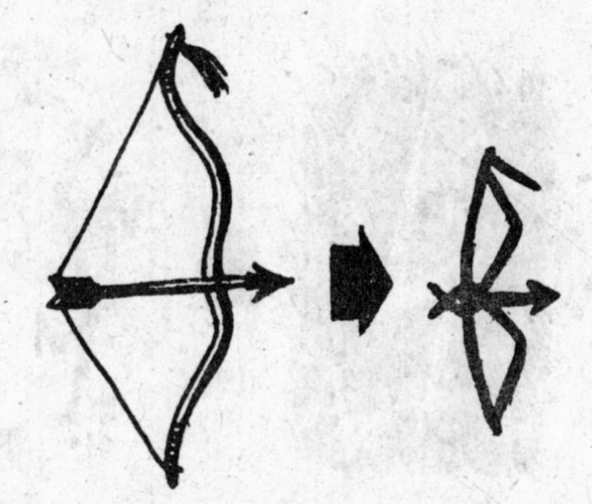

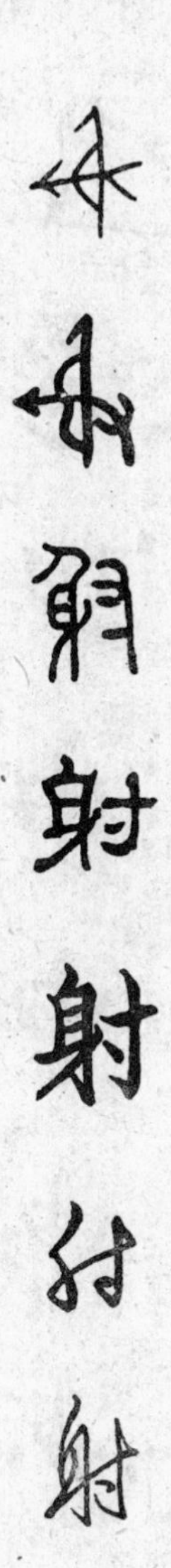

In oracle bone inscriptions, graphically it was an arrow to be shot from the bow. In bronze inscriptions, 又, hand, was added. In small seal characters, 弓 evolved into 身, and 又 evolved into 寸 forming 射.

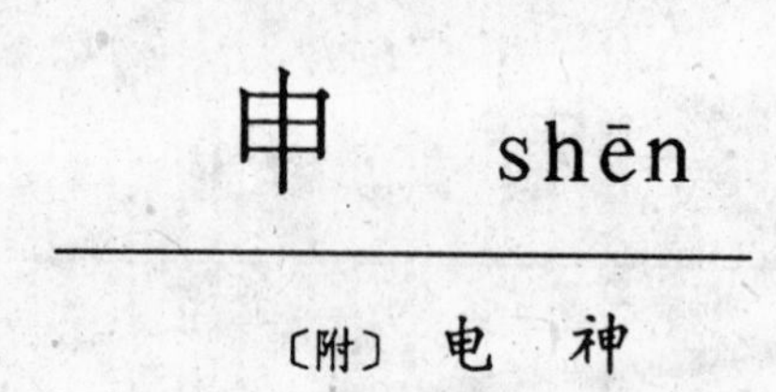

申 shēn

〔附〕电 神

It is the original form of 电. Graphically, it is the curved lightning flashes appearing in the clouds. The ancient people believed lightning was the manifestation of god. Hence, 神 was represented by 申. Later, 示 was added to form 神, and 雨 was added to form 電.

身 shēn

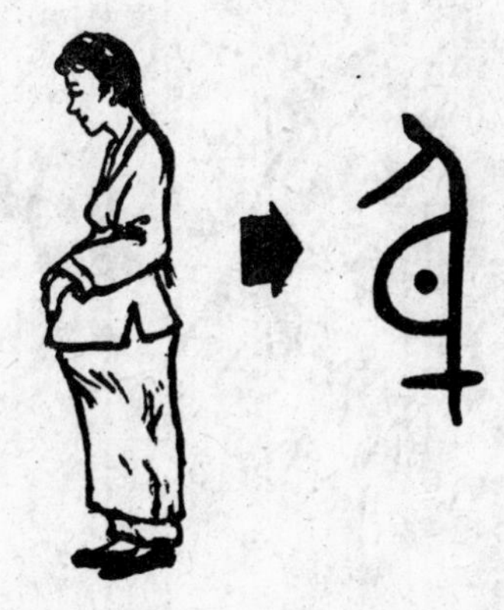

Its original meaning was "pregnancy." Graphically, it is a woman standing with her belly protruding and the dot on it is a self-explanatory symbol representing the fetus. Later, it extended to mean "health," "self," "in person," etc.

沈 shěn

〔附〕沉

沈 and 沉 are in the same form. Its original meaning was 沉没, to sink and disappear. In oracle bone inscriptions, it was an ox (or a sheep) being drowned in the stream. In bronze inscriptions, it was the form of man with fetters being drowned.

生 shēng

Graphically, it is a seedling from the earth. Hence, its original meaning was "to grow" or "to sprout." It also extends to mean "to bear a child," "life," etc.

升 shēng

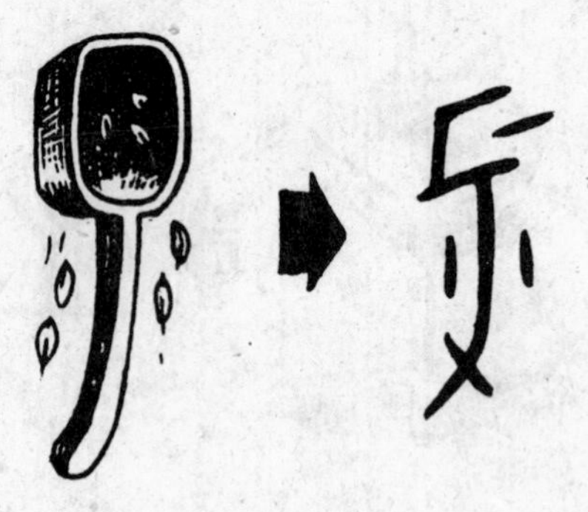

As a unit of measurement, it is a liter or one-tenth of a 斗, ten liters. In oracle bone and bronze inscriptions, 升 and 斗 were almost in the same form (see Case 斗). Their difference lay only in the short horizontal plane(s) in the spoon of the former symbolizing the paddy.

圣(聖)shèng

〔附〕 听

Originally, it indicated "a clever man." Later, it indicated "a man of wisdom and virtue." Graphically, it is composed of 人, 耳 and 口, signifying a man with sharp ears and tongue. In ancient books, it was interchangeable with 听.

尸 shī

Graphically, it is a sitting man as viewed from the side. Its original meaning was "a dead man being worshiped with sacrificial offerings." It also indicates "corpse" and is written 屍 with this meaning. It is interchangeable with 夷, a name for a nationality in ancient times.

食 shí

〔附〕饲

Its original meaning was "food." Graphically, it is a food container. Generally, it is used as a verb, indicating 吃, "to eat." It is pronounced sì, interchangeable with 饲 when it means "to give food to somebody to eat."

旹 旹 時 時 時 时 時 时

时(時)shí

As a pictophonetic character, its original meaning was "season" (of the four seasons of the year). Its initial form was 旹, of which 日 indicates meaning and 㞢 (i.e. 之) indicates the sound. Later, it evolved into 時 of which 日 indicates meaning and 寺 indicates the sound.

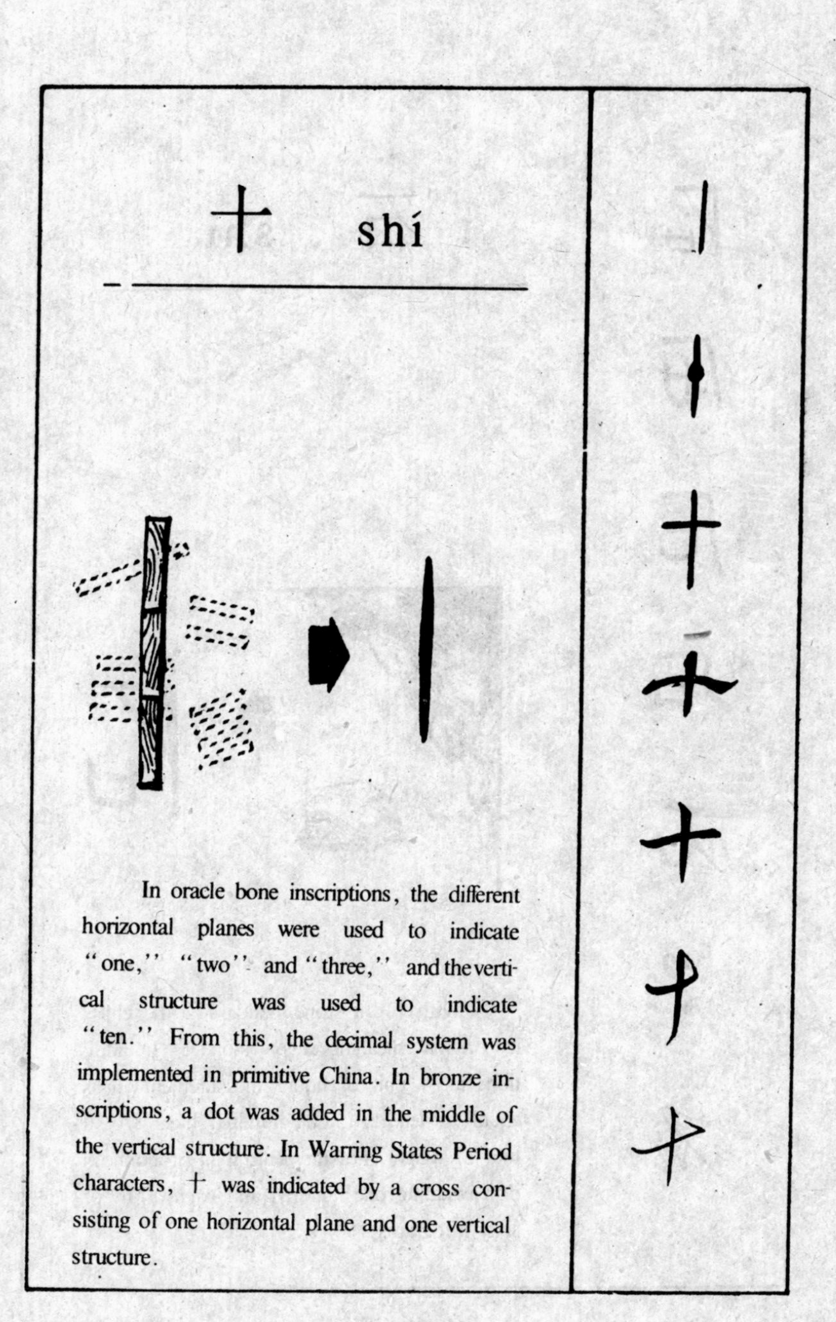

十 shí

In oracle bone inscriptions, the different horizontal planes were used to indicate "one," "two" and "three," and the vertical structure was used to indicate "ten." From this, the decimal system was implemented in primitive China. In bronze inscriptions, a dot was added in the middle of the vertical structure. In Warring States Period characters, 十 was indicated by a cross consisting of one horizontal plane and one vertical structure.

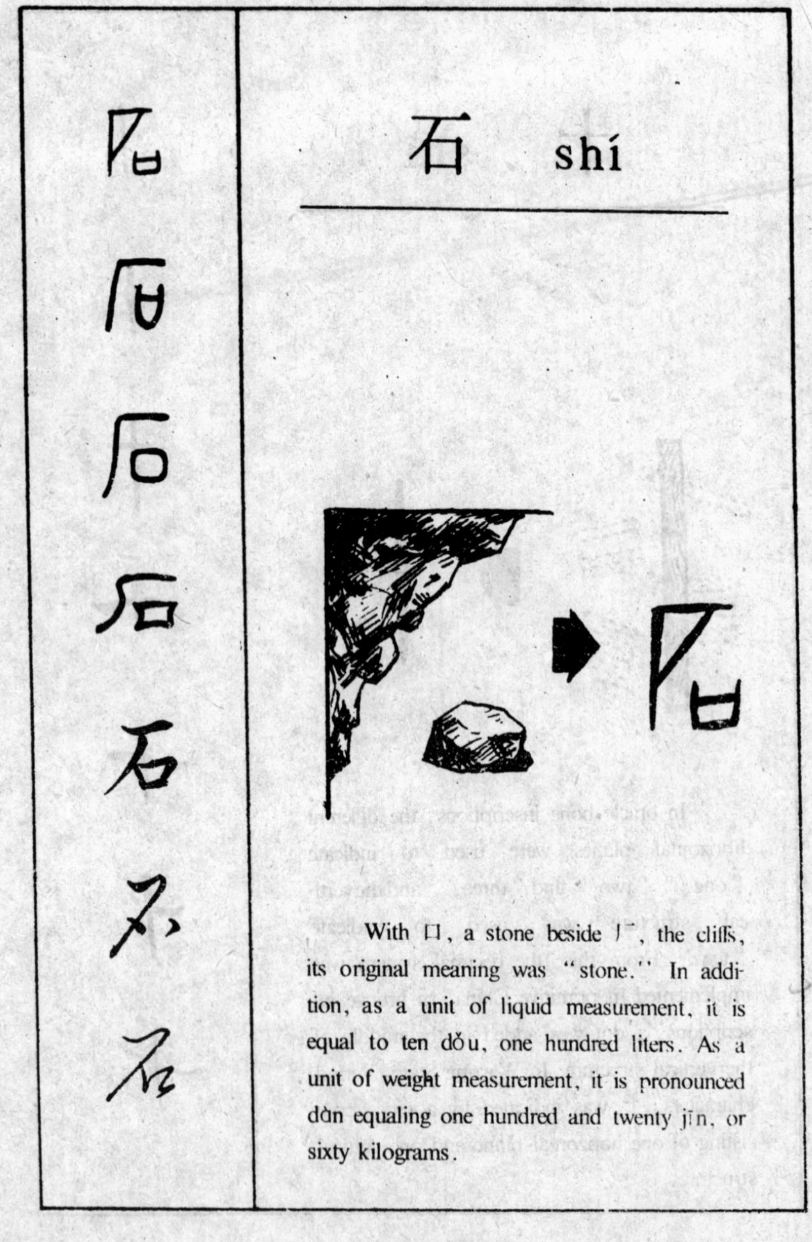

石 shí

With 口, a stone beside 厂, the cliffs, its original meaning was "stone." In addition, as a unit of liquid measurement, it is equal to ten dǒu, one hundred liters. As a unit of weight measurement, it is pronounced dàn equaling one hundred and twenty jīn, or sixty kilograms.

史 shǐ

〔附〕吏使事

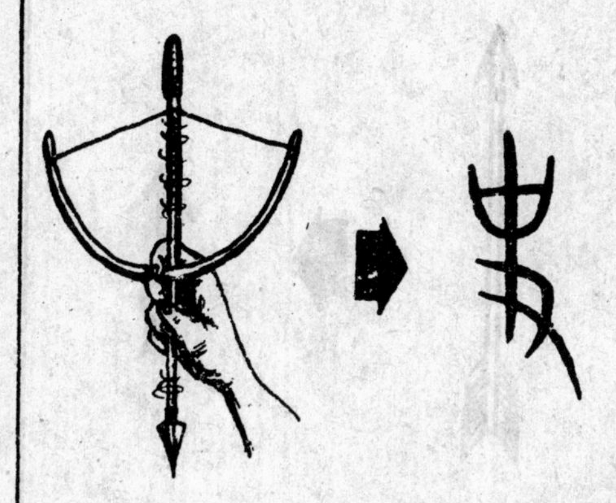

Its original meaning was "the official in charge of chronicles" or "an historian." In primitive times, the chronicle officials were responsible for divination. So a hand holding a bow drill (to mark the oracle bones to seek the divine guidance) indicates this official. Actually 史, 吏, 使 and 事 originate from the same form. Later, they became different in form as well as in meaning.

矢 shǐ

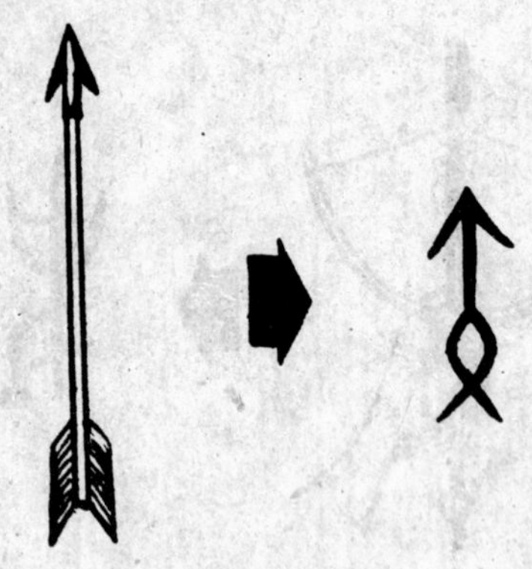

Its original meaning was "arrow." In ancient writings, obviously it was the form of an arrow: the upper part is the arrowhead, the middle is the shaft and the lower part is the tail. Today, the idiom 有的放矢, "to shoot the arrow at the target" is still in use.

豕 shǐ

Its original meaning was "pig." Its form in oracle bone inscriptions was like a pig with its head turned upward, its tail turned downward and the middle part symbolizing the fat body. The comparison with 犬 reveals the different features of the two animals in which the tail of "dog" bends upwards and its body is very thin.

示　shì

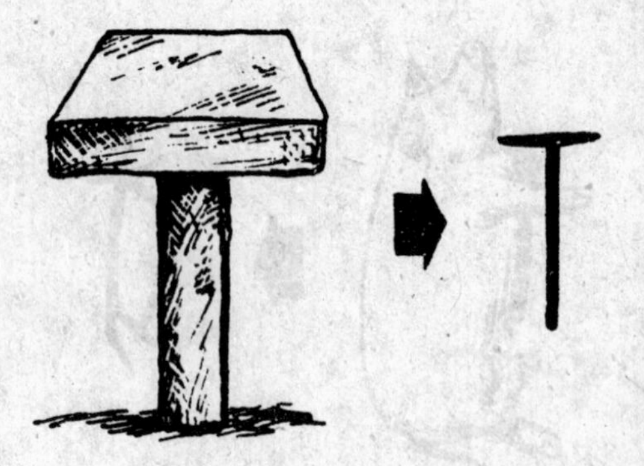

Originally, it was the stone table for offering ceremonial sacrifices to the gods. Later, it evolved into 示 (qí, also 祇), and it was very easily mistaken as 示 (shì). Characters with the radical 示 always pertain to ritual ceremonies, worship or prayer.

氏 shì

From its forms in Warring States Period characters, graphically it was a wood post with a dragon-shaped or snake-shaped totem above, which was the symbol of a clan. Its original meaning was "the title for the clan," which was enjoyed by aristocrats exclusively in ancient times.

首 shǒu

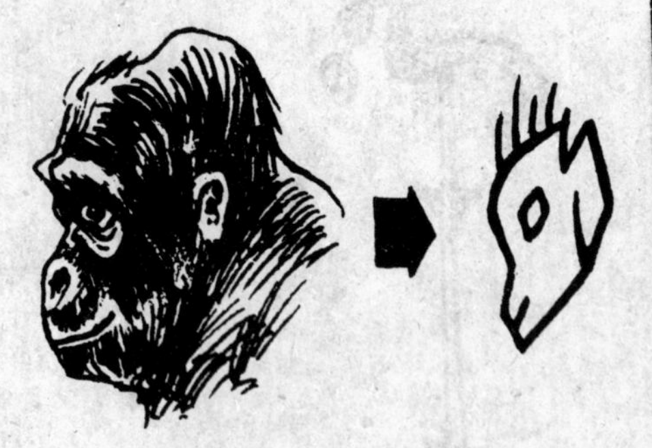

Graphically, it was the head of a beast (rather than a man) in oracle bone inscriptions. In bronze inscriptions, one eye and the hair were used to symbolize the head.

受 shòu

〔附〕授

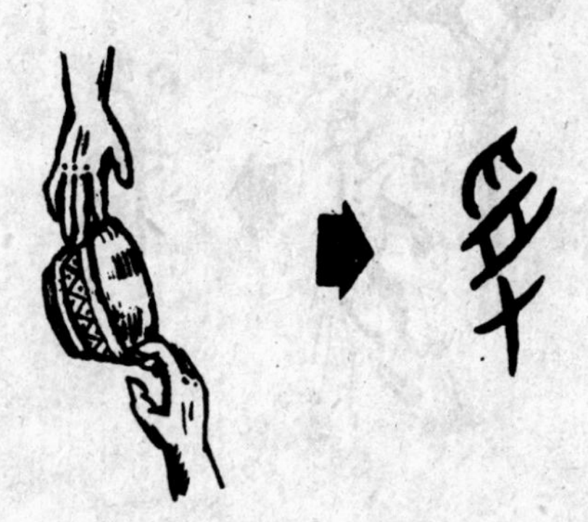

In oracle bone inscriptions, graphically it was a man's hand sending a plate (see 凡 and 盘) to another man's hand, signifying "to give" (授) and "to receive" (受) at the same time. In ancient books, 授 and 受 were written in the same form.

兽(獸)shòu

〔附〕 狩

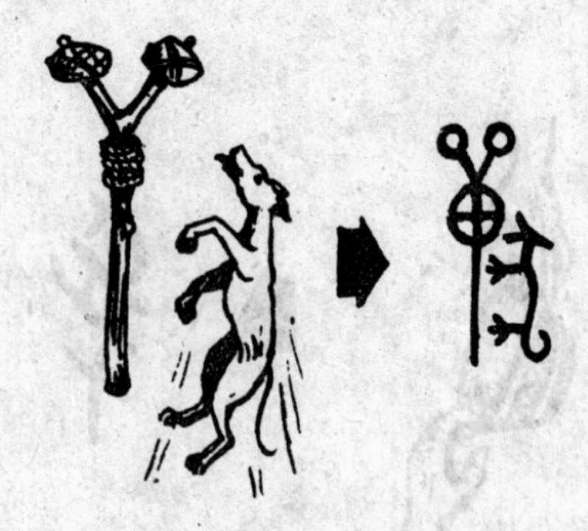

The left part of this character, 单 (see Case 单) is the weapon used to capture wild animals, while the right part is a hunting dog. Hence, its original meaning was "to hunt." Later, it evolved into 狩. And the game of the hunt became 獸, of which the simplified version is 兽.

黍 shǔ

Unlike a paddy, the spike of broomcorn millet is dispersed, hence its form in oracle bone inscriptions was obvious. In addition, water is near the stalk in some forms of this character, indicating that it can be used for brewing wine.

蜀 shǔ

〔附〕 蠋

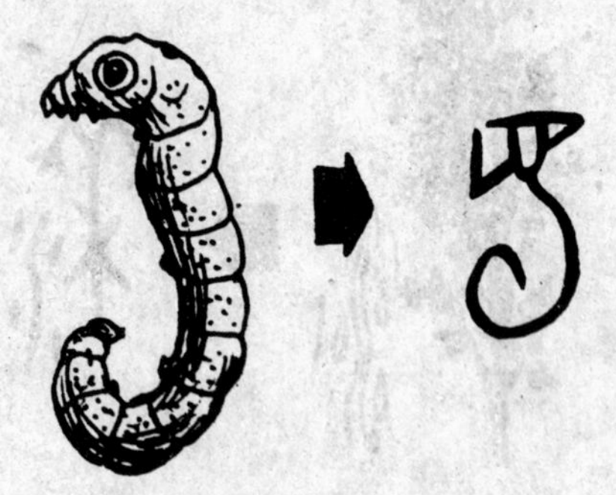

Its original meaning was "moth or butterfly larva." As a pictograph in oracle bone inscriptions, it emphasized the big eyes and the curved body of a worm. In bronze inscriptions, the radical 虫 was added to form 蠋, zhú. Later, it was used for special name.

戍 shù

Graphically, it is a soldier (人) holding a weapon (戈). Hence, its original meaning was "soldier guarding the front." Today, the phrases 卫戍, 戍边, etc. are still in use.

束 shù

Its original meaning was "to bind." It also means "a handful" or "a bundle of." Graphically, it is a rope binding the firewood (or cotton sack in some forms). Today, 束缚，一束，约束 and other phrases are in use.

水 shuǐ

As a pictograph, the winding part in the center indicates flowing water and the dots on the sides signify drops of water or waves. In ancient books, it was also used to indicate "stream" and "river."

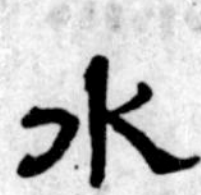

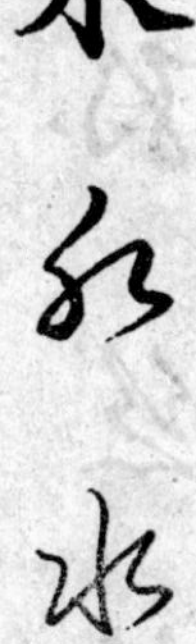
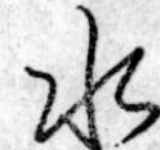

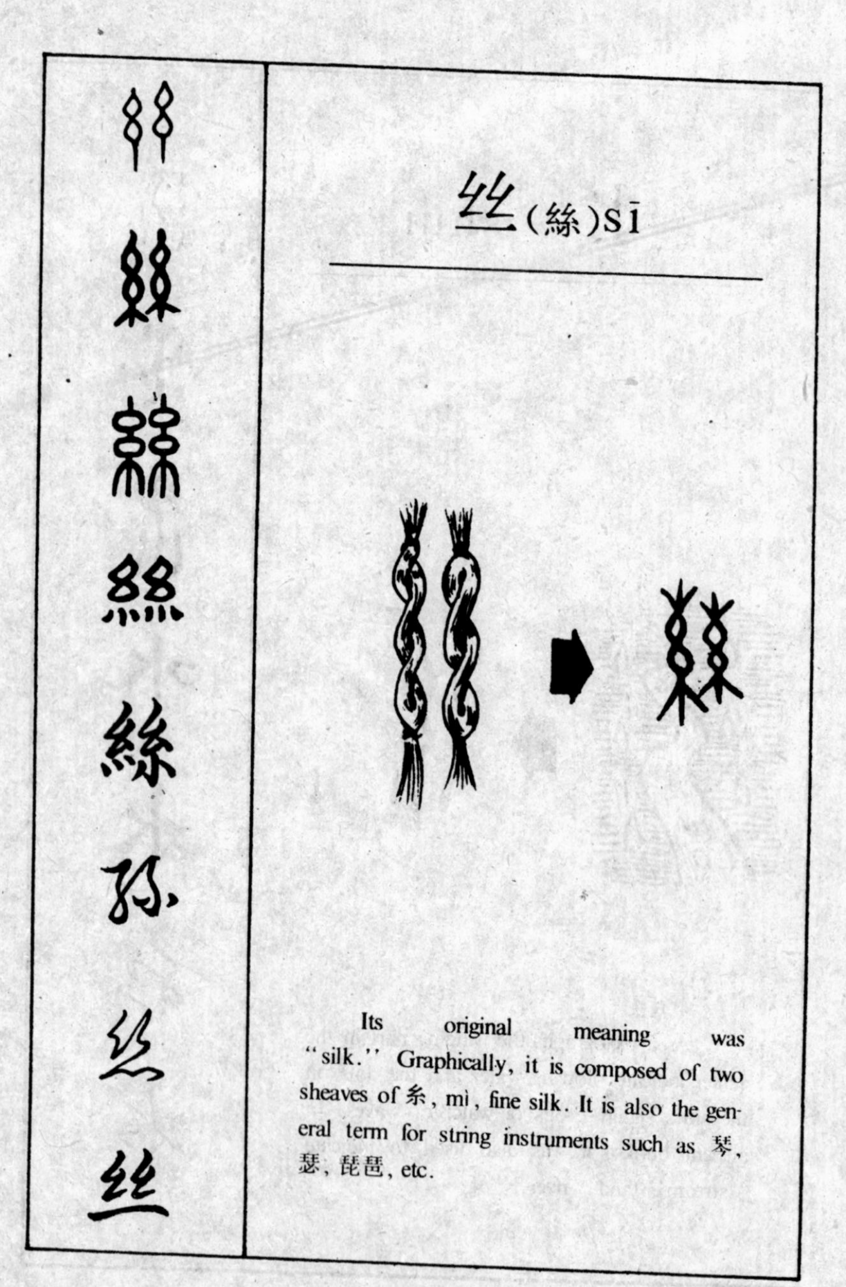

丝(絲)sī

Its original meaning was "silk." Graphically, it is composed of two sheaves of 糸, mì, fine silk. It is also the general term for string instruments such as 琴, 瑟, 琵琶, etc.

司 sī

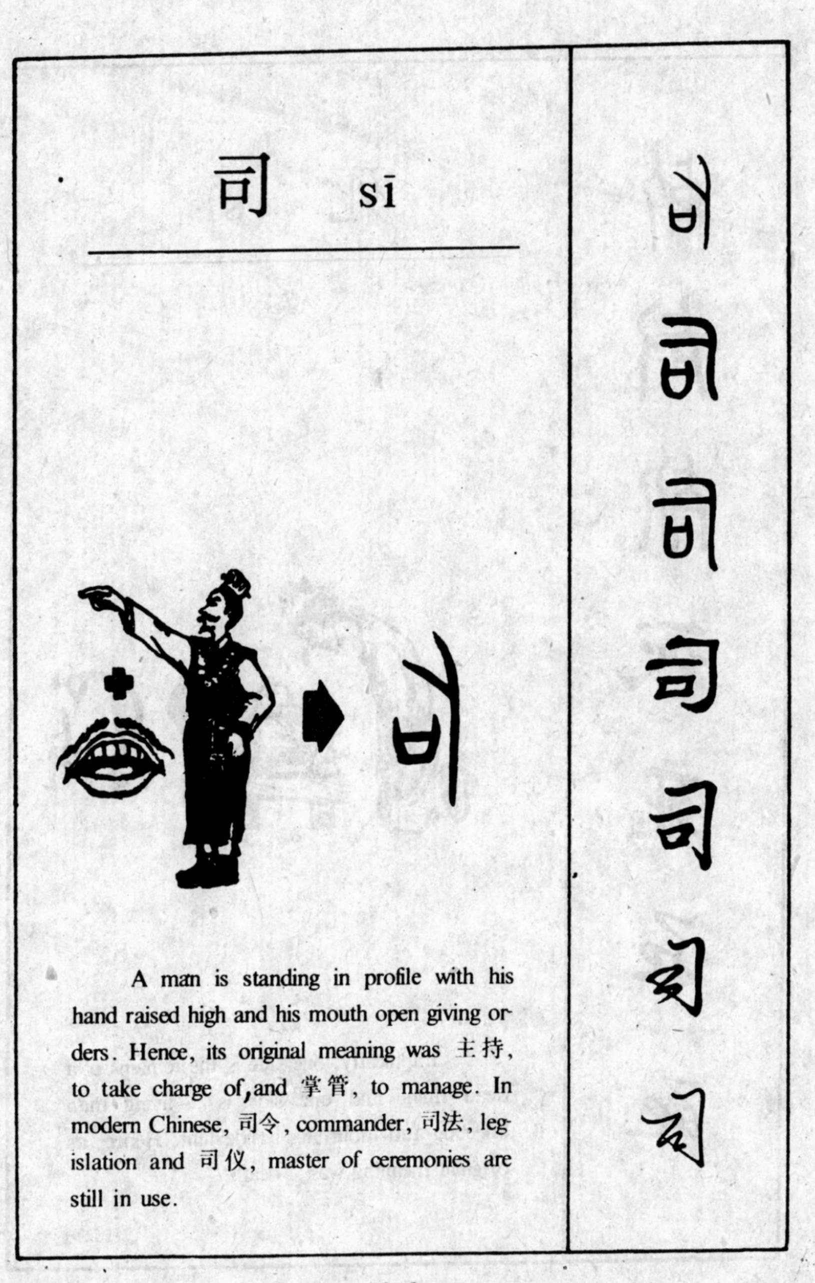

A man is standing in profile with his hand raised high and his mouth open giving orders. Hence, its original meaning was 主持, to take charge of, and 掌管, to manage. In modern Chinese, 司令, commander, 司法, legislation and 司仪, master of ceremonies are still in use.

死 sǐ

Graphically, one side is the remains of a dead man, and one side is a living man kneeling and mourning beside him. Hence, its original meaning was "death."

四 sì

In oracle bone and bronze inscriptions, the four horizontal planes indicated the number "four." Later, 四, which graphically meant "to breathe," was loaned to indicate "four" and thence 呬 (xì) was coined to mean "to breathe."

祀 sì

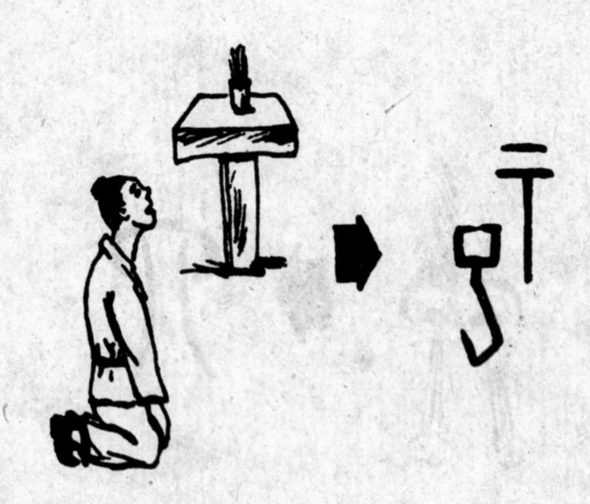

Graphically, a man is kneeling and worshipping before the sacrificial altar (see Case 示). Hence, its original meaning was "to kneel and worship gods or ancestors." The radical 巳 is a phonetic symbol.

夙 sù

Its original meaning was "early." Graphically, a setting moon in the sky and a man laboring with his hands formed 夙 in oracle bone and bronze inscriptions. It extends to mean 旧, 平素, e.g. 夙愿, will and wish, 宿怨, lasting hatred.

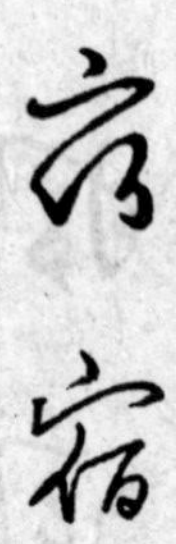

宿 sù

Its original meaning was "a lodging." Graphically, in a house a man is sleeping on the bamboo mat of which the lines can be seen clearly. Later, for the sake of writing convenience, the man and the mat were separated.

索 suǒ

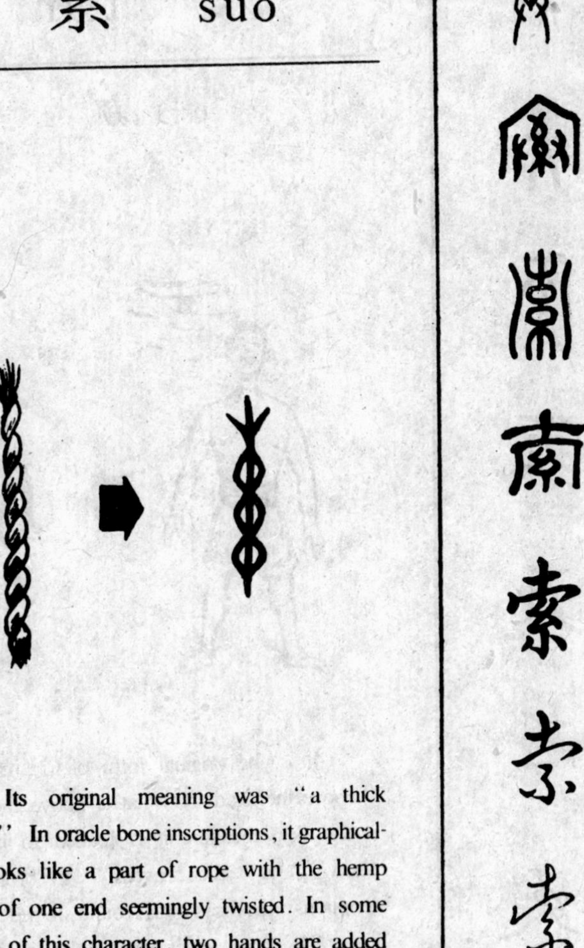

Its original meaning was "a thick rope." In oracle bone inscriptions, it graphically looks like a part of rope with the hemp fiber of one end seemingly twisted. In some forms of this character, two hands are added signifying making rope by twisting hemp fibers between the palms.

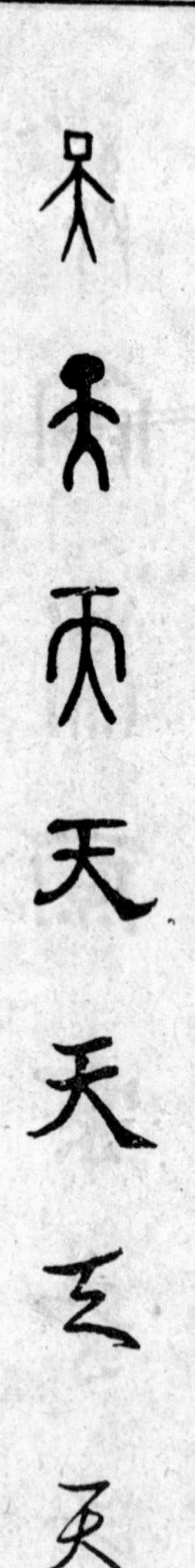

天 tiān

〔附〕颠

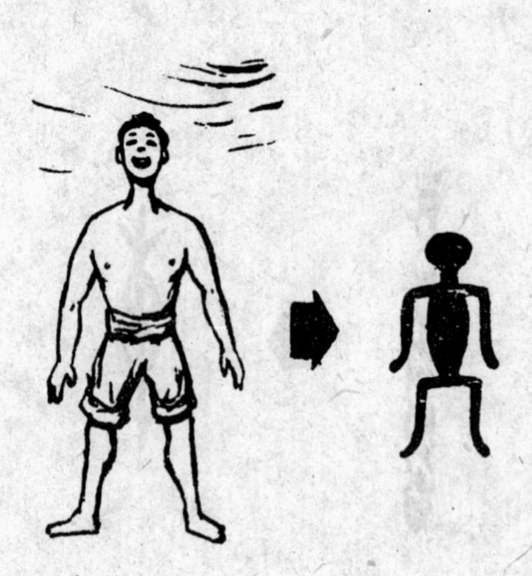

It is the original form of 颠, meaning "above the head." What is above the head is the sky, therefore it is loaned to indicate "sky" and "the heavens." In bronze inscriptions, the head was round-shaped, while in oracle bone inscriptions, the head was marked with a square or a horizontal plane for the sake of inscribing convenience.

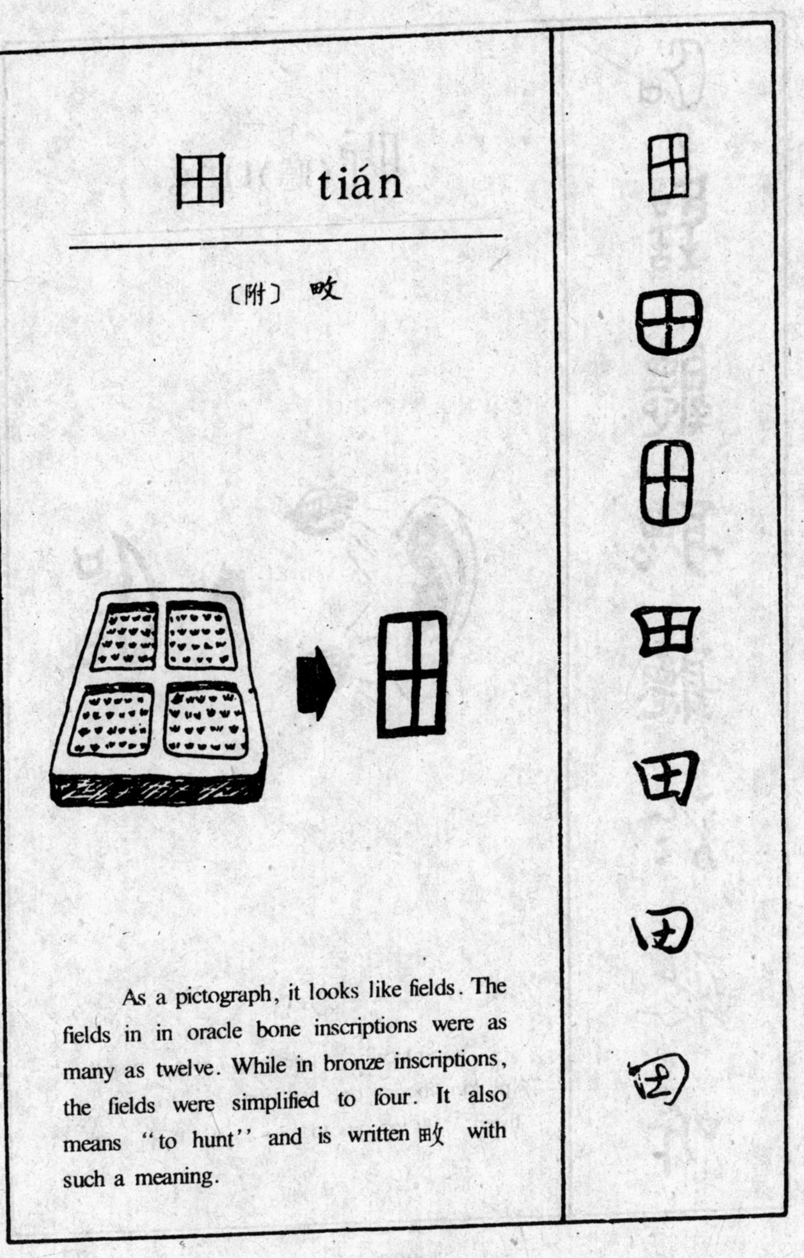

田 tián

〔附〕畋

As a pictograph, it looks like fields. The fields in in oracle bone inscriptions were as many as twelve. While in bronze inscriptions, the fields were simplified to four. It also means "to hunt" and is written 畋 with such a meaning.

聽

聽

听

听(聽)tīng

Graphically, one or two mouths speaking beside one ear signifies "to hear or listen." It extends to mean 听从, 听任, etc.

同　tóng

The upper part of this character is 凡, indicating "all" and the lower part is 口, indicating "to speak." Since it signifies all with one voice, its original meaning was "common," or "resemblance."

徒 tú

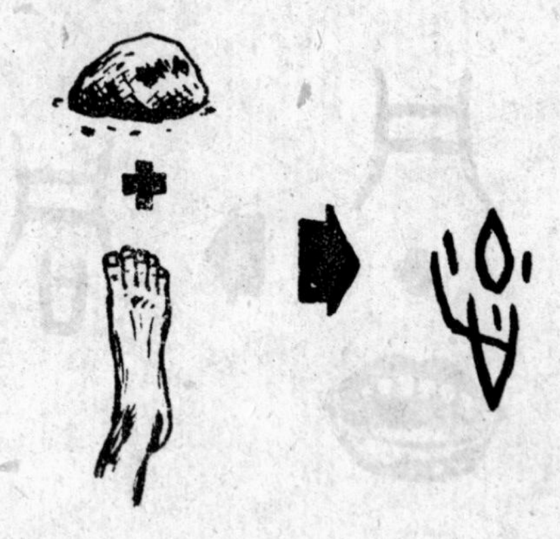

Its original meaning was "to walk." In oracle bone inscriptions, the upper phonetic 土 and lower graphic 止 constituted this character. Since bronze inscriptions, the radical 彳, to walk, was added. Now 徒步, to walk, is still in use.

土 tǔ

As a pictograph, graphically it is a dust heap. In its early graphs and bronze inscriptions, the delineation was in thick lines, while in oracle bone inscriptions, it was in fine lines for the sake of inscribing convenience.

兔 tù

As a pictograph, it is a vivid delineation of a rabbit: long ears, agile body, short legs and a tail. Later, it ceased to resemble a rabbit.

屯　tún

〔附〕 纯

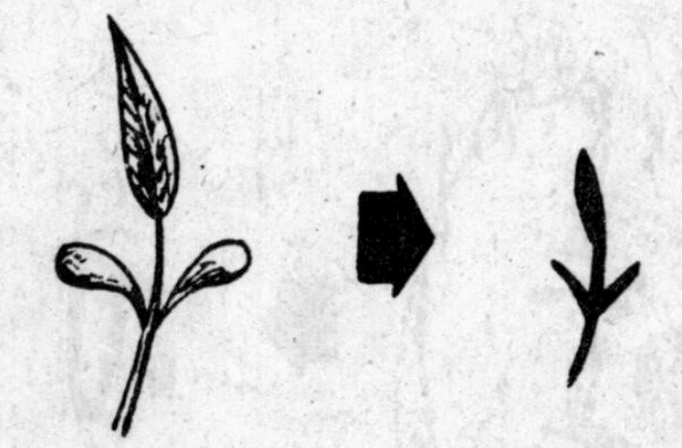

It is the original form of 春, which in oracle bone inscriptions was written as 屯. Graphically, it is a seedling sprouting out of the earth. In bronze inscriptions, it was loaned to be 纯, silk. Later, it mostly indicated "to assemble," "to station troops," etc.

豚 tún

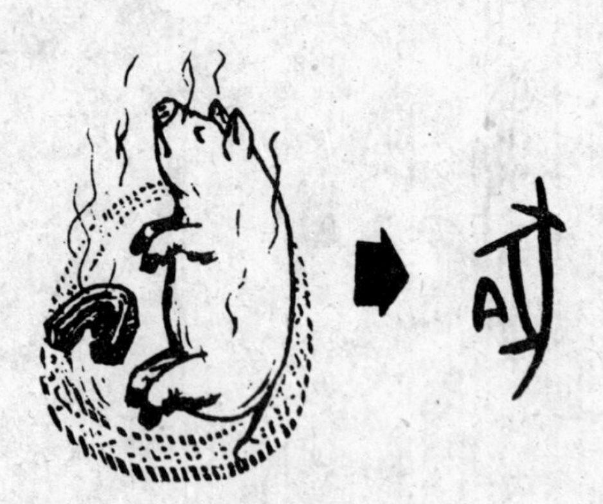

Its original meaning was "a piglet." It was composed of 豕, pig, and 月, meat, in oracle bone inscriptions, while in bronze inscriptions 又, hand, was added, symbolizing a pig raised to be eaten.

妥 tuǒ

〔附〕 绥

Graphically, a huge hand pushes down a kneeling woman, indicating "to control." Hence, its original meaning was "stable" and "firm." Later, it was written as 绥 when with such a meaning.

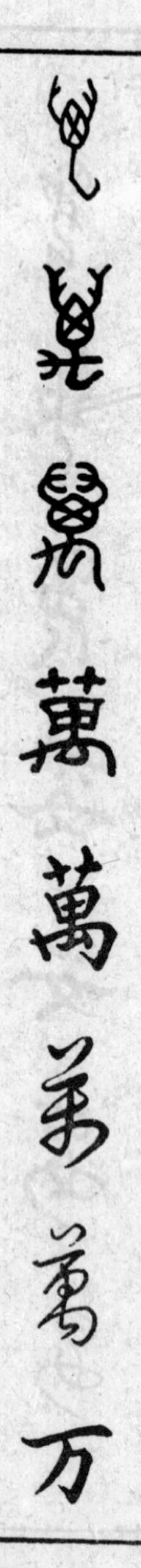

万(萬)wàn

〔附〕 虿

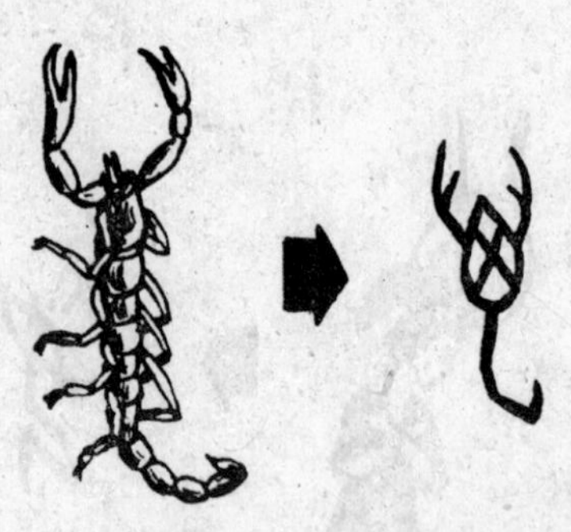

Its original meaning was "scorpion." In oracle bone and bronze inscriptions, it was vivid portrait of a scorpion with body and limbs. Later, it was loaned to be the numeral ten thousand, and was written as 蠆 (虿, chai). The simplified version "万" came in use during the Han Dynasty.

王 wáng

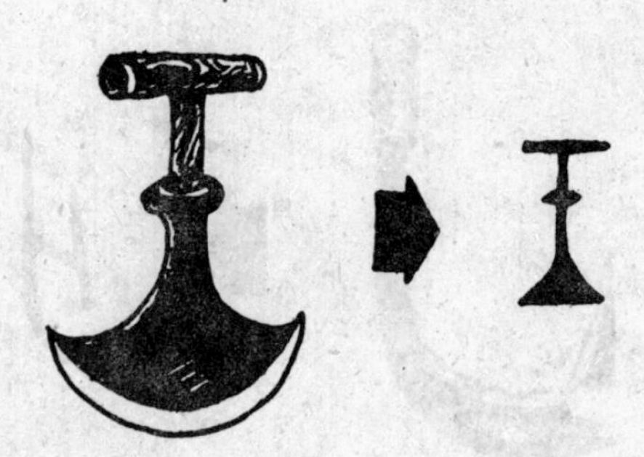

As its original form, graphically this character is a huge ax with shaft on the top and wide blade on the bottom, symbolizing power and authority. Hence, 王 was the title for the highest rulers in ancient times, i.e. king.

亡 wáng

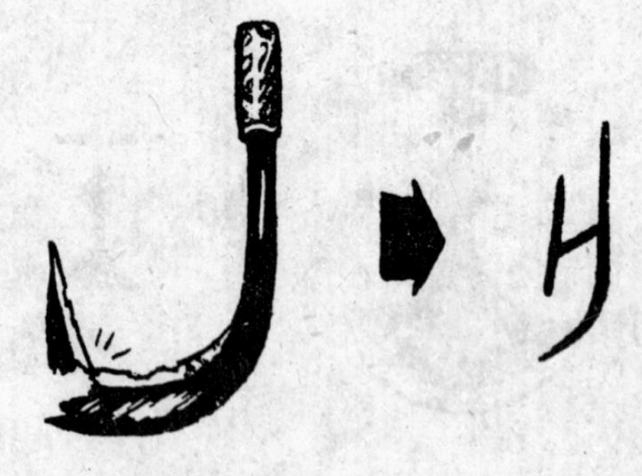

Graphically, it is like a broken sickle, which is useless. It extends to mean "to die," or "to destroy." In ancient writings, it was loaned to be 无, indicating "nothing," "no," etc.

往 wǎng

Its original meaning was "to go." In oracle bone inscriptions, the upper part of this character was 止, foot, indicating meaning and the lower phonetic symbol 王, king. The radical 彳 was added since the time of bronze inscriptions.

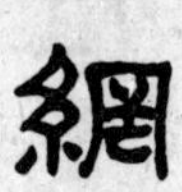

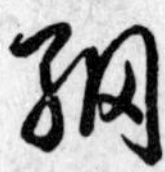

网(網)wǎng

〔附〕罔

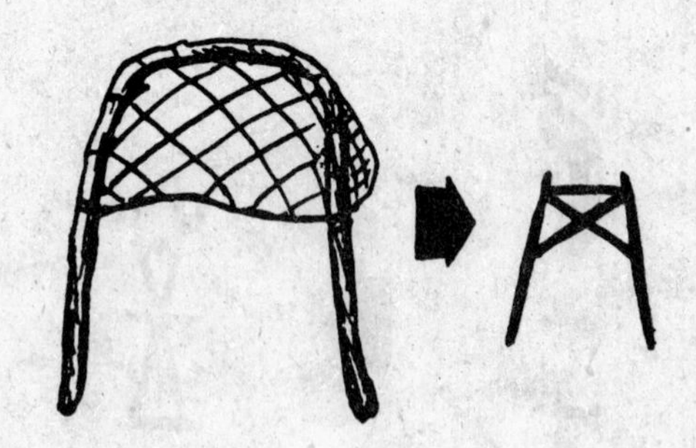

Its ancient graph was a net with two sticks for capturing birds and beasts. Later, the phonetic symbol 忘 was added and formed 罔. Eventually, 糸 was added to form 網. Its simplified version is its ancient form.

望 wàng

Its original meaning was "to look into the distance." In oracle bone inscriptions, graphically it was a man standing on the ground and looking into the distance with open eyes. In bronze inscriptions, the moon shape was added to stress the meaning. 望 can be written as 朢.

为(為)wéi, wèi

Graphically, it is a hand leading an elephant to make it serve the man (see Case 象). Hence, its original meaning was "to do."

韦(韋)wéi

〔附〕 違

It is the original form of 違, indicating "contrary." In oracle bone inscriptions, the square in the middle of this character signifies the town people living in a community; the two feet at the upper and lower part respectively symbolize walking towards opposite directions. In ancient books, it was interchangeable with 卫.

尾 wěi

A tail-shaped ornament is added to the buttocks of a man. This is a way primitive people imitated animals or indicated the totem when they danced or marked ceremonial occasions.

卫（衛）wèi

In early bronze inscriptions, a town in the graph was surrounded by the feet of patrolling soldiers. Later, it used the phonetic symbol 韋 and the graphic symbol 行 as radicals.

未 wèi

Graphically, a tree with a lot of leaves. Hence, its original meaning was "abundant." Later, it was loaned to indicate the eighth of the twelve Earthly Branches. And its meaning changed to "no," "not yet," etc. with its original meaning no longer in existence.

畏 wèi

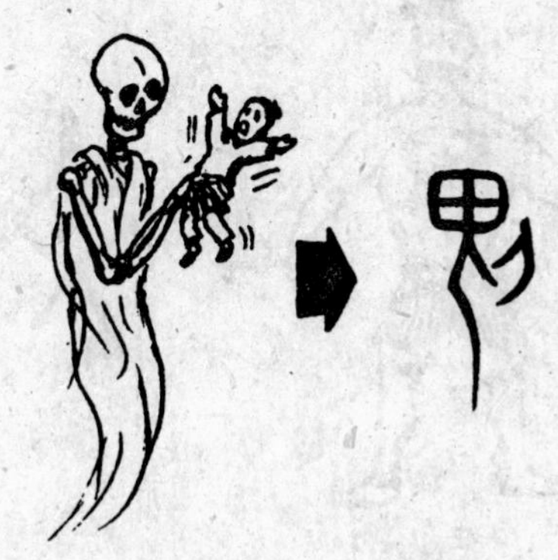

It is a frightening thing that a ghost (see Case 鬼) holding a club is chasing after and capturing a living man. Hence, its original meaning was "to be afraid" or "fear." It extends to mean "to be in awe."

文 wén

Its original meaning was skin tattooing. Its primitive graph was a man with designs tattooed on his chest or back.

闻(聞)wén

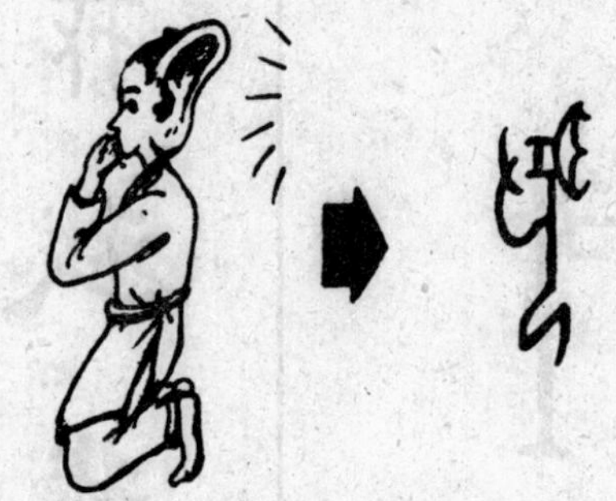

Graphically, a person is kneeling down with a hand covering his mouth and his exaggerated ear listening carefully. Hence, its original meaning was "to hear." Later, it was used to mean "to smell."

我 wǒ

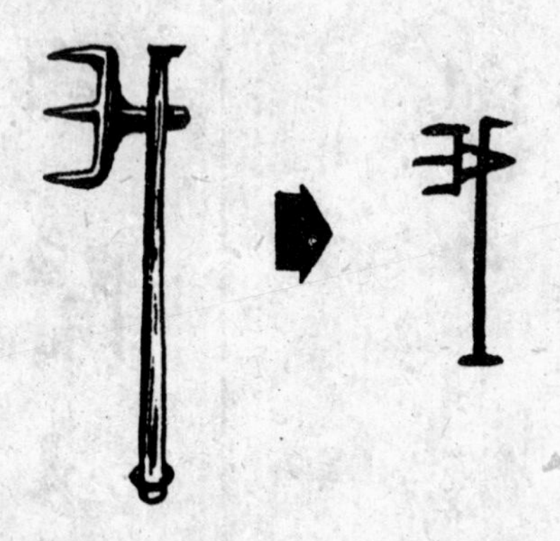

Its original meaning was an ancient weapon with a long shaft and three sharp points. Since oracle bone inscriptions, however, it was loaned to indicate the first person, "I," with the original meaning no longer in existence.

巫 wū

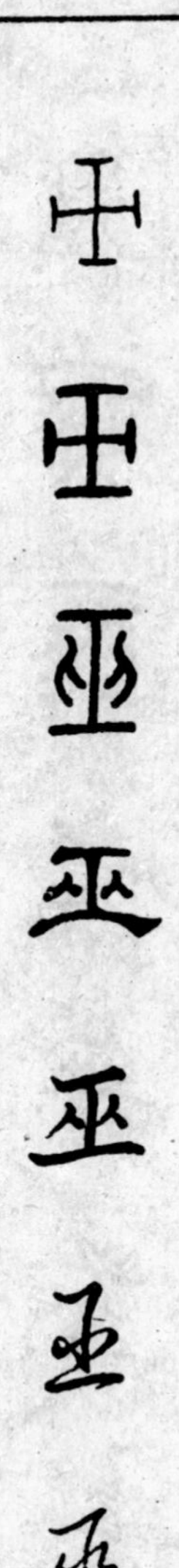

In primitive times, the person playing the role of messenger between man and gods or ghosts was called 巫. In oracle bone and bronze inscriptions, graphically it was bamboo strips laid in cross which was the prop for the diviner.

舞 wǔ

〔附〕无

Graphically, it is a person dancing with ox tails in her hands. Later, it was loaned to indicate 無 (无), nothing. The form of two feet 舛 were added later creating the character 舞, "to dance."

武 wǔ

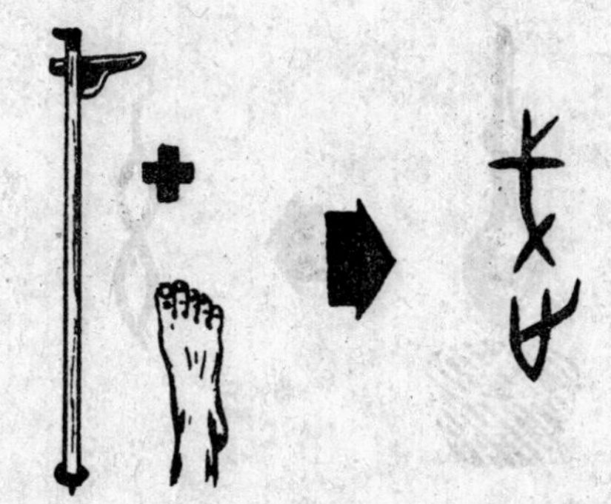

The upper part of this character 戈, a weapon in ancient times, and the lower part 止, foot, together mean "to take the weapon to go to battle." Hence, its original meanings were the general term for military affairs, strategy and power.

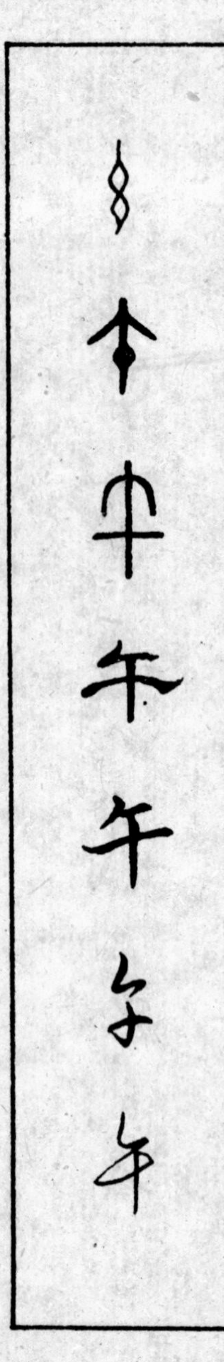

午 wǔ

〔附〕杵迕忤

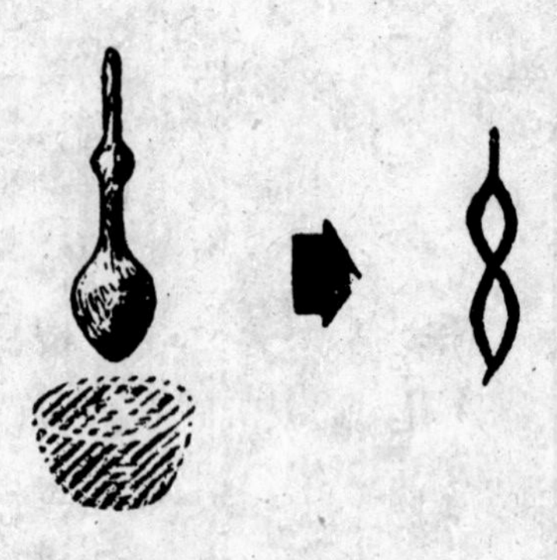

As a pictograph, graphically it is a pestle used to husk rice. It is the original form of 杵. Later, it indicated the seventh of the Twelve Earthly Branches and 杵 was coined, which is now pronounced chǔ. It is interchangeable with 迕 and 忤, wǔ, to go against, counter.

五 wǔ

Using horizontal planes to indicate the numerals from one through four is very convenient, i.e. 一, one, 二, two, 三, three, and 四, four. From the number five on, it becomes very difficult to employ this method. Given this limitation, the crossed plane × or 㐅 are used to signify "five."

戊 wù

Originally, it was a pictograph. Graphically, it is crescent shaped ax with a wide blade, a weapon in primitive times. Later, it was loaned to indicate the fifth of the Ten Heavenly Stems with the original meaning no longer in existence. Reference can be found in 戈 , 戍, 戎, 戒 and others.

勿 wù

〔附〕 物

Graphically, a knife is peeling or cutting away useless vegetable roots signifying "to abandon." This was the original meaning of this character. It is loaned for use in 物.

昔 xī

Its original meaning was "previous" or "past." In primitive times, floods were a frequent occurrence. Therefore, the form of flood and the radical 日 are used to indicate time in the past.

西 xī

〔附〕 栖

Its original meaning was "to perch" with the graph of a bird perching on a nest, which does not appear in oracle bone and bronze inscriptions. The bird was added to its form in small seal characters. When the sun is setting in the west the birds begin taking rest and perch on their nests. Therefore, it indicates "west."

析 xī

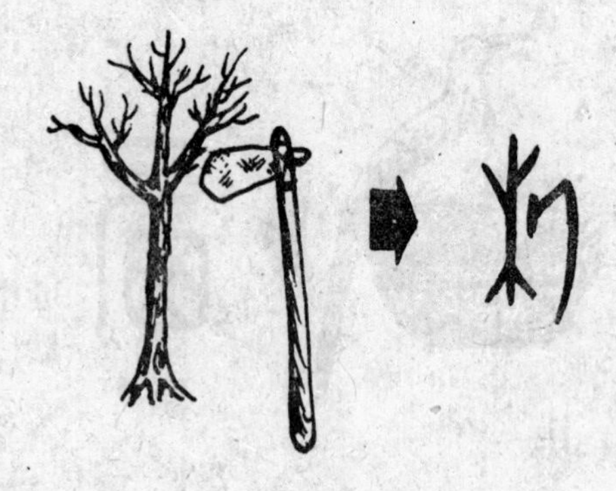

Composed of 木, wood (see Case 木), and 斤, ax (see Case 斤), it originally meant "to split with an ax." Later, it extended to mean 分析, to analyze, 辨析, to distinguish, etc.

奚 xī

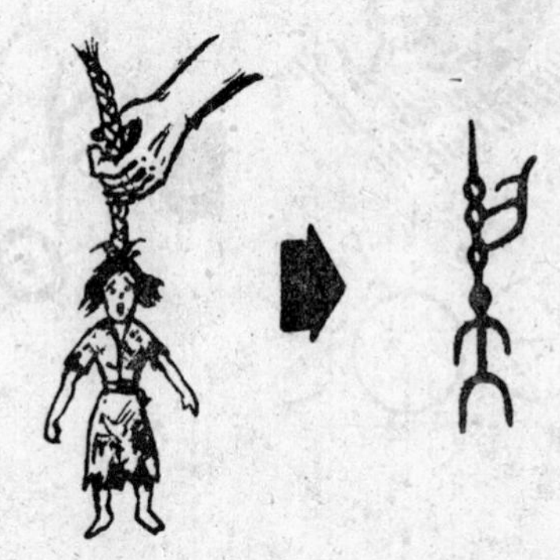

Graphically, the head of a person is tied with a rope and is led by a huge hand. Hence, its original meaning was "slave," woman slave in particular. Later, it was used to be the interrogative "why" or "where."

习(習)xí

Its original meaning was "the bird flies many times." In oracle bone inscriptions and the chǔ jiǎn of Warring States Period, its upper part was 羽, the wings, and the lower part were 日, indicating the bird is flying. It later evolved into 白.

喜 xǐ

It is composed of 壴, drum (see Case 鼓 and 彭), and 口, mouth. Playing the drum and laughing with open mouth are the signs of "happiness."

系 xì

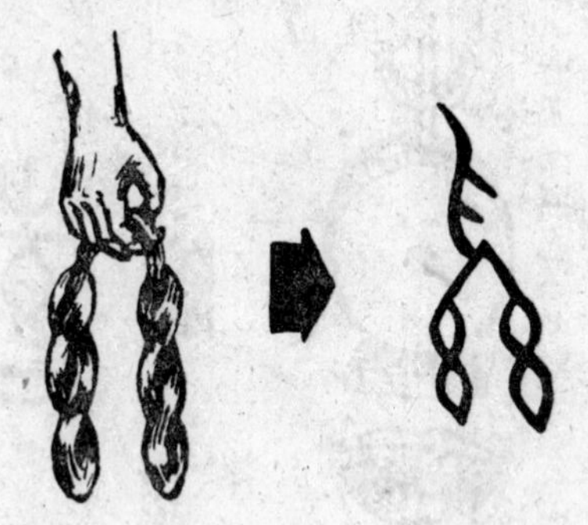

Graphically, a hand is holding two or three bundles of silk. Its original meaning was "to connect." It is interchangeable with 繫. It also means "to inherit," "generation," "lineage," etc. 繫 and 系 are combined and simplified to 系.

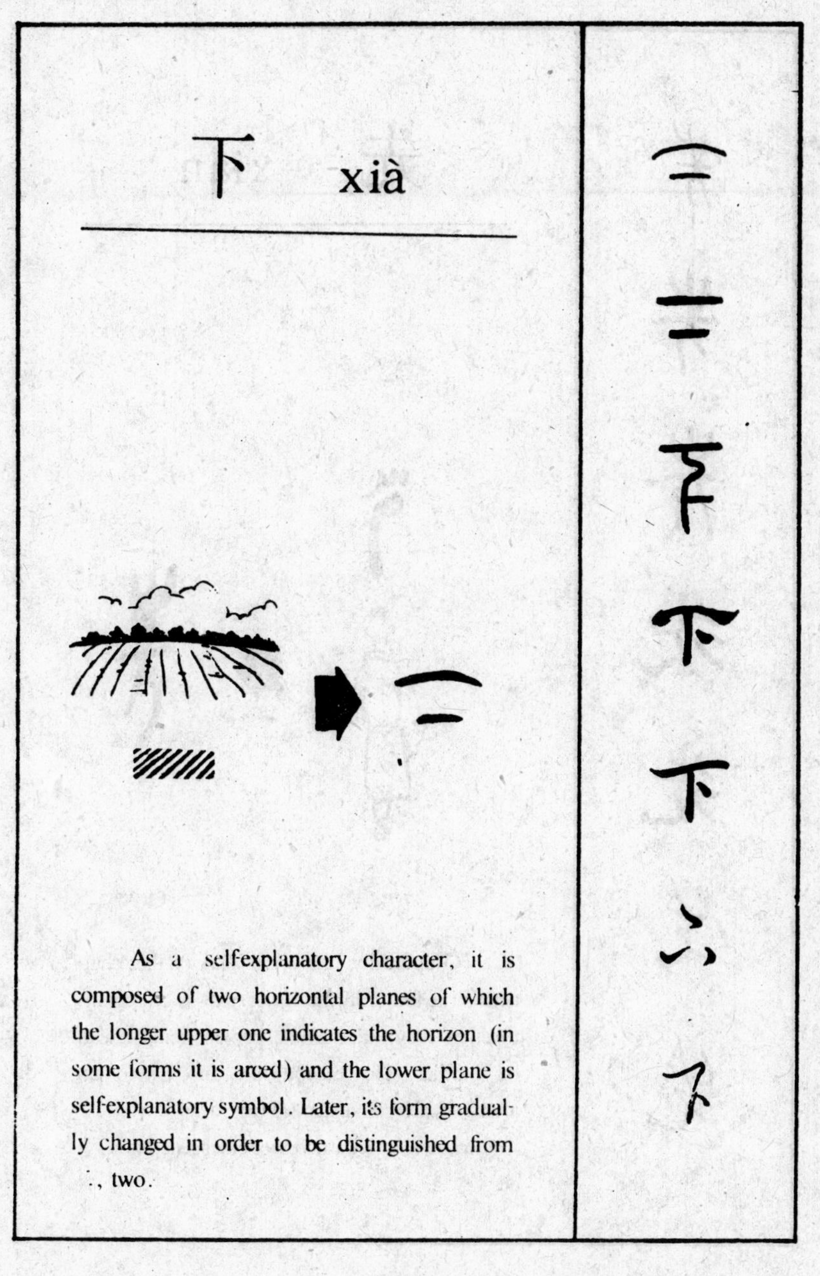

下 xià

As a selfexplanatory character, it is composed of two horizontal planes of which the longer upper one indicates the horizon (in some forms it is arced) and the lower plane is selfexplanatory symbol. Later, its form gradually changed in order to be distinguished from :, two.

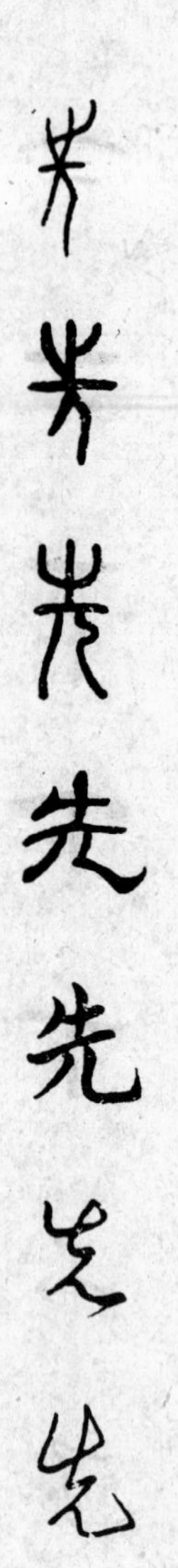

先 xiān

Graphically, the upper part of this character is a foot and the lower part is a person, together they indicate one person going ahead of another. Hence, the idea of 先, to go ahead. Later, it extended to mean "past," "ancestor," "the deceased elder generation," etc.

咸 xián

Graphically, a 戌, huge ax (see Case 戌) is used to smash 口, indicating goods (see Case 品 and 多). Its original meaning was "all." It later came to mean "salty."

陷 xiàn

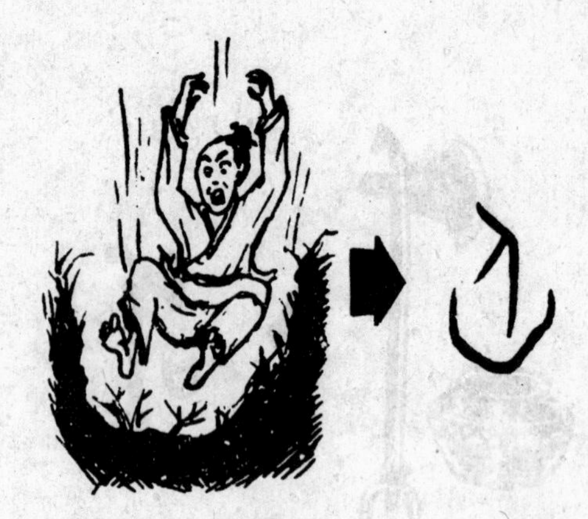

Originally, it was 口. Graphically, a person is falling into a pit in oracle bone inscriptions. In bronze inscriptions 臽, an opening, was added on the top of the pit and pointed stakes were added on the bottom

献(獻)xiàn

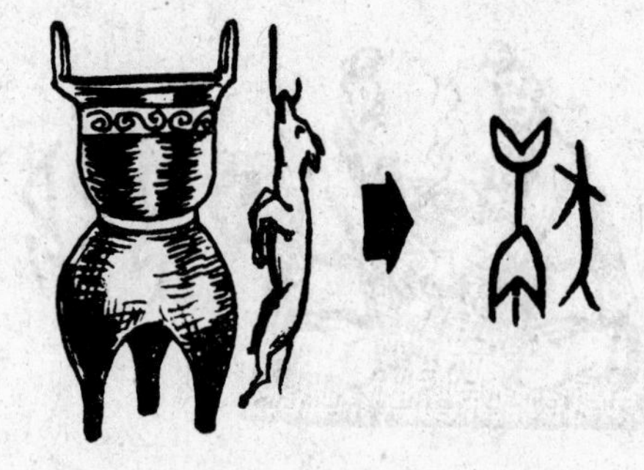

Originally, it was composed of 鬳, 犬, i.e. 甗, yǎn, a primitive cooker and 犬, dog. The dog was cooked in a cooker and offered to the clan temple. Hence, its original meaning was "to offer sacrifice." It extends to mean 奉献, to offer as a tribute.

乡(鄉)xiāng

〔附〕飨　卿　响

鄉 is the original form of 饗 (飨). It means "to treat guests with wine and food." Graphically, it is two persons kneeling with a container of food between them. It is interchangeable with 乡, 响, and 卿.

相 xiāng, xiàng

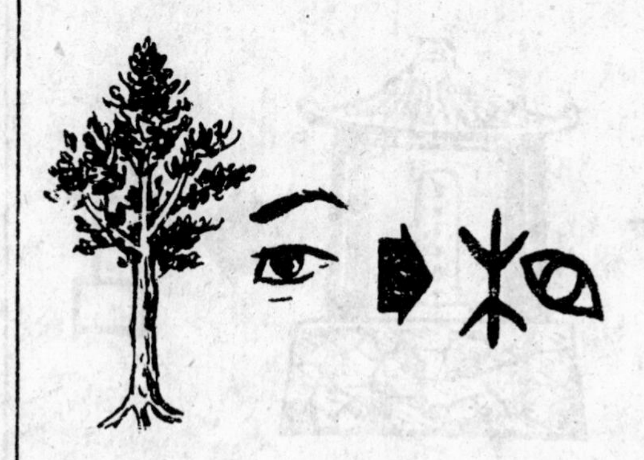

Its original meaning was "to take a careful look," or "to observe" with the pronunciation of xiàng (fourth tone). Graphically, it is an eye carefully observing a tree. It also means "mutual," with pronunciation xiāng (first tone).

享 xiǎng

〔附〕亨 烹

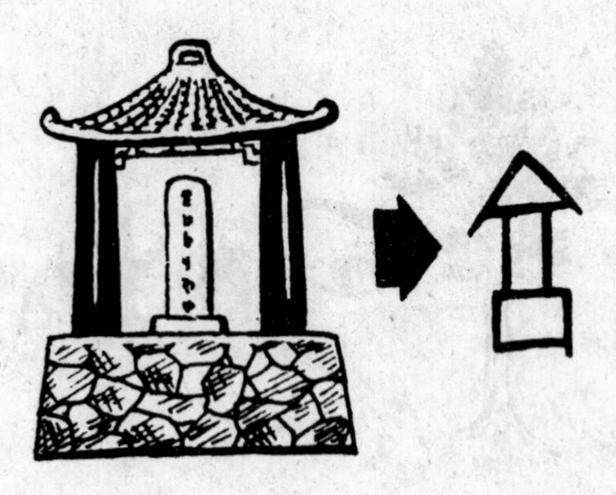

Originally, it was 亯. Graphically, it looks like a clan hall. Hence, its original meaning was "the sacrificial offerings are offered to ancestors or gods." Later, it extended to mean "to appreciate" and "to enjoy." It is interchangeable with 亨 and 烹.

向 xiàng

Its original meaning was the window facing the north. It extended to mean "towards," and "past," etc. Later, 嚮 was coined with the same meaning as 向. Today, they are combined and simplified to 向.

象 xiàng

It is a pictograph. The long nose and thick body of the elephant are stressed in the graph.

小 xiǎo

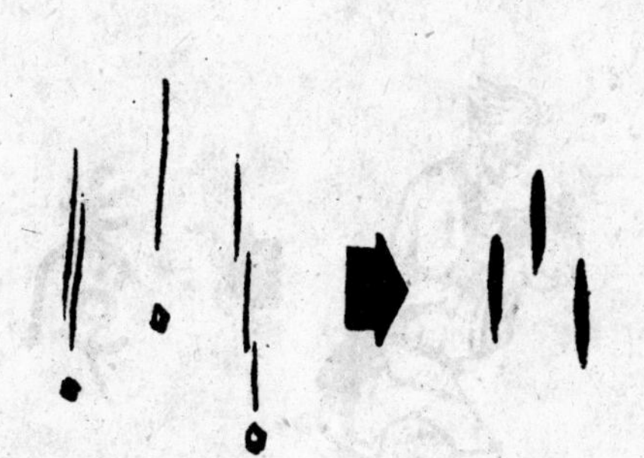

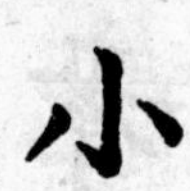

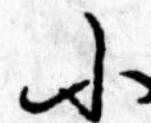

Graphically, it consisted of three short vertical structures in oracle bone and bronze inscriptions which represented tiny grains of sand, signifying "small." Later, it evolved into its present form. In ancient books, it was interchangeable with 少.

孝 xiào

Graphically, a child is carrying an old man with sparse hair on his back. This is the sign of filial piety. See Case 老 and 考.

心 xīn

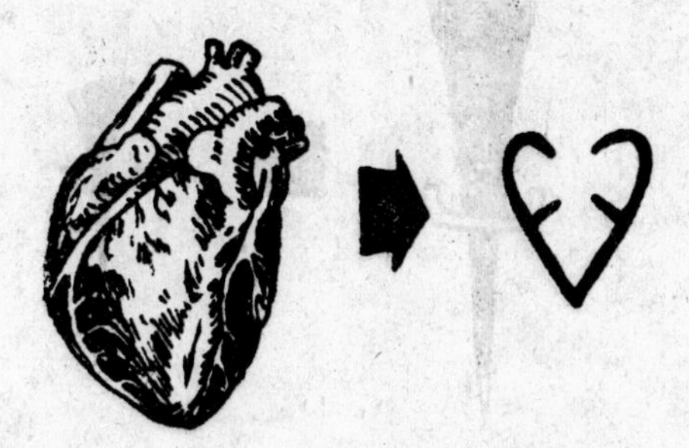

As a pictograph, it was the form of a heart in oracle bone inscriptions. Later, its form began to shift away from a pictographic representation. In official script, its form was very far removed from the original.

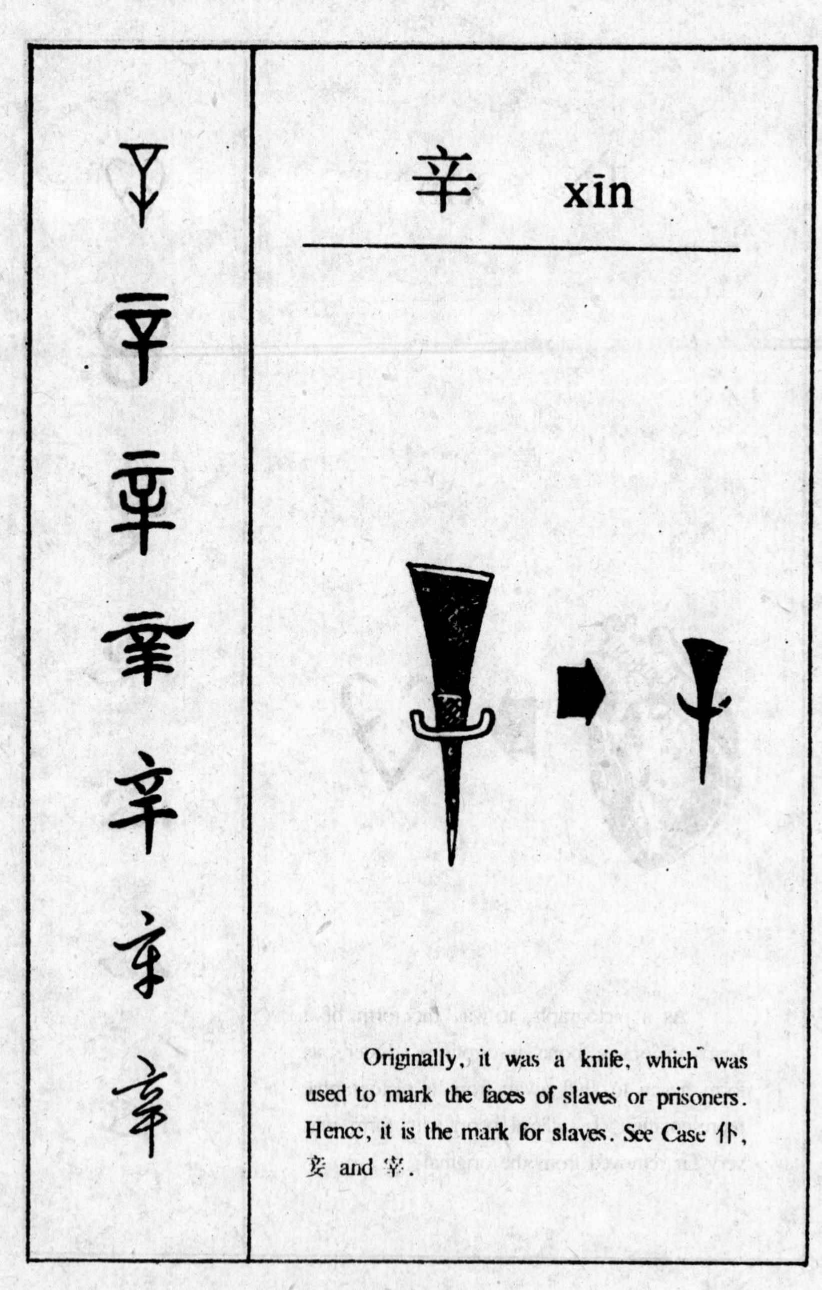

辛 xīn

Originally, it was a knife, which was used to mark the faces of slaves or prisoners. Hence, it is the mark for slaves. See Case 仆, 妾 and 宰.

新 xīn

〔附〕 薪

It is the original form of 薪. Graphically, it is composed of the phonetic symbol 辛 and the indicative symbol 斤, ax (see Case 斤).

星 xīng

It consists of several 日-shaped or 日-shaped stars in the sky on the upper part and the phonetic symbol 生 on the lower part. Here, 日 is not the sun but a star. See Case 晶.

兴(興)xīng, xìng

Graphically, several hands are raising a big plate in the air (see Case 凡). Hence, its original meaning was "to raise." It also means "to get up."

行 xíng, háng

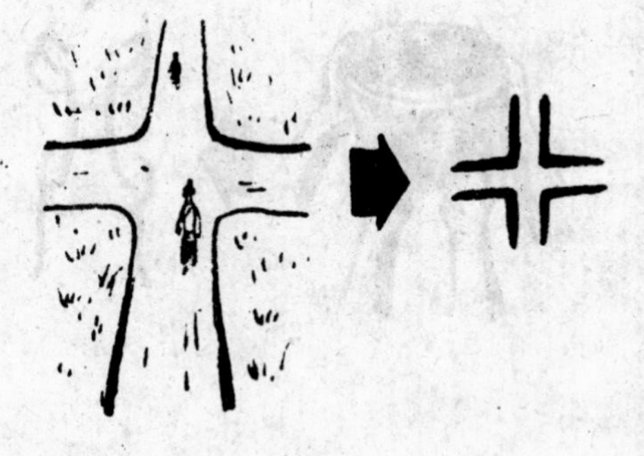

Graphically, it is an intersection. Hence, its original meaning was "road," pronounced háng. Later, it was mostly used to mean 行走, "to walk," xíng.

兄 xiōng

〔附〕 况

In ancient times, the elder brother could order his younger brother to do anything he wanted, so the big open mouth is added on the top of 人 to indicate the meaning "elder brother." In ancient books, 兄 may replace 况 (況).

休 xiū

Graphically, a man is taking rest under a tree. Hence, its original meaning was "to rest." Later, it extended to mean "to stop," "perfect," "don't," etc.

羞 xiū

〔附〕 馐

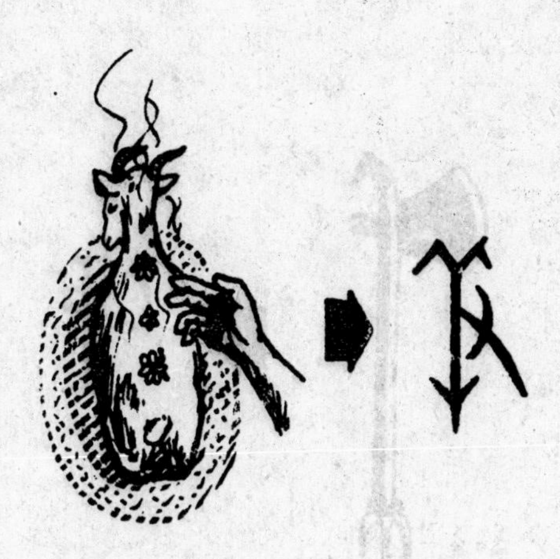

It is the original form of 馐 and originally meant "delicacies." Graphically, it is a hand tearing mutton to prepare for a meal. It also means "to devote."

戌 xū

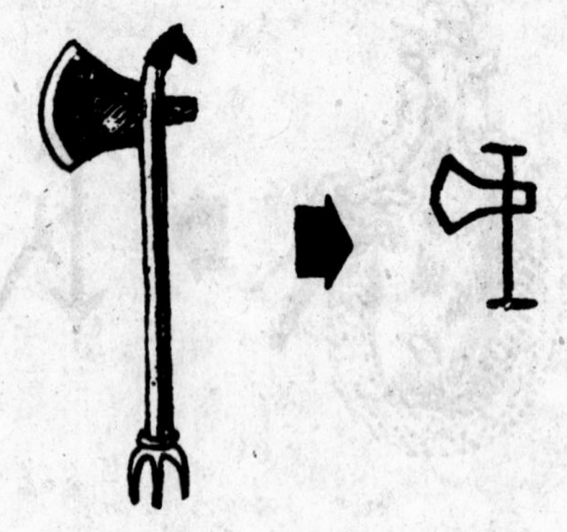

Originally, it was the name of an ancient weapon. Graphically, it is an ax with a long shaft and wide blade. Later, it was loaned to indicate the eleventh of the Twelve Earthly Branches with its original meaning no longer in existence. See Case 戈, 戊, 戍, 戎, and 戒.

畜 xù, chù

〔附〕 蓄

It is the original form of 蓄. Its early form consisted of 糸 and 田 symbolizing the harvest of silk and crops. Today, it mostly indicates poultry and livestock with the pronunciation chù. It is pronounced xù in 畜牧, livestock farm, 蓄养, to raise livestock, 畜产, livestock production , etc.

宣 xuān

Its original meaning was "the large palace hall of the ancient kings and emperors." 宀 indicates the palace chamber, while 亘, xuān, is the form of flying clouds, symbolizing the hugeness of the palace.

旋 xuán

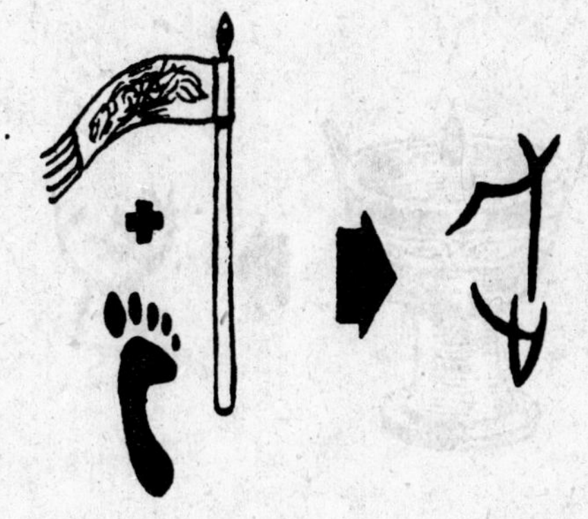

Composed of a flag waving on the top of a flagpost and the form of foot under the flag, it signifies the army is returning in great triumph, today written as 凯旋.

血 xuè, xiě

The dot in the middle of 皿, goods container, indicates the blood of the livestock killed and sacrificed in ceremonial rituals. Offering the blood of livestock to the ancestors or gods is called 血祭.

旬　xún

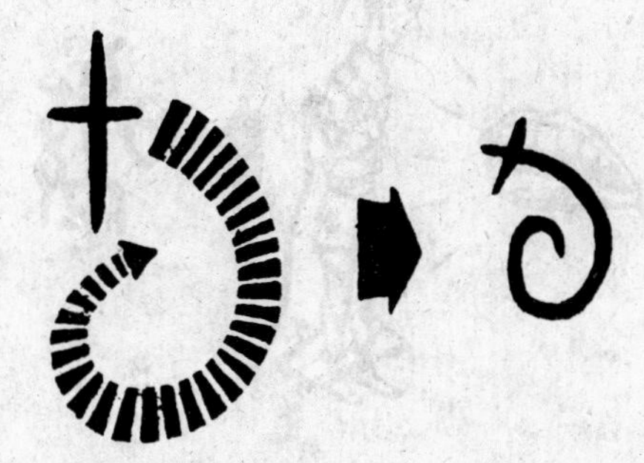

Its original meaning was "ten days." Primitive people used the Ten Heavenly Stems to keep time. 旬 is the time it takes 甲 (十-shaped, see Case 甲) to revolve to its original position.

讯(訊)xùn

Graphically, the prisoner's hands are tied behind his back, his feet are shackled and a big mouth in front is questioning him. Hence, its original meaning was "to interrogate."

亚(亞)yà

Its original meaning was "clan temple." Graphically, it is a compound of buildings facing four directions. It extends to mean "official titles." Later, it was mostly used to mean "inferior," "second class," e.g. 亚军, the second place winner.

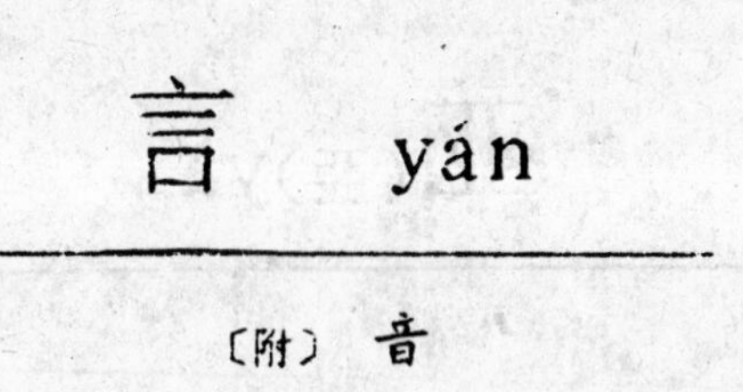

In early oracle bone inscriptions, it was the form of a tongue extending from a mouth The short horizontal plane is the self-explanatory symbol. It can replace 音, voice or sound. in oracle bone inscriptions.

炎 yán

〔附〕 焰

Its original meaning was "the roaring flames" or "to burn." Graphically, it is fire on fire, indicating fierce burning. In ancient books, it can replace 焰, yàn, flames.

央 yāng

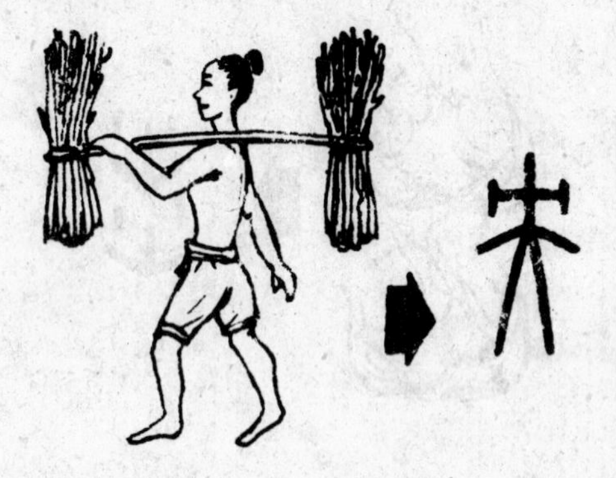

Graphically, a man is shouldering a pole with loads on either end. As his shoulder is in the middle of the pole, its original meaning was "middle." It also means "end."

羊 yáng

〔附〕 祥

Graphically, it is a front-viewed sheep head with the horns bent downward (compare with Case 牛) and a pointed mouth on the bottom. It is loaned for use in 祥, e.g. 吉羊 (祥), auspicious.

阳(陽)yáng

Originally, it was 阝丁 in oracle bone inscriptions. Graphically, it is the sun rising to the height of the stone table on which sacrificial offerings are offered to the gods. In bronze inscriptions, 彡 was added to indicate the sunshine. Later, the radical 阜, mountain, was added to symbolize the sun rising from behind the mountain.

扬(揚)yáng

In oracle bone inscriptions, it was the same form as 扬. In bronze inscriptions, the form of a man kneeling and raising his two hands forward was added, thus conveying the meanings "to raise" and "to praise."

养(養)yǎng

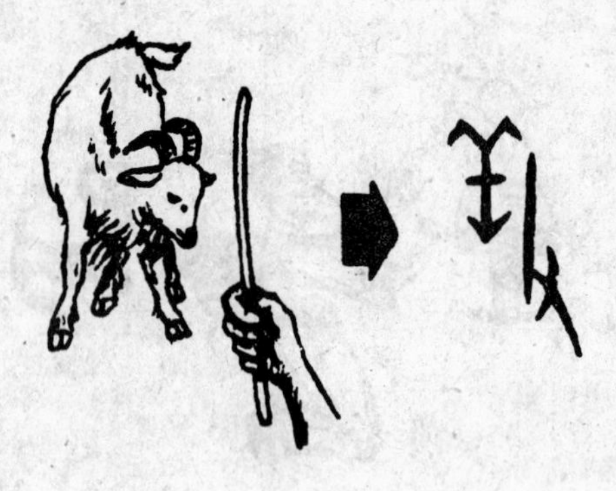

In oracle bone and bronze inscriptions, its form was a hand with a whip herding a sheep. Hence, its original meaning was "livestock herding." Later, it extended to mean "to bear children," "to breed," "to recuperate," etc.

夭 yāo

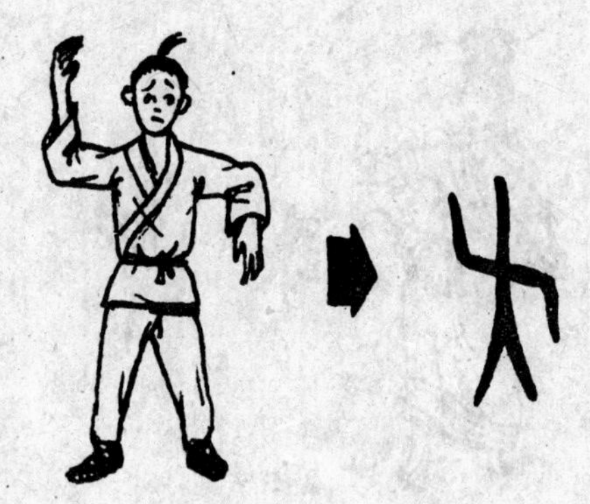

Its original meaning was "to bend." Graphically, it is a man with bent arms. Later, it extended to mean "to die young," e.g. 夭折.

〔附〕 腰

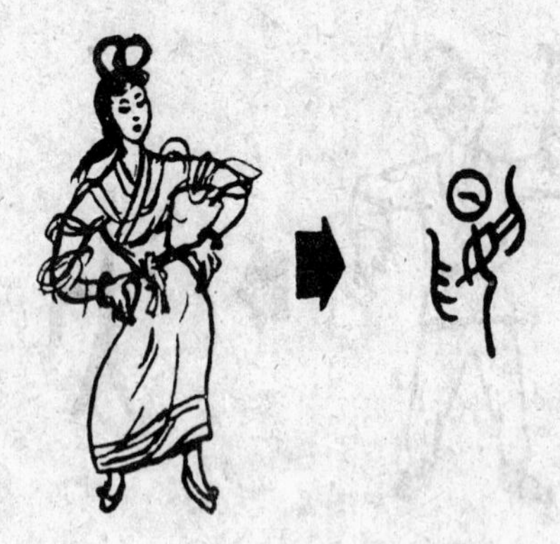

Its original meaning was 腰, "waist." In oracle bone inscriptions, it was like a woman with arms akimbo. Her head was initially 目-shaped, but later changed to 日 or 西 since bronze inscriptions.

野 yě

Its original meaning was "vicinity," or "fields." As an ideograph, in oracle bone and bronze inscriptions, it was composed of 林, woods, and 土, earth. In small seal characters, it became pictophonetic with 里 (田 and 土) indicating meaning and 予 (予 and 野 are pronounced the same) indicating sound.

页(頁)yè

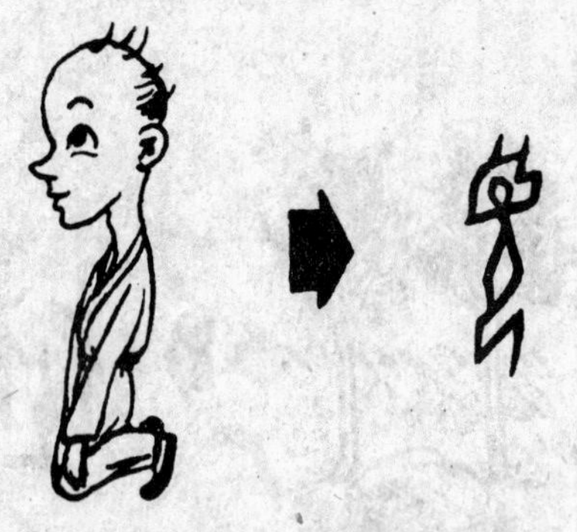

Its original meaning was "head." Graphically, in oracle bone inscriptions it is a man with a huge head and big eyes. Since bronze inscriptions, it has gradually changed, becoming more and more dissimilar. But the meaning of the radical 页 is linked with "head" in meaning.

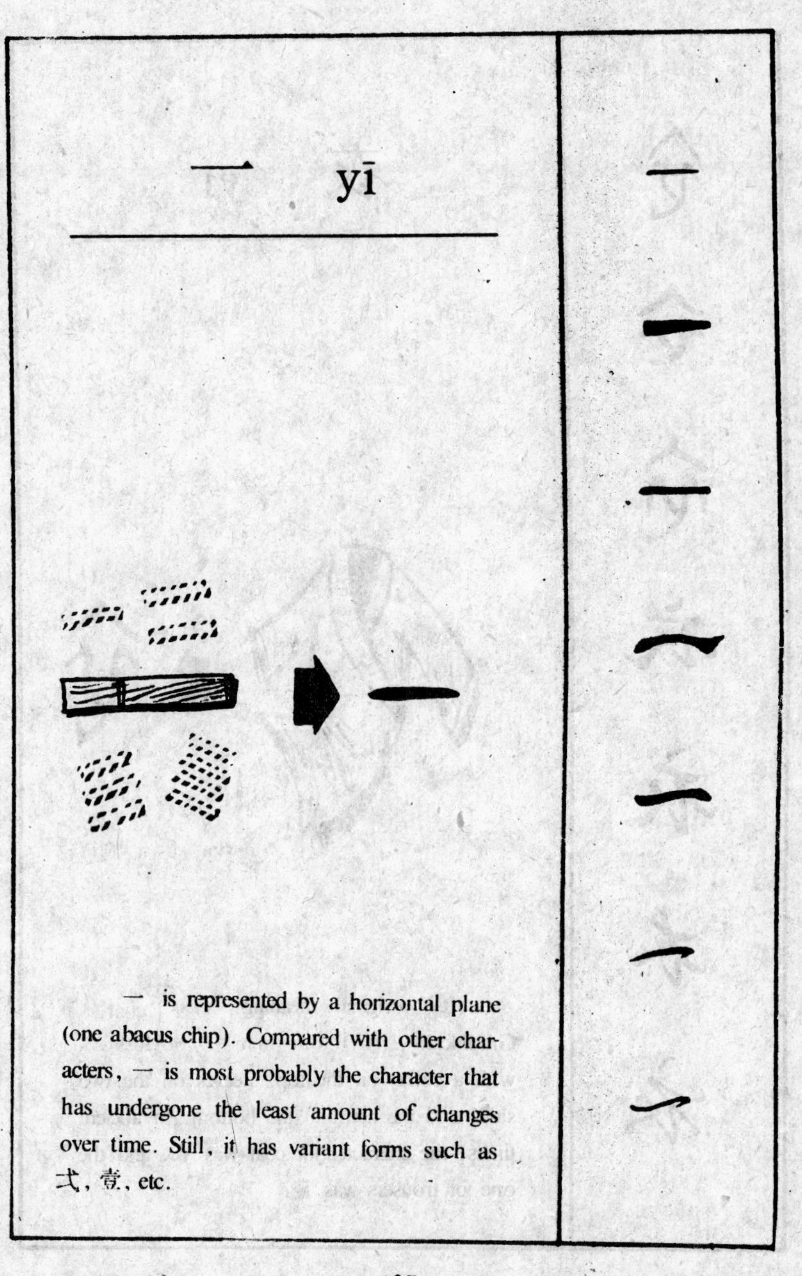

一 yī

一 is represented by a horizontal plane (one abacus chip). Compared with other characters, 一 is most probably the character that has undergone the least amount of changes over time. Still, it has variant forms such as 弌, 壹, etc.

衣 yī

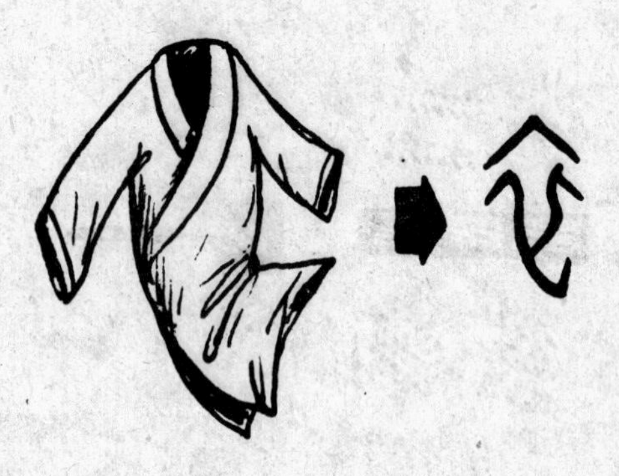

Its original meaning was "coat." Graphically, it is an item of clothes, with a collar on the top, sleeves on the two sides and the hem at the bottom. In ancient times, the character for coat was 衣, and the one for trousers was 裳.

夷 yí

Originally, it was the name for a nomadic nationality. In oracle bone inscriptions, 尸 was used for 夷 (see Case 尸). In bronze inscriptions, it was the form of a man armed with a 矰, zēng, a short arrow tied with a silk rope, which was a common style of dress among nomadic people at the time.

疑　yí

〔附〕 凝

Its original meaning was "puzzled" or "to hesitate." In oracle bone inscriptions, graphically it was a man with a cane standing at a crossroad and wondering which direction to go. In bronze inscriptions, 牛 was added to indicate a man is puzzled and wondering what to do because he lost his ox. In ancient writings, it was interchangeable with 凝.

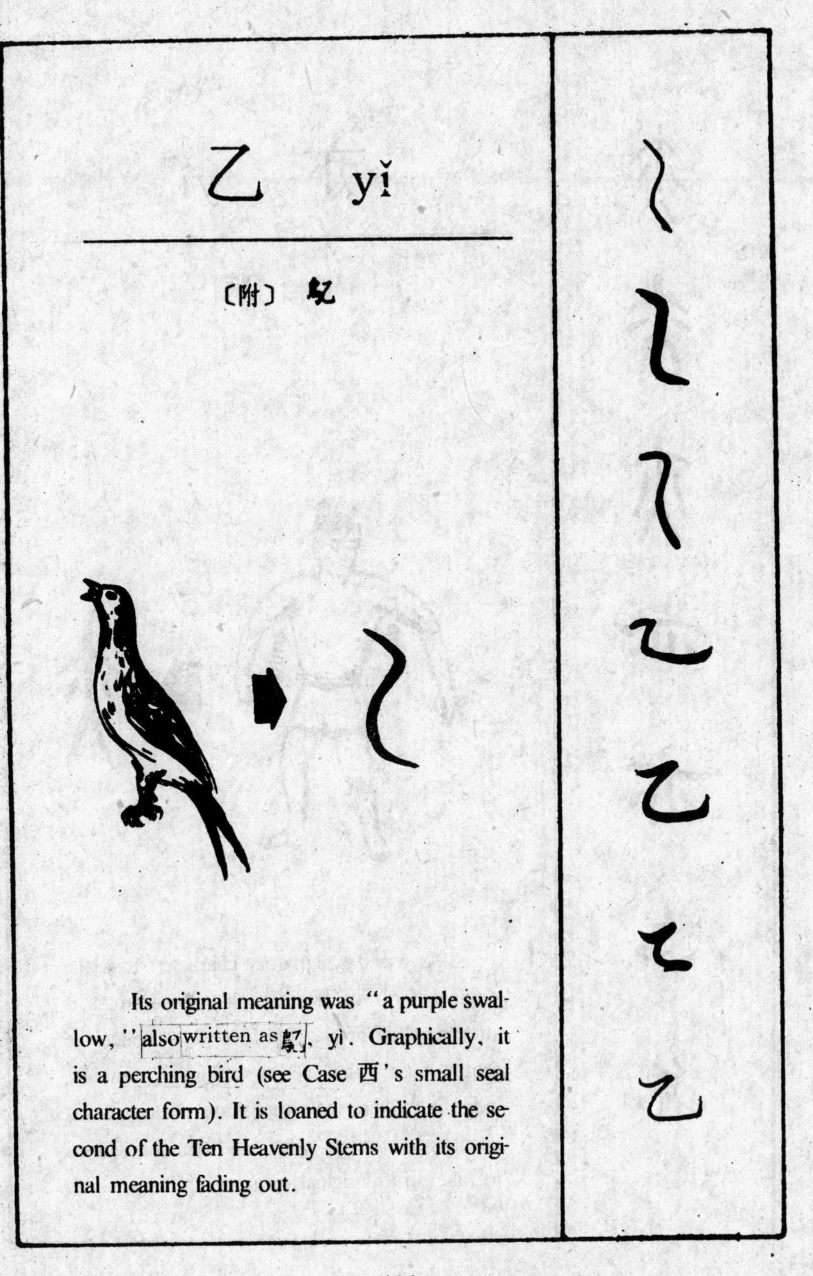

乙 yǐ

〔附〕 鳦

Its original meaning was "a purple swallow," also written as 鳦, yì. Graphically, it is a perching bird (see Case 西's small seal character form). It is loaned to indicate the second of the Ten Heavenly Stems with its original meaning fading out.

亦 yì

〔附〕 腋

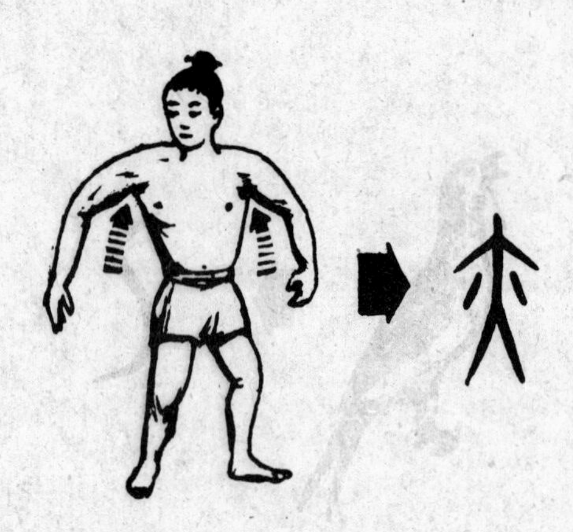

As a self-explanatory character, it is the original form of 腋. Graphically, a man is stretching his arms. The two dots under the armpits are the self-explanatory symbols, indicating where the armpits are. Later, it was used as a function word, and 腋 was coined to take on its original meaning.

邑 yì

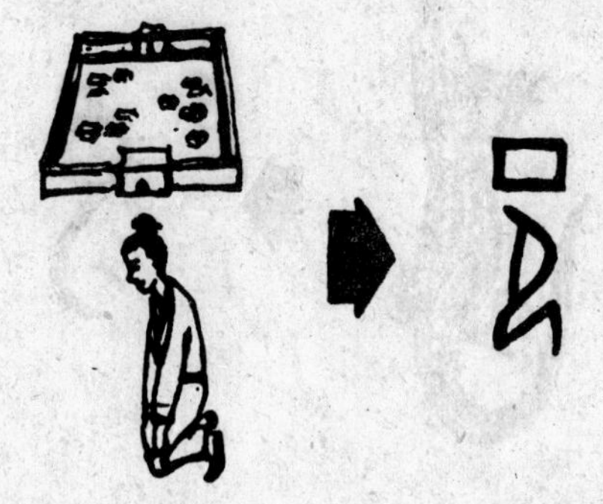

Originally it meant "the place where people live in a community." Graphically, its upper part is square indicating a city; the lower part is a man sitting on a mat indicating to settle down in a place. It extended to mean "state capital," "fief" and "city."

易 yì

〔附〕 蜴 賜 锡

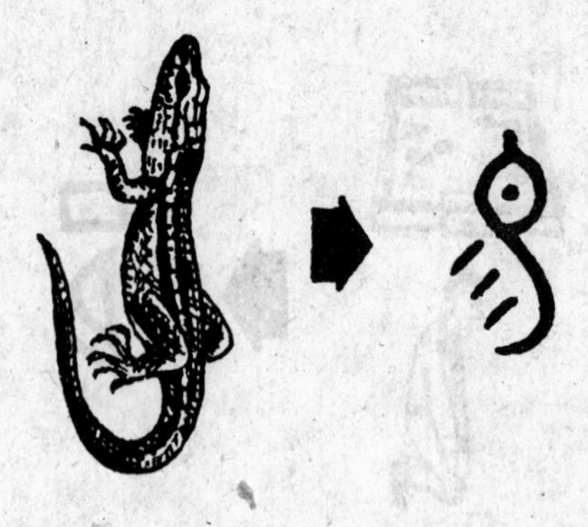

It is the original form of 蜴. In bronze inscriptions, it was loaned to be 賜 (or 锡). Later, it was loaned to mean "to change," "to exchange," "business deal," etc.

异(異)yì

Graphically, it is the form of man's body with a ghost head (see Case 鬼) and two stretched hands. Its original meaning was "unique" and "ghostlike."

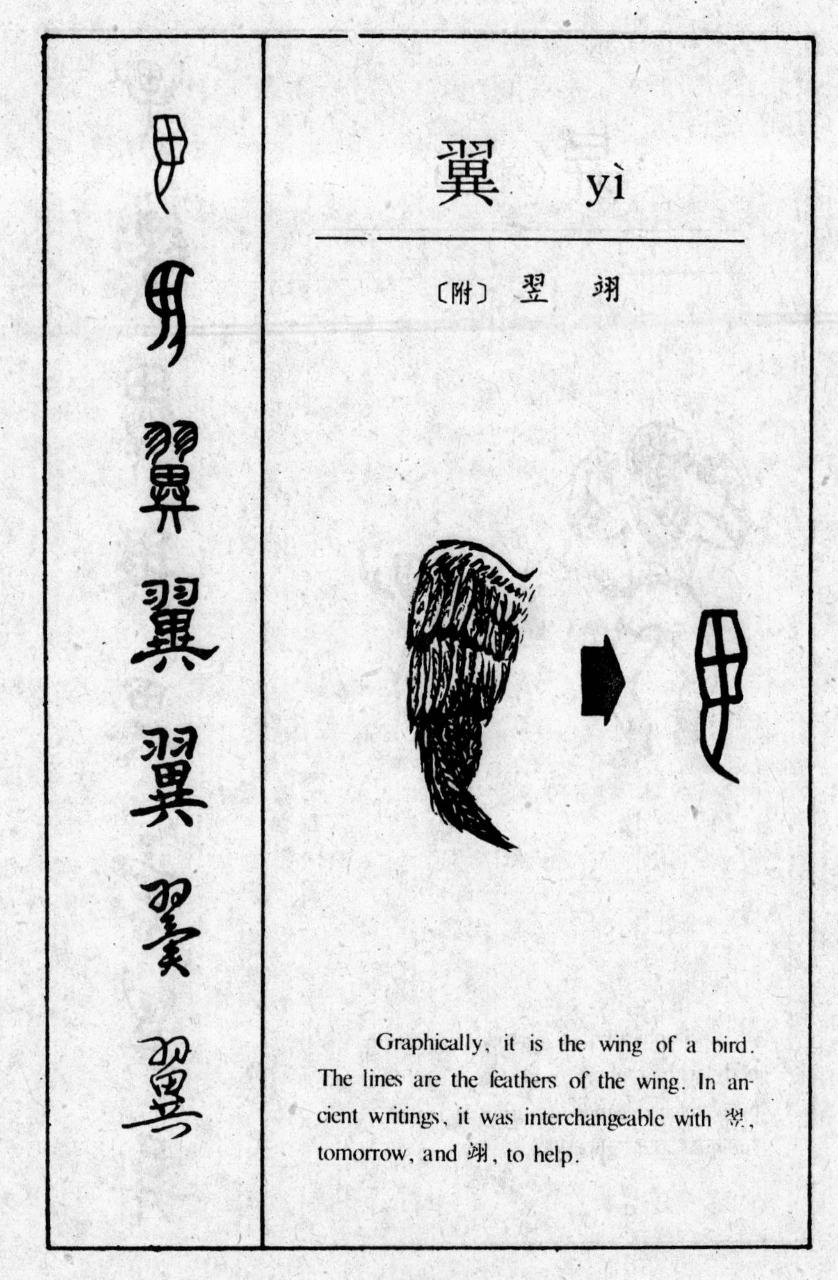

翼 yì

〔附〕 翌 翊

Graphically, it is the wing of a bird. The lines are the feathers of the wing. In ancient writings, it was interchangeable with 翌, tomorrow, and 翊, to help.

义(義)yì

〔附〕 仪

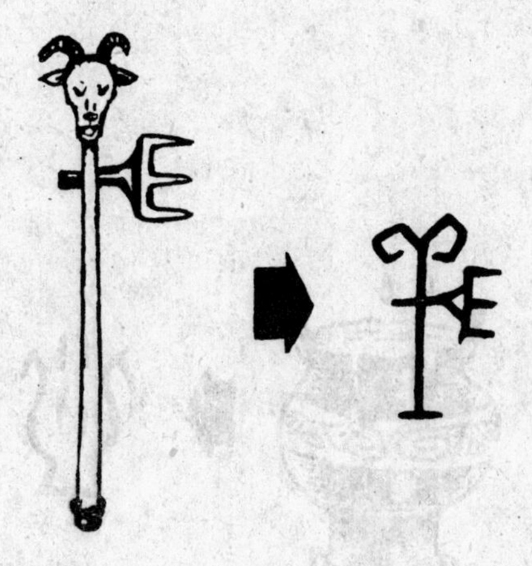

It is the original form of 仪. Graphically, it is a sheep's head impaled on a trident-shaped weapon with long shaft (see Case 我), symbolizing "power and prestige." Later, the phonetic radical 我 was added.

義 義 義 義 義 義 义

益　yì

〔附〕溢

It is the original form of 溢. Graphically, it is water in a container overflowing. Hence, its extended meaning was "rich," "abundant," "increase," "more," "advantages," etc.

艺(藝)yì

Its original form was 埶. In oracle bone inscriptions, its form was a man kneeling down on the ground and planting a small tree carefully. In bronze inscriptions, 土 was added to further stress the meaning of "plant." In modern Chinese, it also means "horticulture."

艺

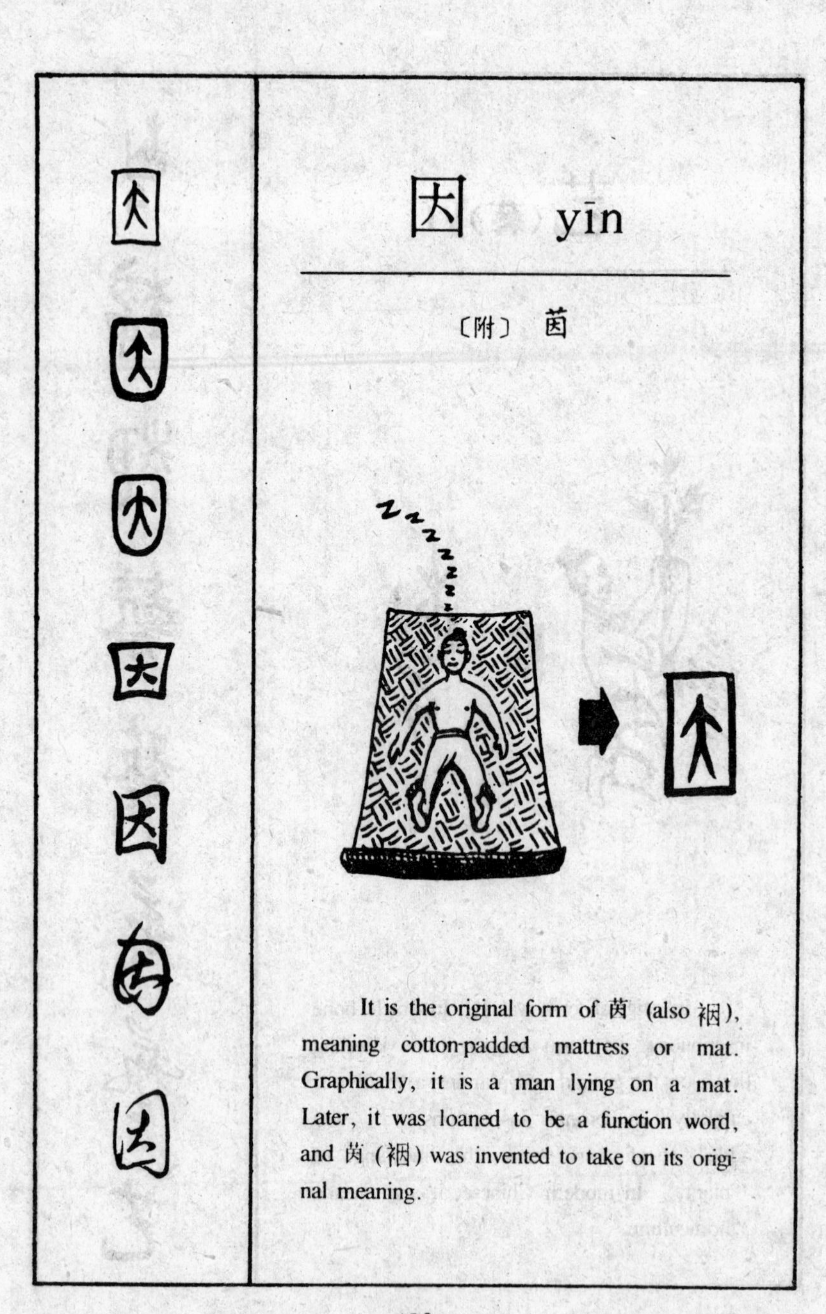

因 yīn

〔附〕 茵

It is the original form of 茵 (also 裀), meaning cotton-padded mattress or mat. Graphically, it is a man lying on a mat. Later, it was loaned to be a function word, and 茵 (裀) was invented to take on its original meaning.

殷 yīn

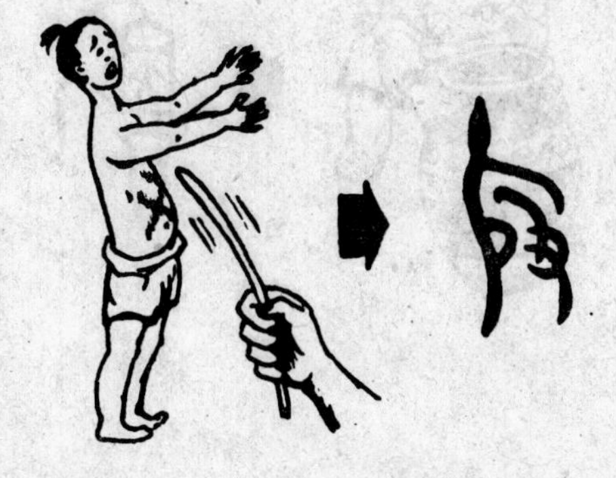

Graphically, it is a man being beaten by a stick. Hence, its original meaning was "sorrow." It also means "flourishing" and "multitudinous." It is written as 慇懃 when it means 殷勤, solicitous."

饮（飲）yǐn

In oracle bone inscriptions, it was a man holding a jar of wine (see Case 酉), bending his head, opening his mouth and extending his tongue. In bronze inscriptions, its form was simplified, and the phonetic 今 (its regular script form is 歙, a variant form of 饮) was added.

饮

尹 yǐn

Graphically, it is a hand holding a scepter which symbolizes the power to control the common people. Hence, its original meaning was "to rule." It also indicates the high officials in ancient times, e.g. 令尹.

印 yìn

〔附〕抑

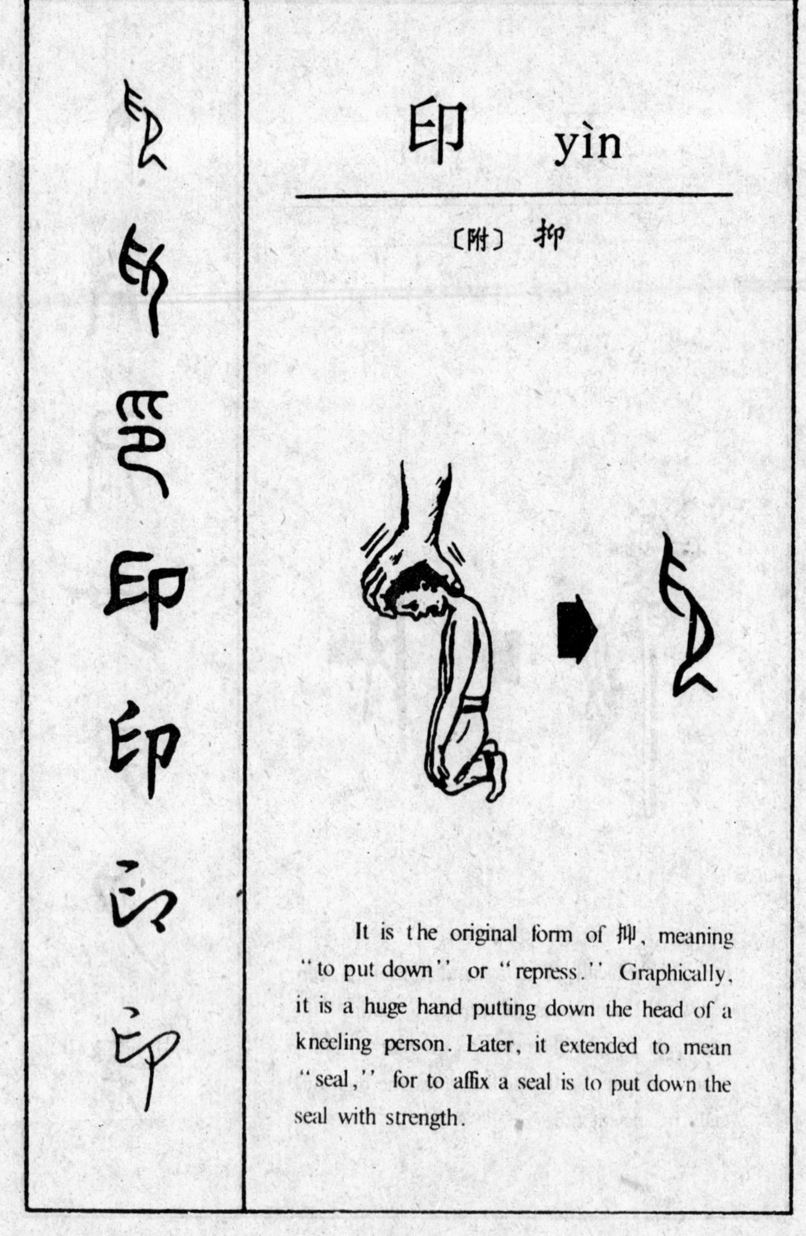

It is the original form of 抑, meaning "to put down" or "repress." Graphically, it is a huge hand putting down the head of a kneeling person. Later, it extended to mean "seal," for to affix a seal is to put down the seal with strength.

婴(嬰)yīng

〔附〕 撄　缨

Its original meaning was "neck ornaments." In oracle bone inscriptions, graphically it was a lady holding a cluster of shells (see Case 朋). Later, it indicated "a girl infant." It is interchangeable with 撄 and 缨.

庸 yōng

〔附〕墉

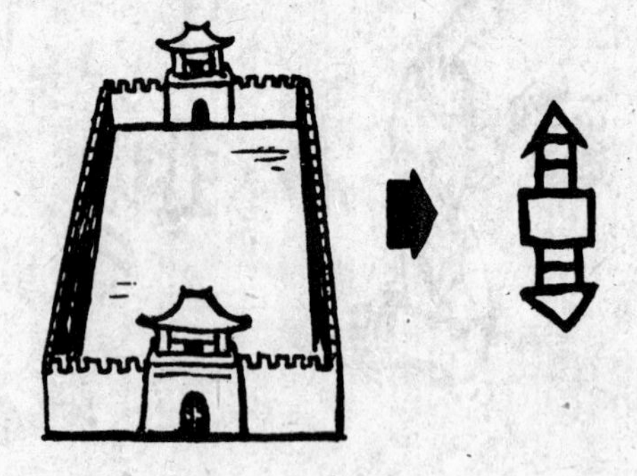

Its original form was 𩫖, the original form of 墉, meaning "city" or "city wall." In oracle bone inscriptions, the central part of 𩫖 was the square-shaped city, and the two ends were two opposite towers. In bronze inscriptions, it had another form 庸 composed of 庚 and 用.

永 yǒng

〔附〕派 咏

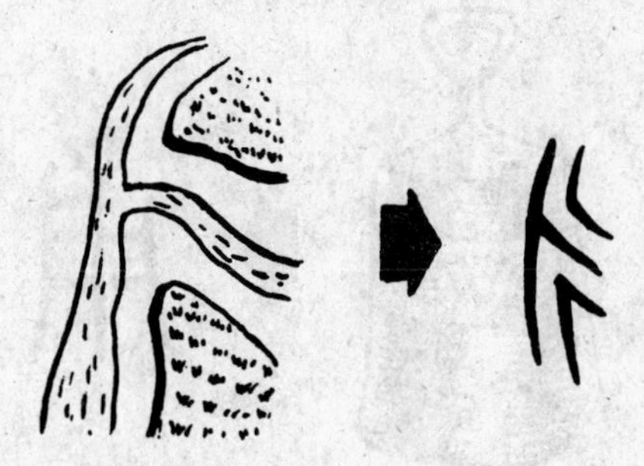

Graphically, it is a main river with many branches. Originally, 永 and 𠂢 (the original form of 派, meaning "branch") were written in the same form. Just like the inexhaustible flowing waters of the great rivers, its meaning was "everlasting." It is interchangeable with 詠 (咏).

用 yòng

〔附〕甬 镛 桶

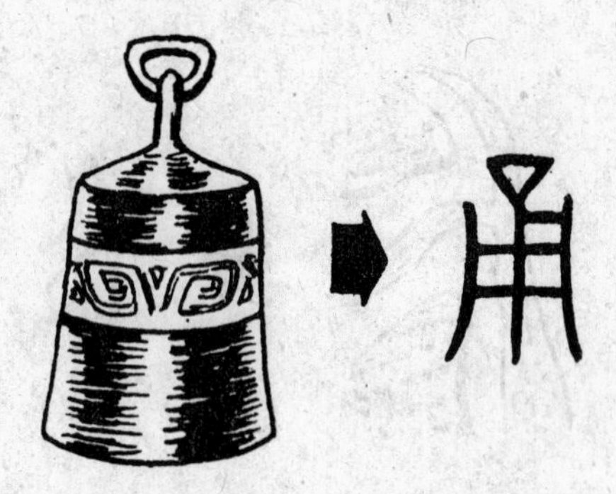

It is the original form of 甬, meaning a great bell. Graphically, it is the form of a bell. It is interchangeable with 镛. 甬 is also interchangeable with 桶, a primitive container.

幽 yōu

〔附〕黝

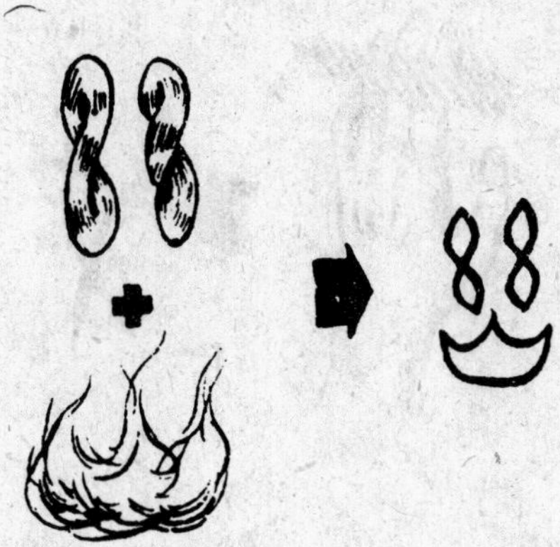

The upper part of this character is 絲 (the original form of 丝, silk) and the lower part is 火, fire. The flames are as thin as silk, hence the original meaning "small fire." It extended to mean "dim," "tranquil," etc. It is interchangeable with 黝, yóu, meaning "black."

尤 yóu

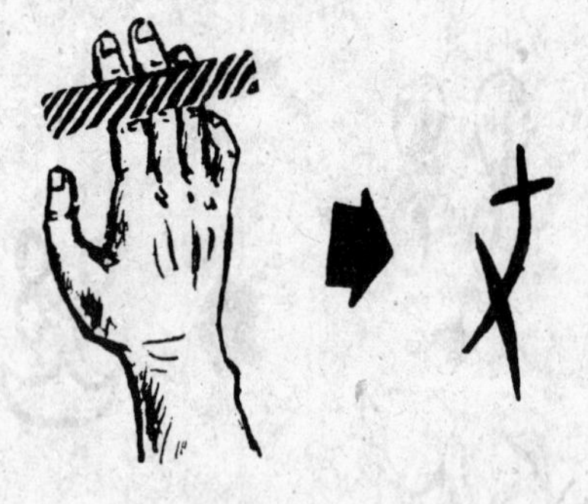

In oracle bone inscriptions, it was graphically represented by 又, hand, and on the upper part of it a crossed short horizontal plane, which indicates the thing which should not be done (much like the universal kill sign ⦸). Hence, its original meanings were "crime" and "mistake." It extended to mean "to blame," "to attribute to" and others.

有 yǒu

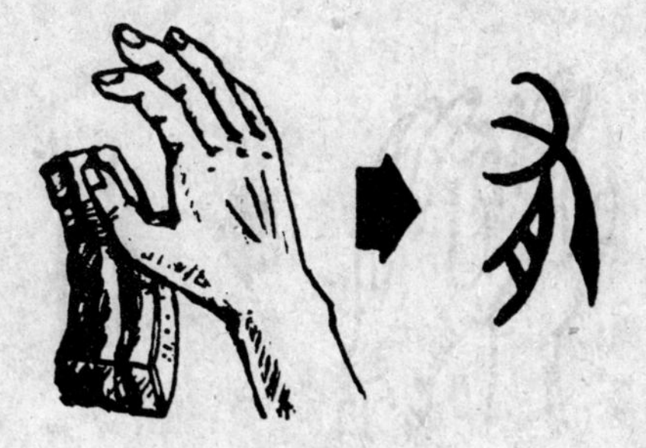

有

In oracle bone inscriptions, 有 was
resented by 又 and 㞢 . In bronze
tions, the radical 月, meat, was
lower part of this character. Its
ing was “to acquire” or “t

𠬝 𠬚 𠬛 友 友 友

友 yǒu

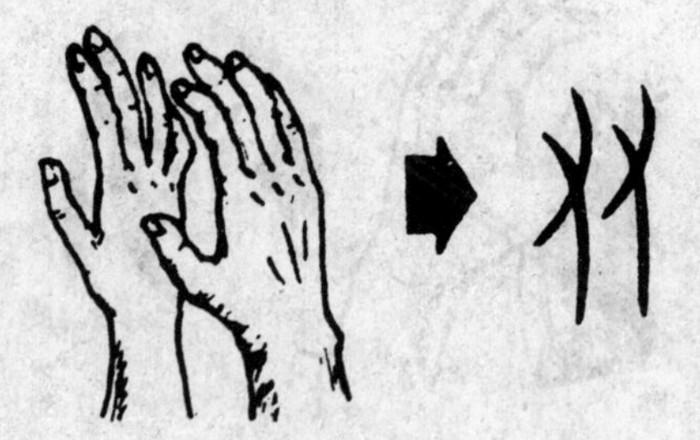

Graphically, two people's right hands are together, signifying "friends," 朋友. In ancient writings, 朋 meant "to collude with," a connotation which 友 does not share.

酉　yǒu

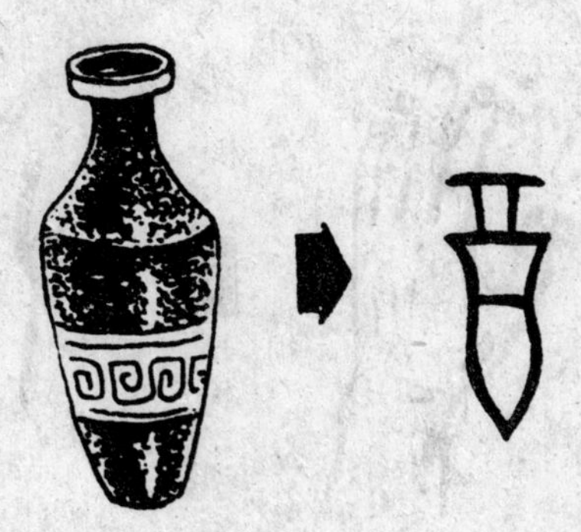

It is the original form of 酒. Graphically, it is a wine jar. Later, it was loaned to indicate the tenth of the Twelve Earthly Br
with the original meaning fading ou
characters with radical 酉, its o
ing can still be sensed.

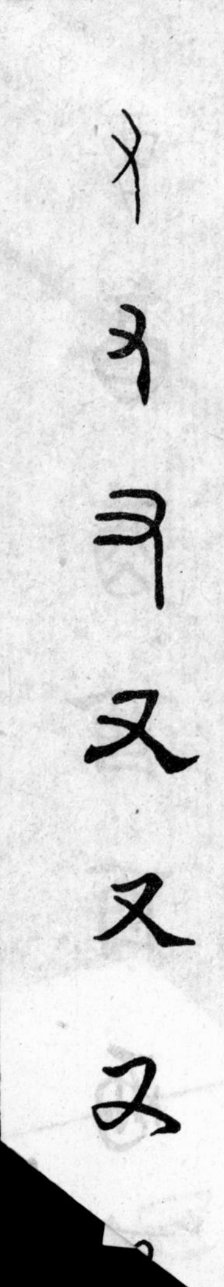

又 yòu

〔附〕右 佑

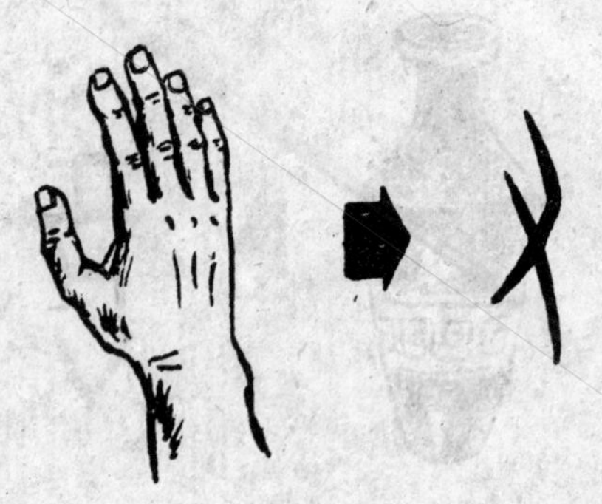

It is a right hand, which is not a graph but a simplified symbol. In oracle bone and bronze inscriptions, it was loaned to be 右, right (as opposed to left), 祐 (佑), to bless, and 有, to have.

 yòu

Its original meaning was "vegetable garden" and "orchard." In oracle bone i
scriptions, as a pictograph, it was like a s
shaped field with separated ridges. I
inscriptions, it changed to a picto
acter with the radical 囗 and
有.

鱼(魚)yú

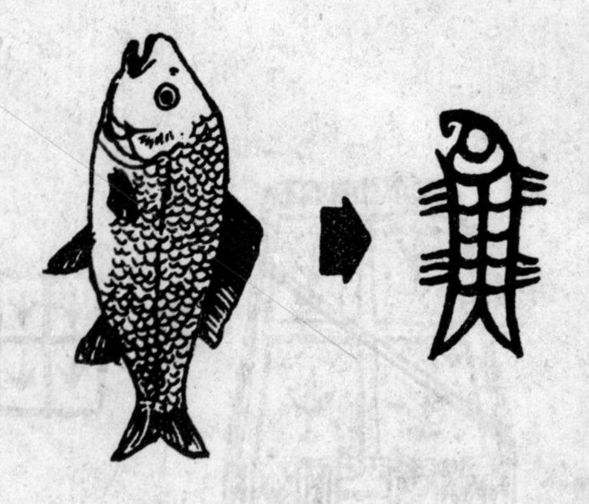

Graphically, it is the vivid delineation of a fish with head, body, scales and fins. Gradually, it became a pictographic character no longer resembling a fish with "" (fire) indicating the caudal fin.

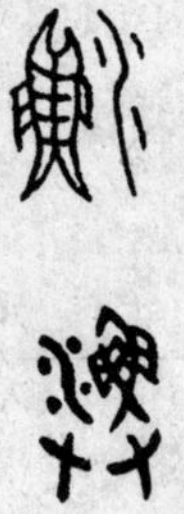

渔(漁)yú

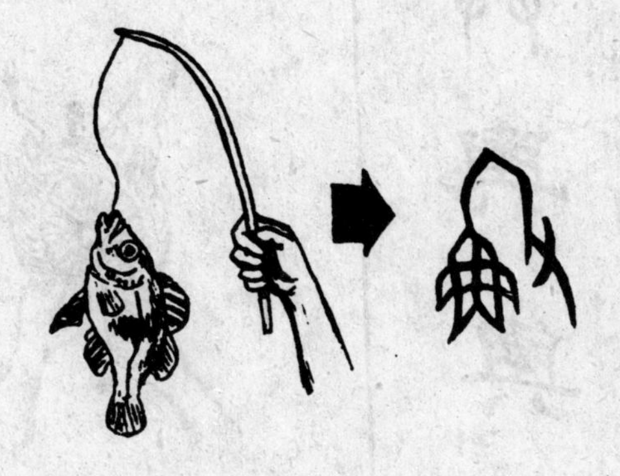

In oracle bone and br

it had several forms: a fi

er; a fish caught by

pole, line and ho

net. And the

as four.

fish.''

舆(輿)yú

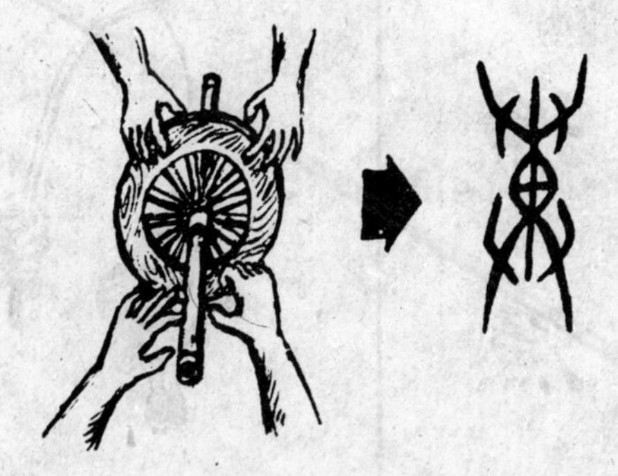

Its original meaning was "cart maker." Graphically, it is a wheel with four hands around it, symbolizing making a cart. Later, it mostly indicated "cabin" and all vehicles. It extended to mean the public. 舆论 is "public opinion."

雨 yǔ

In oracle bone inscriptions, the upper horizontal plane indicated the sky, and the various dots below symbolized rainfall. S[illegible] bronze inscriptions, its form has s[illegible] changed. In regular script, it is [illegible] trace its original form, excep[illegible] points.

羽 yǔ

In oracle bone inscriptions, it was the vivid delineation of two feathers. Hence, its original meaning was "the long hair on the wings." It eventually extended to mean "birds" and "the wings of birds." It also indicates "feather on the arrow."

玉 yù

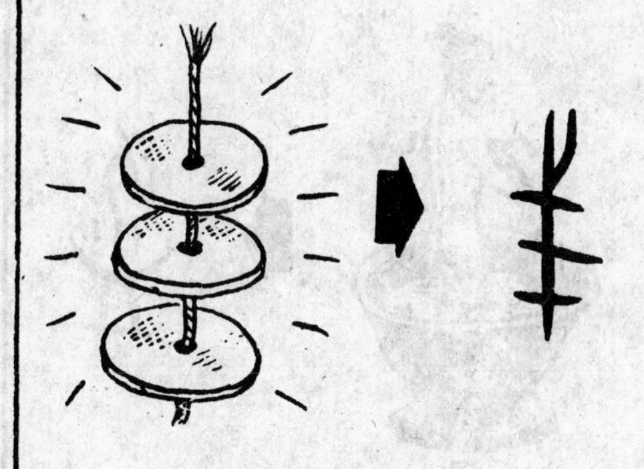

In oracle bone inscriptions, its form was like a string of jades. In bronze inscriptions and small seal characters, like 王, its form was three horizontal planes and one vertical structure. The difference between 玉 and 王 lies in that in the former the three planes are of the same length, while in the latter they are not. Since the time of official scripts, a dot has been added.

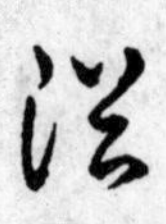

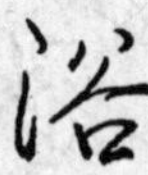

 yù

In oracle bone inscriptions, its form was a bathing man standing in a big basin with drops of water on his body. In bronze inscriptions, this character is not available. During the Warring States Period chǔ bó shō (book copied on silk unearthed in Hubei and Hunan Provinces) this pictophonetic character first began to be used with the radical 水 and phonetic symbol 谷.

御 yù

〔附〕驭

Graphically, a man is holding a horsewhip. Hence, its original meaning was "to drive a cart drawn by horses." Interchangeable with 驭, it extended to indicate "of or relating to the emperor." Later, it also came to mean "to defend," mostly in the form of 禦. 御 and 禦 are combined and simplified to 御.

育 yù

〔附〕毓　后

Graphically, it is the form of a woman with an infant and some water beside them, indicating 生育, to bear a child. Originally, it was written the same as 毓. It was interchangeable with 后 in oracle bone inscriptions.

聿 yù

〔附〕笔

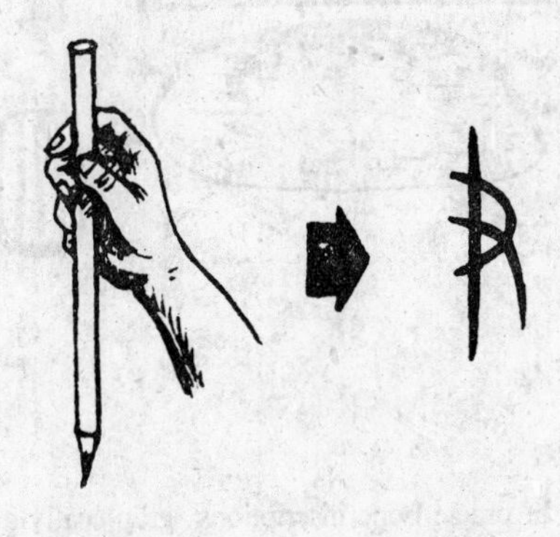

It is the original form of 筆(笔). In oracle bone and bronze inscriptions, graphically it was a hand holding a brush. Later, it was used as an auxiliary word. The radical 竹 was then added to form the character 筆, brush.

渊(淵)yuān

In oracle bone inscriptions, graphically it was a big pond with the three lines indicating water. Since bronze inscriptions, the radical 水 has been added. Hence, its original meaning was "deep pool" and "water with ripples." It extended to mean "deep and far," e.g. 渊博, deep and profound knowledge.

元 yuán

〔附〕 兀

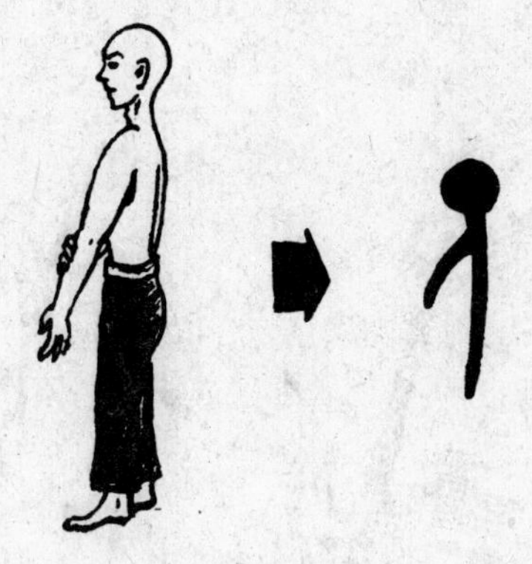

Its original meaning was "head." Graphically, it is the profile of a man, which in oracle bone inscriptions, was represented by one or two short horizontal planes for the sake of carving convenience. In bronze inscriptions, the round dot indicated the head. In ancient books, it was interchangeable with 兀.

爰 yuán

〔附〕 援

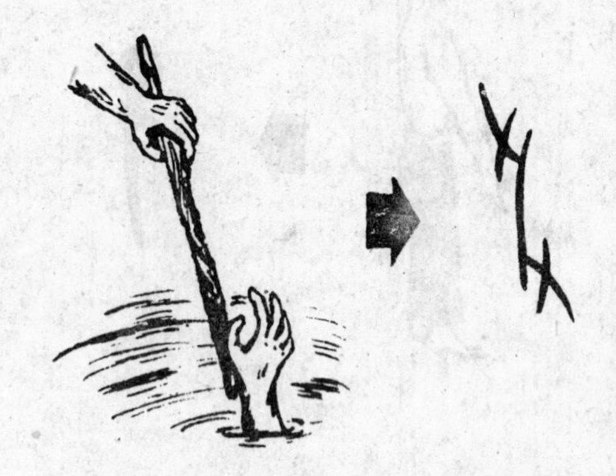

It is the original form of 援. In oracle bone inscriptions, it was a hand extending a stick to the hand of another person, indicating "to save and support." Since it was loaned to be a function word, 援 was coined to take on its original meaning.

员(員)yuán

〔附〕 圓

It is the original form of 圓. Graphically, it is a tripod with the upper part as a circle indicating the round opening of a tripod. Later, 圓 was invented to be distinguished from 员.

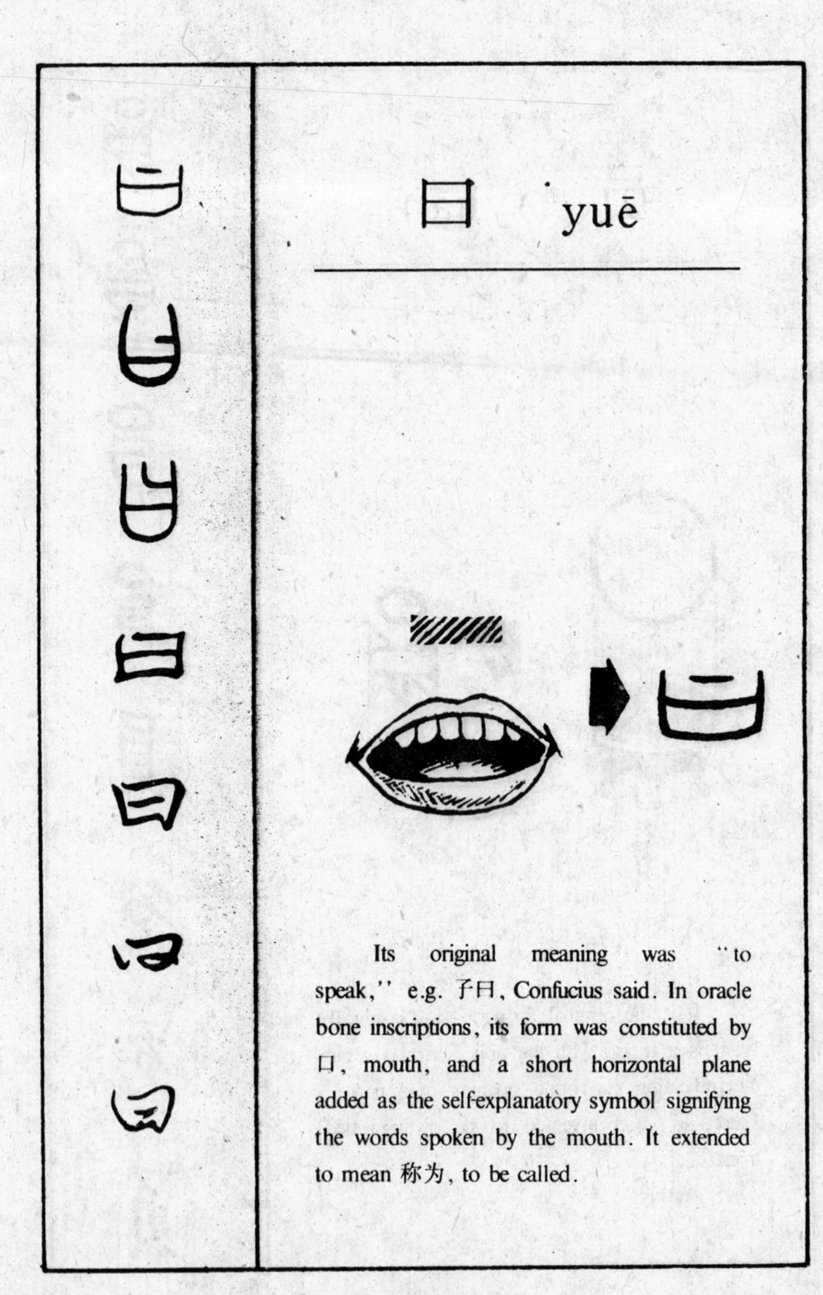

曰 yuē

Its original meaning was "to speak," e.g. 子曰, Confucius said. In oracle bone inscriptions, its form was constituted by 口, mouth, and a short horizontal plane added as the self-explanatory symbol signifying the words spoken by the mouth. It extended to mean 称为, to be called.

月 yuè

〔附〕 夕

Graphically, it is a crescent, which mostly appears at night. Hence, it indicates 夕, evening, night. In oracle bone and bronze inscriptions, it was interchangeable with 夕. Since small seal characters, their meanings began to diverge from one another.

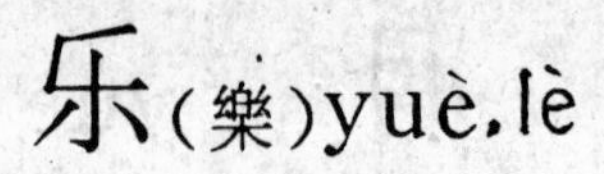

乐(樂)yuè,lè

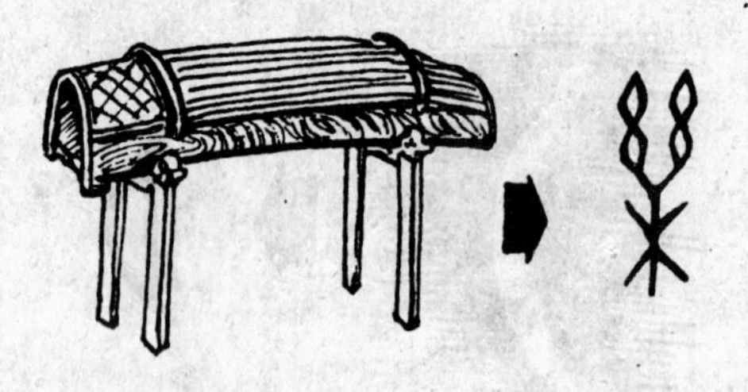

Its original meaning was "musical instrument." It also indicates "music." Originally, it was composed of 木, wood, and 丝, silk bowstring, for a stringed instrument. Later, 白, plucked instrument, was added. It extended to mean "to delight."

云(雲)yún

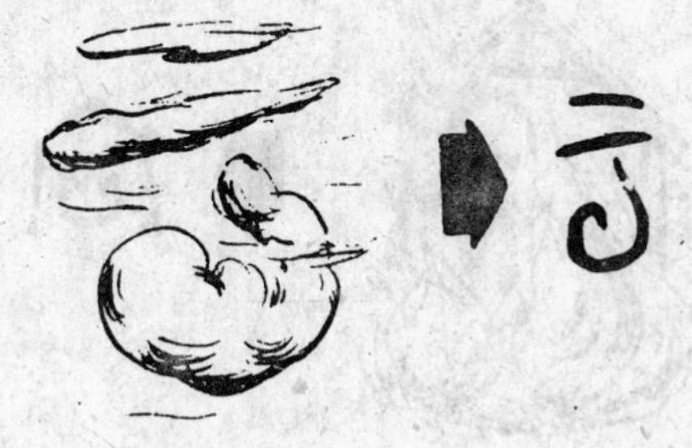

As a pictograph, it consists of two short horizontal planes indicating the cloud layers and a hook symbolizing cirrus clouds. Since it was loaned to mean 说, to say, 雲 was invented to convey its original sense. The simplified version resumed its primitive form then.

雲 雲 雲 雲 云

灾(災)zāi

In oracle bone inscriptions, there were three forms of 灾, calamity: 𠕒, the calamity of fire (house on fire); 巛, flood, (like the form of flood); and 𢦏, war (a weapon decapitating a man). In regular script, it is written in three ways: 灾, 災, and 烖. Today, they are combined to be 灾.

宰 zǎi

Graphically, a knife used for torture in a house (see Case 辛) indicates that the slaves with marks are laboring in the house. Hence, its original meaning was "slave." It also indicates the slave master.

再 zài

In oracle bone inscriptions, its form is a fish and the horizontal planes added on the ends signifies one plus one. Hence, its original meaning was "twice" or "second time." Since bronze inscriptions, its form has changed a lot and it is difficult to trace back to its original meaning.

在 zài

As a pictophonetic character with few strokes, it is composed of the radical 土 and the phonetic 才. Hence, its original meaning was "to exist" or "to live." It extended to mean "be located in" and the like.

臧 zāng

〔附〕藏

Its original meaning was "slave." Graphically, it is weapon 戈 piercing the eye of a man and making him blind. In ancient times, this was one of the cruel ways employed to make people slaves. It is also interchangeable with 藏, cáng.

昃 zè

Its original meaning was "the sun setting in the west." Graphically, it is a man standing in the slanting sunshine. Some forms of the man are also very slanted making it seem like the shadow of the man in the setting sun.

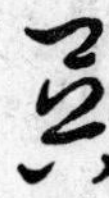

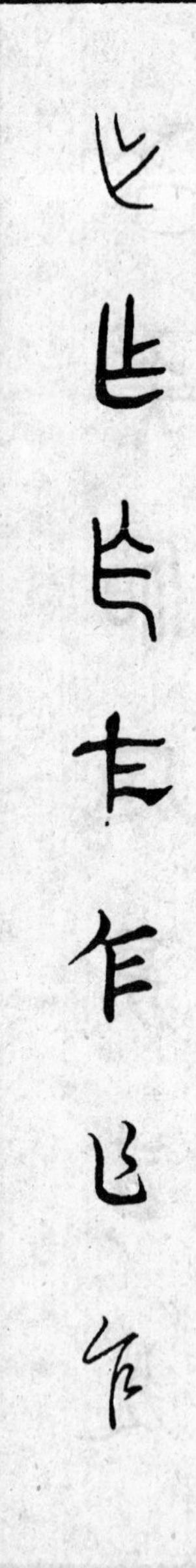

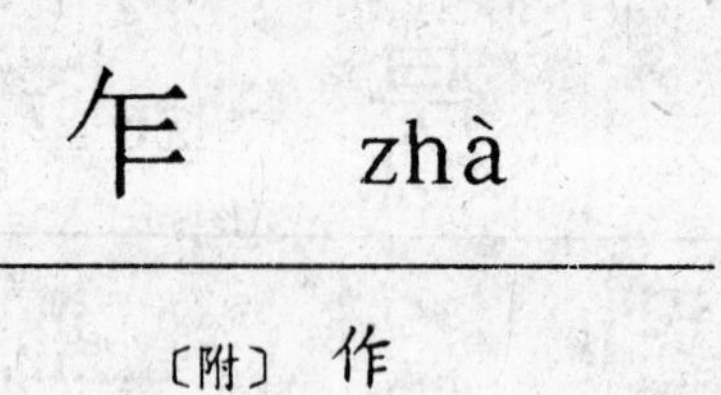

乍 zhà

〔附〕作

It is the original form of 作. Graphically, it is like the front of a garment in oracle bone inscriptions, indicating "tailoring." In the bronze inscriptions of the Shang and Zhou dynasties, mostly it was in the form of 乍.

占 zhān, zhàn

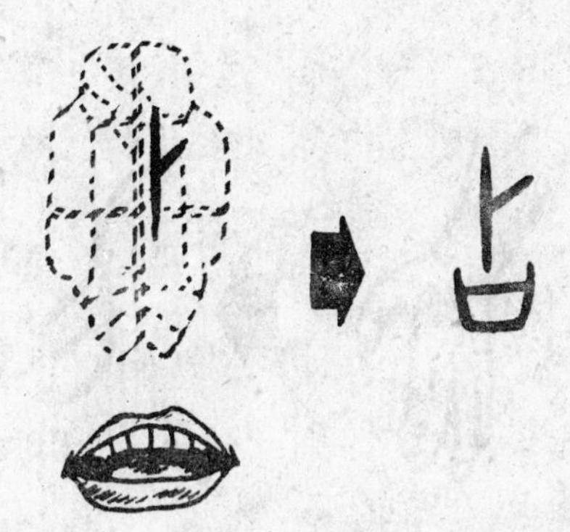

Its original meaning was "to see the omens and know what lies in the future." The upper part of this character is 卜, indicating playing divination, the lower part is 口, indicating to predict the future. Interchangeable with 口, it also means "to own." Today, 占 and 佔 are combined and simplified to 占.

爪 zhǎo,zhuǎ

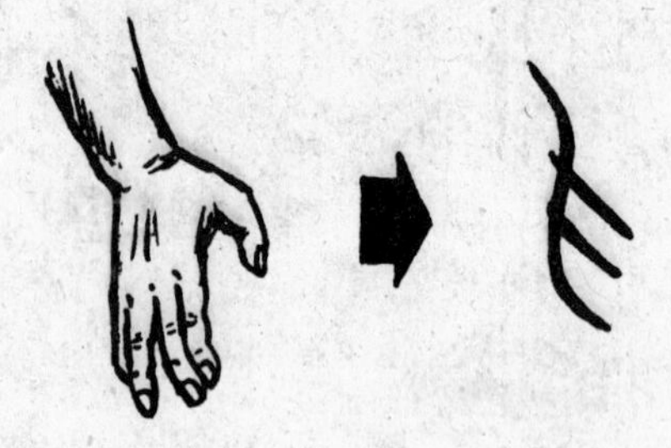

Graphically, it is a hand, which is simplified to three fingers, catching something. Its form with the meaning "hand" can be proved in 采, 为, 爱, 受, 孚, and 妥. Later, it indicated fingernail, toenail and the claw of birds and animals.

召 zhào

〔附〕 招 诏

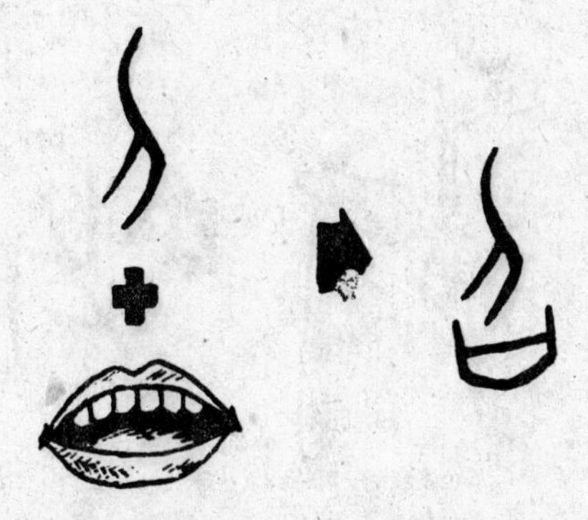

As a pictophonetic character, it is composed of the radical 口 and the phonetic symbol 刀. Its original meaning was 呼唤, "to call." In bronze inscriptions, it had a complex version, which looked like two hands taking 酉, wine, and 月, meat, from a container to entertain the guests. It is interchangeable with 招 and 诏.

折　zhé

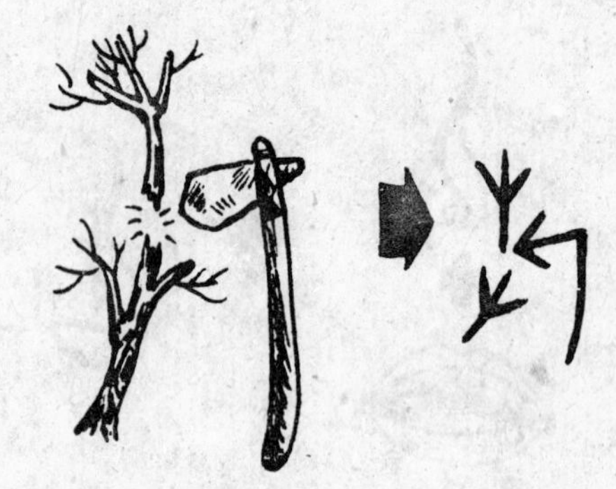

Graphically, a huge ax, 斤, is cutting a tree, 木. Hence, its original meaning was "to break," "to cut down."

贞(貞)zhēn

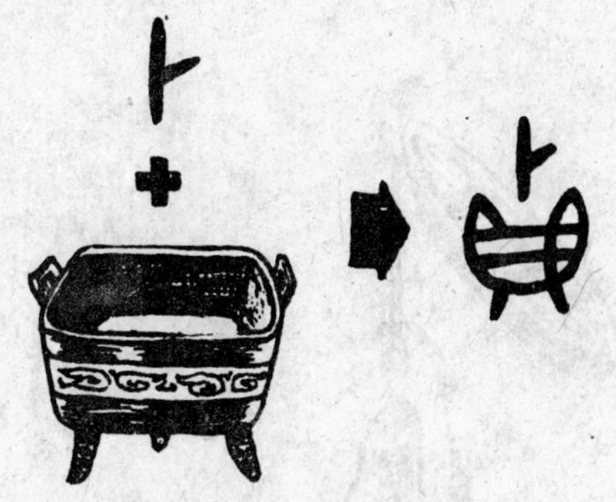

Its original meaning was "to play divination." In oracle bone inscriptions, it was represented by 鼎, tripod. In bronze inscriptions, the radical 卜 was added to indicate playing divination. Its extended meaning is 贞节, chastity, 坚贞, faithful.

朕 zhèn

Graphically, it is two hands holding a pointed stick and repairing the cracks of a broken boat. Hence, its original meaning was "crack" or "crevice." Later, the radical 舟 changed to 月 and the meaning began to indicate 我, I. Since the first emperor in Qin Dynasty, it has been used as the emperor's exclusive address for himself.

正 zhèng

〔附〕 征

It is the original form of 征. Originally, its upper part was a square-shaped town and the lower part was a foot walking "straight" towards the town.

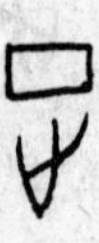

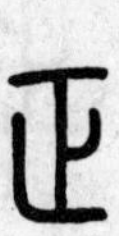

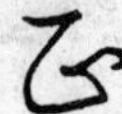

之 zhī

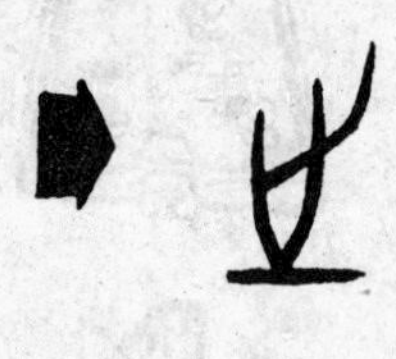

Graphically, it is a foot with a horizontal plane under it indicating the place from where the foot comes from. Hence, its original meaning was "to go" or "to go to some place." Later, it was loaned to be a form word. In oracle bone inscriptions, it was interchangeable with 又 and 有.

直 zhí

〔附〕 值

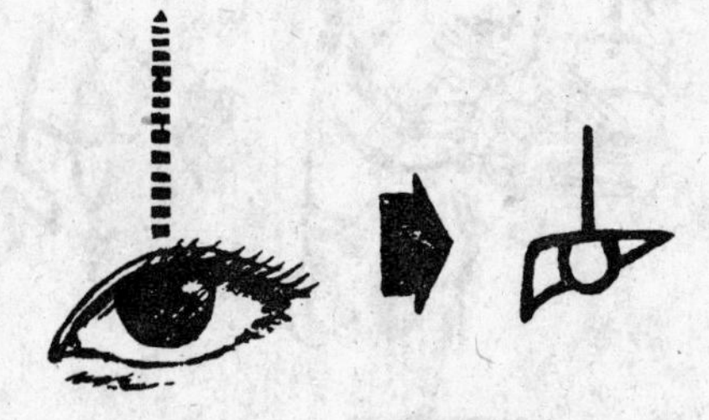

In oracle bone inscriptions, its form was an eye with a vertical line above it. Hence, its meaning derives from the straight line along which the eye can see. In small seal characters, a folded structure was added. In ancient writings, it was interchangeable with 值.

执(執)zhí

In oracle bone inscriptions, it was the vivid delineation of a man with both hands handcuffed. Hence, its original meaning was "to arrest."

止 zhǐ

〔附〕 趾

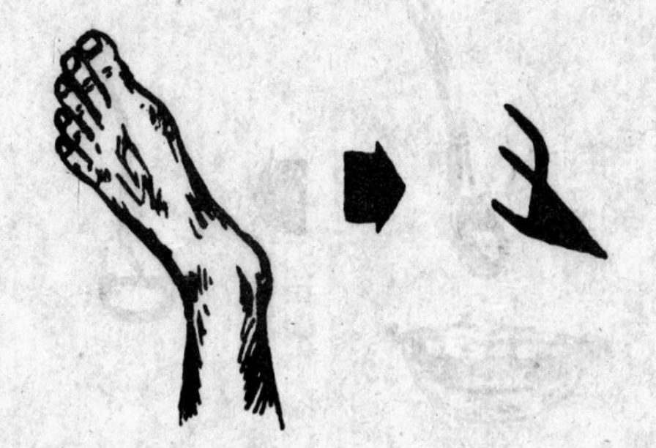

It is the original form of 趾, meaning foot. In oracle bone inscriptions, it was the form of a foot with three toes.

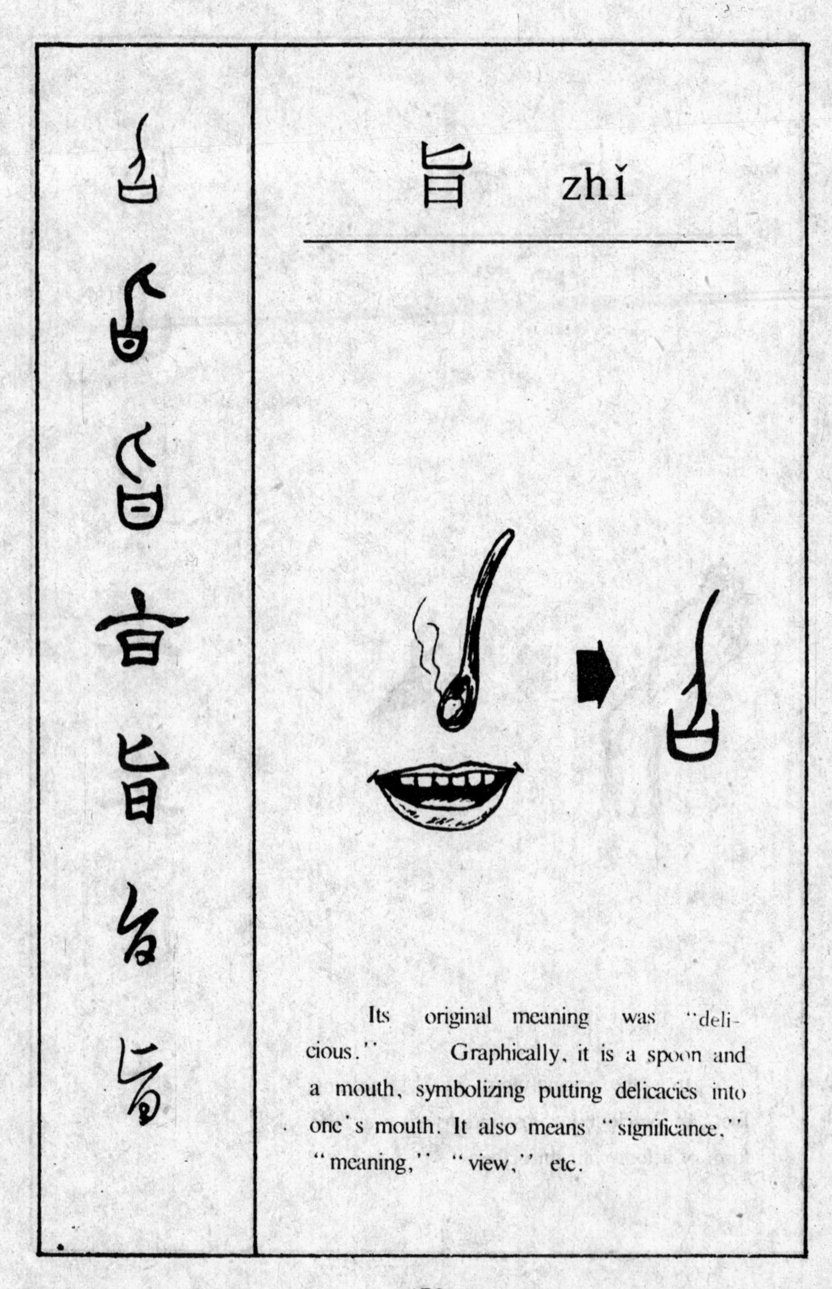

旨 zhǐ

Its original meaning was "delicious." Graphically, it is a spoon and a mouth, symbolizing putting delicacies into one's mouth. It also means "significance," "meaning," "view," etc.

至 zhì

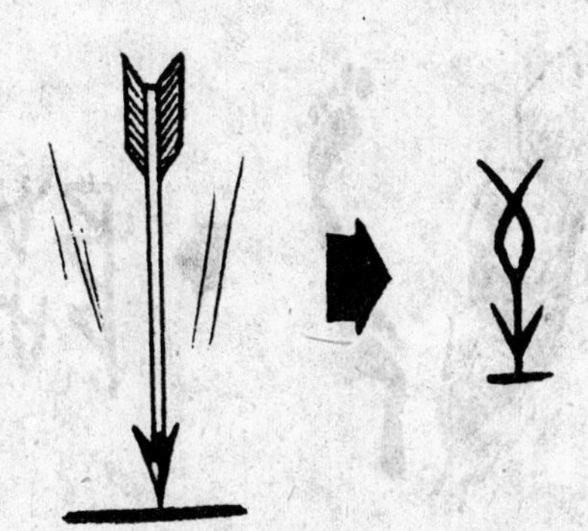

Graphically, it is an arrow with a horizontal line under it indicating the place the arrow falls. Hence, its original meaning was "to arrive."

陟 zhì

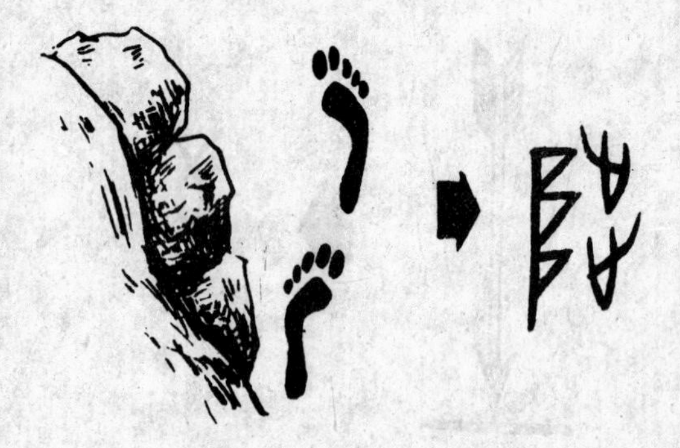

Its original meaning was "to climb mountains" or "to scale heights." Graphically, it is composed of 𠂤 (阜), mountain of earth, and two 止 (趾), the two feet scaling the mountain.

中 zhōng

Graphically, it is a flagpost planted in a circle with a flag waving on it. Hence, its original meaning was "central," "middle," Later, the flag was omitted.

众(衆)zhòng

Its original meanings were "many people," "the masses" and "all of the people." In oracle bone inscriptions, its form was constituted by 日, the sun, and three 人, people (indicating a multitude of people). In bronze inscriptions, 日 was written as 罒 (eye shape).

周 zhōu

In oracle bone inscriptions, its form was a field on which the plants are densely planted, hence the idea of "thorough" or "to spread everywhere." Later, 口 was added and used as a special term, e.g. 周原, a place with rich agricultural production.

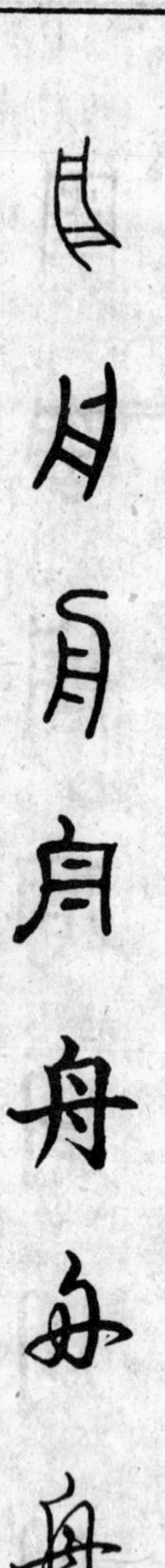

舟 zhōu

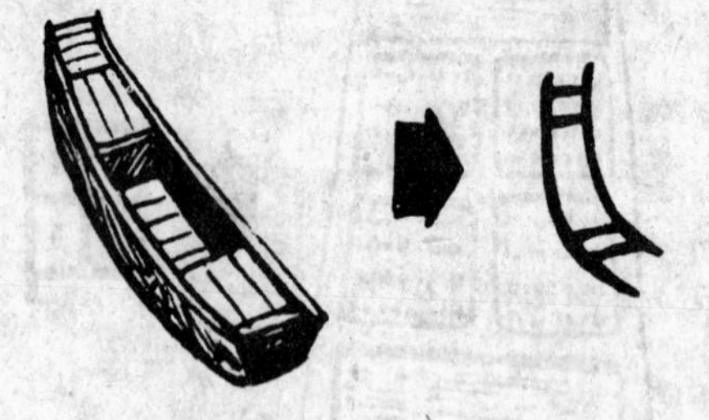

As a pictograph, graphically it resembles a curved boat with horizontal planks across it, hence the meaning "boat." Any character with the radical 舟 is usually close to boat in meaning.

州 zhōu

〔附〕 洲

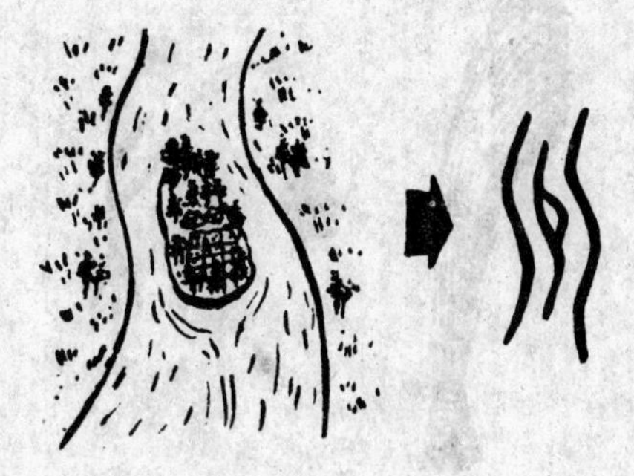

It is the original form of 洲 meaning "land surrounded by water." Graphically, it is a river and the circled part in the flow indicates the piece of land. Later, it was used to be the name of an ancient administrative area. 洲 was invented to convey the original sense.

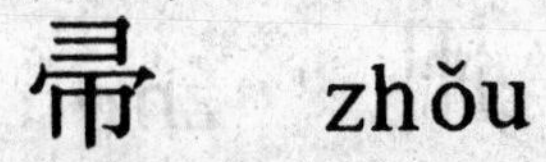

帚 zhǒu

As a pictograph, in oracle bone inscriptions, its form was a broom with the upper part as the broom head, the lower part as the shaft and the middle as the ties. In small seal characters, the lower part altered to 巾.

朱 zhū

Originally, it was the name for a kind of tree. The character acquired the meaning of "red," which was the color of the tree it originally referred to.

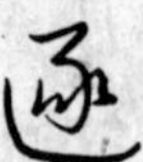

逐 zhú

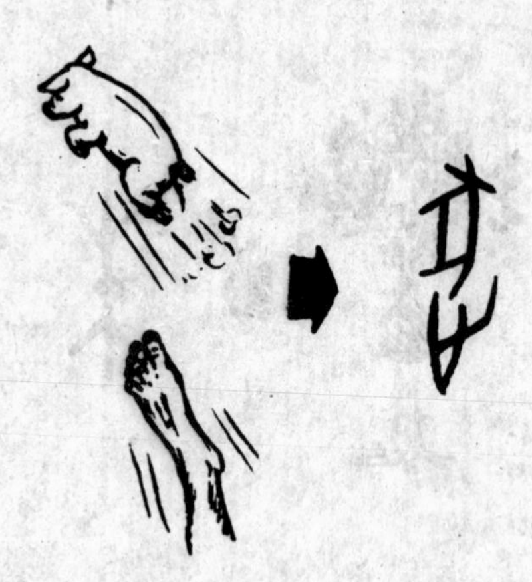

Its original meaning was "to chase." In oracle bone inscriptions, with the upper part as 豕, pig, and the lower part as 止, foot, it symbolized a man chasing after a pig. In bronze inscriptions, 彳 was added on 止, constituting the semantic symbol 辵, chuò, indicating running.

祝 zhù

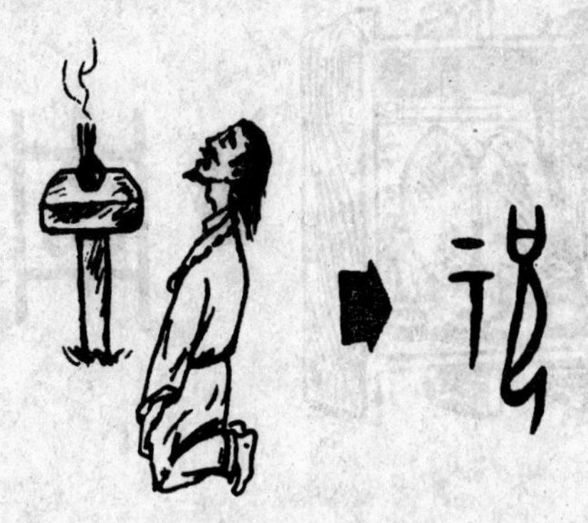

Its original meaning was "a person who is praying during the sacrifice offering ritual." It is also used as a verb, indicating "to pray." Graphically, it is a man kneeling down beside a stone altar praying with a big open mouth.

贮(貯)zhù

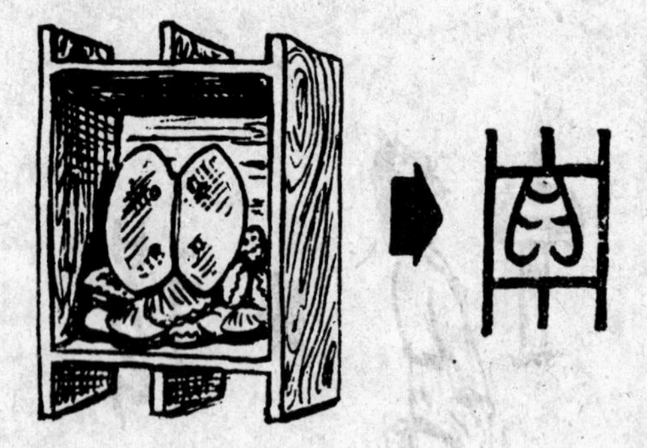

Its original meaning was "to accumulate" or "to deposit." Graphically, it is a wooden box containing 贝, cowries, symbolizing wealth. Later, 贝 was taken out of the box.

铸(鑄)zhù

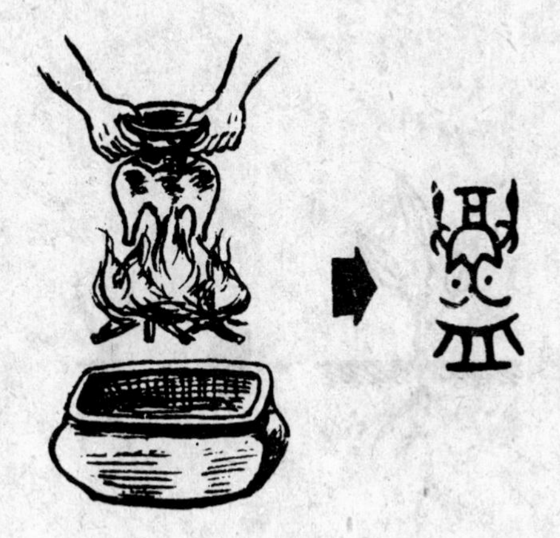

Originally as an ideograph, it was graphically two hands holding 鬲, a container, melting metals on a fire and then pouring it into the 皿, mode, below. Later, it changed to a pictophonetic character with the graphic symbol 金 and the phonetic symbol 寿.

耑 zhuān

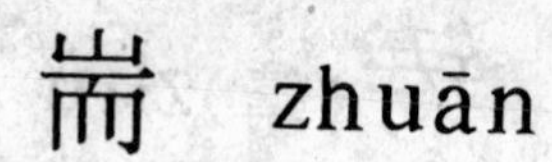

〔附〕端 专

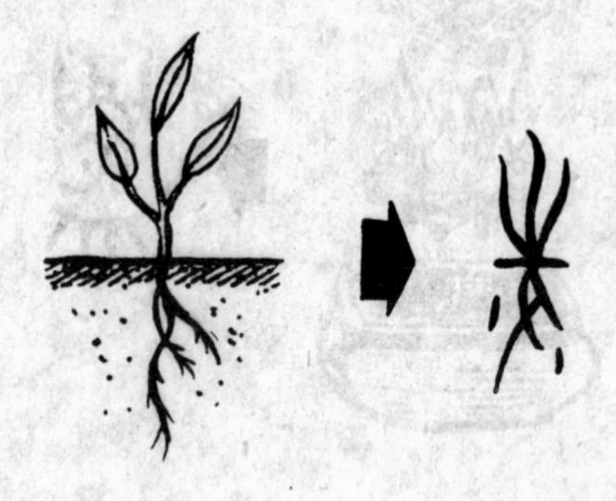

It is the original form of 端. Graphically, it is a seedling sprouting tender leaves and soft roots. It extended to mean "the pointed top." Later, it was mostly used to be 专.

妆(妝)zhuāng

〔附〕装

Its original meaning was "to decorate" or "to make up." As a pictophonetic character it is composed of the graphic symbol 女 and the phonetic symbol 爿, qiáng, with many variant forms. In ancient writings, sometimes it was written as 装.

追 zhuī

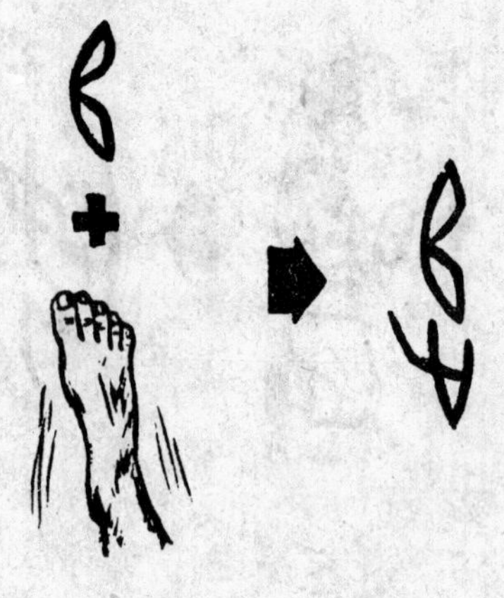

As a pictophonetic character, it is composed of the graphic 止, foot, and the phonetic 𠂤, duī, the original form of 堆, "heap," in oracle bone inscriptions. Since bronze inscriptions, the graphic radical has been written as 辵, chuò.

隹 zhuī

〔附〕唯

It is the general term for a bird with a short tail. Actually, in ancient Chinese characters there exists little difference between 隹 and 鸟. Graphically, it is the form of a bird. In oracle bone and bronze inscriptions, it was loaned to be used in place of 唯 at the beginning of a sentence to indicate the tone of expression.

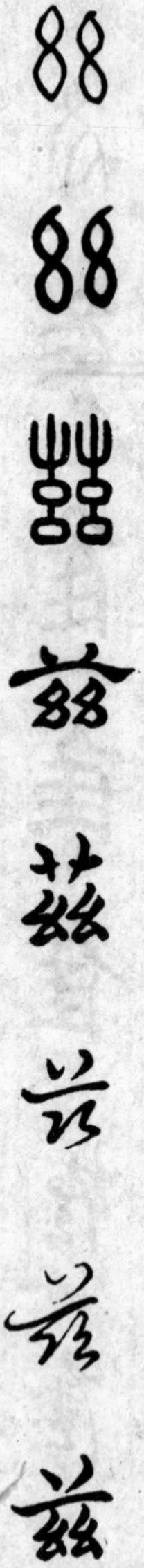

兹 zī

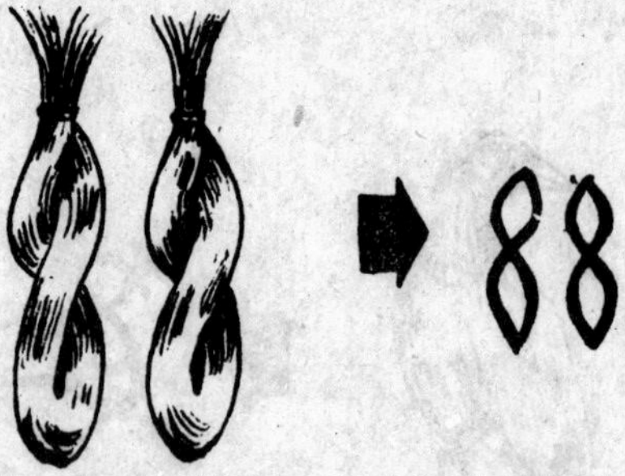

In oracle bone and bronze inscriptions, it was identical with 丝 (the original form of 丝, silk). The radical 艸 was added to it in small seal characters to make the distinction. Mostly, it is used as an indicative adverb, meaning "this."

子 zǐ

In both oracle bone inscriptions and bronze inscriptions, it had two forms: one was a baby with head and hands and two legs wrapped in swaddling clothes; the other was a baby with a big head and hair and two legs bending upwards. The former one is simple while the latter one is complex.

子

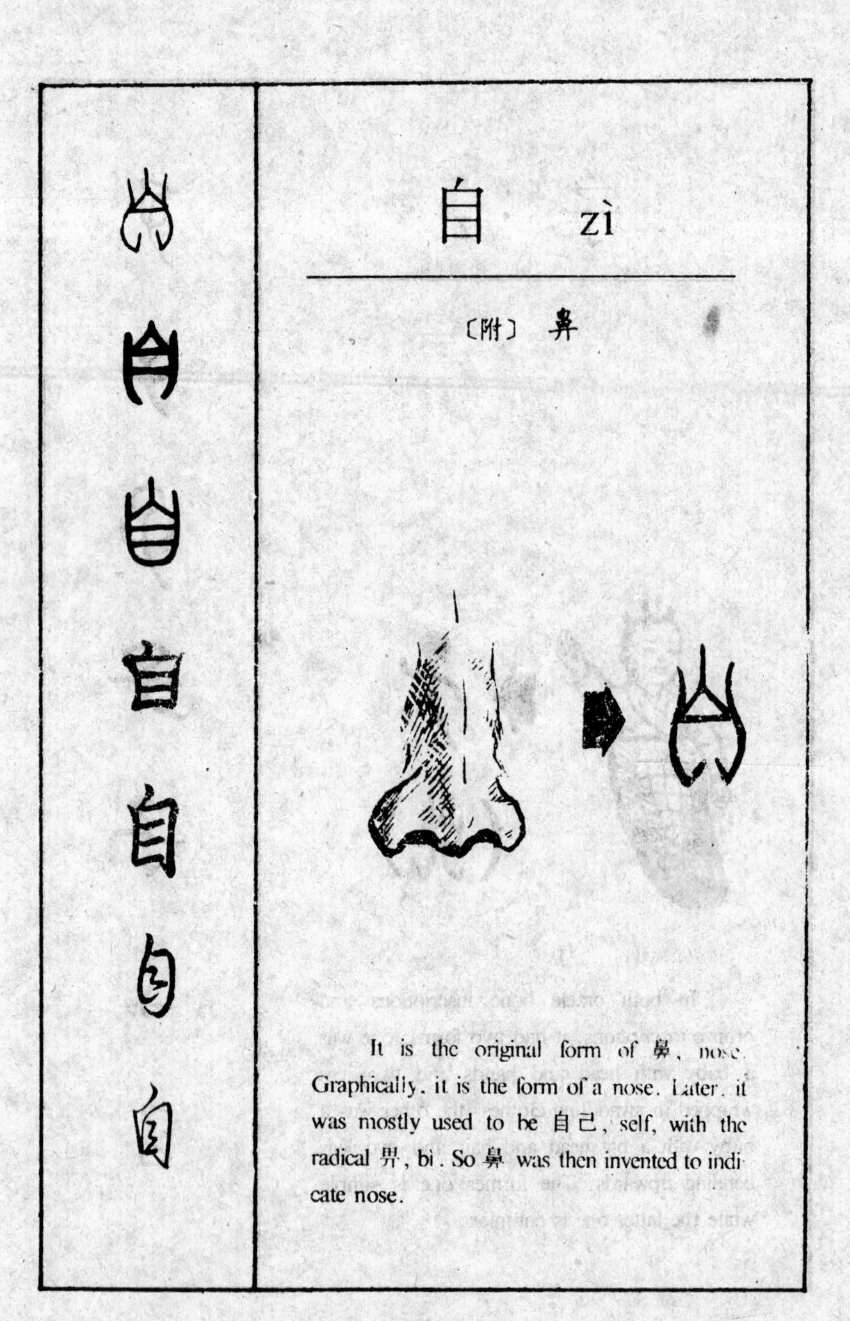

自 zì

〔附〕 鼻

It is the original form of 鼻, nose. Graphically, it is the form of a nose. Later, it was mostly used to be 自己, self, with the radical 畀, bi. So 鼻 was then invented to indicate nose.

宗 zōng

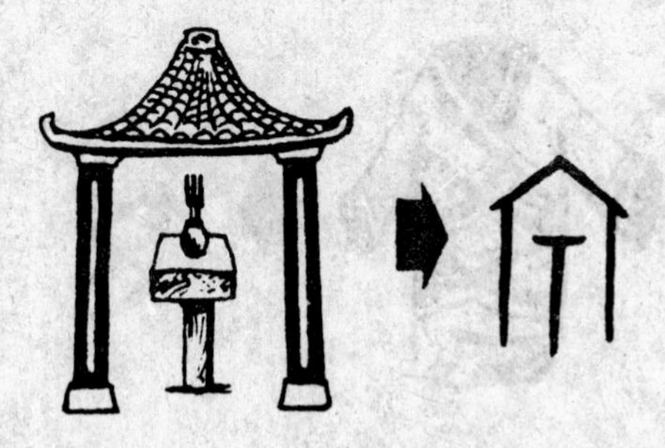

Its original meaning was "clan temple" or "clan hall," the place where ancestors are worshipped and offered sacrifice. Graphically, it is composed of 宀, a building, and 示, the sacrificial table in the building. It extended to mean "ancestors" and "clan."

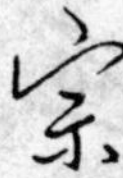

〔附〕 褚

Graphically, it looks like a uniform. Originally, it meant the marked uniform worn by slaves and soldiers. It is also written in the form of 褚, zhǔ. Later, it mostly indicated "soldier."

足 zú

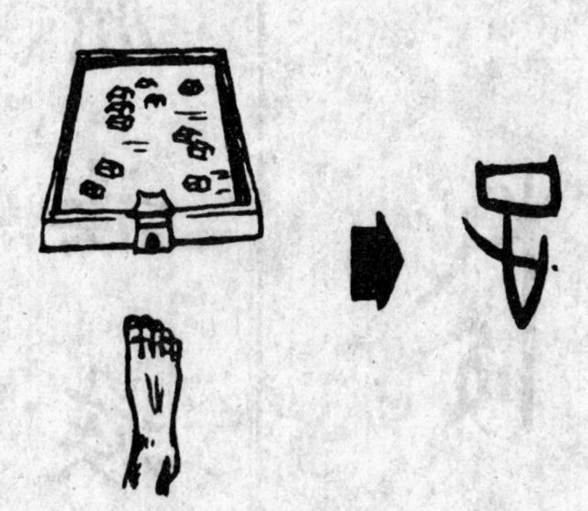

In oracle bone inscriptions, it was in the same form as 止 (see Case 止). Its other form is like a man's leg and foot. In regular script, it is 疋, shū, not the variant form of 匹.

族 zú

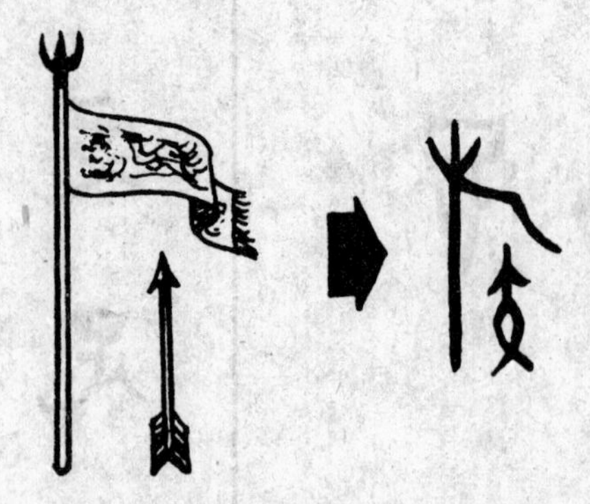

Graphically, it is a flag with an arrowhead under it indicating arms in ancient writings. In primitive times, people of the same clan always fought against enemies under the clan flag. In the Zhou Dynasty, 100 families formed one 族.

祖 zǔ

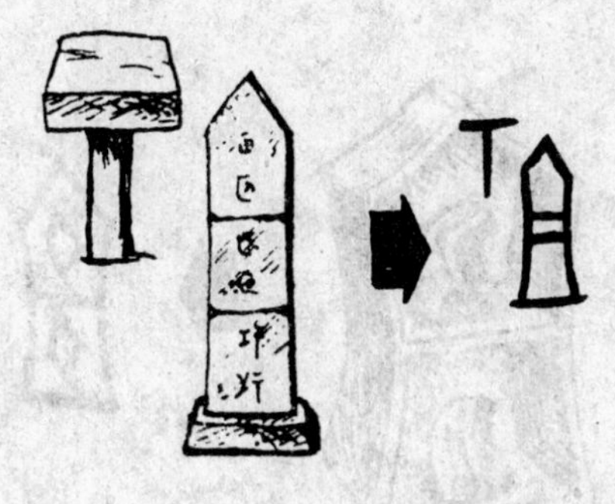

In ancient writings, 祖 and 且 were in the same form. With the radical 示 in oracle bone inscriptions, it originally meant "clan temple." It extends to mean "ancestors" and "grandfather."

俎 zǔ

〔附〕 宜

It is a wooden ceremonial utensil laid at the sacrifice offering or banquets. Later, it extended to indicate the chopping block. Graphically, it is two pieces of meat on the sacrificial table. 俎 and 宜 were in the same form in ancient writings.

尊 zūn

〔附〕 樽

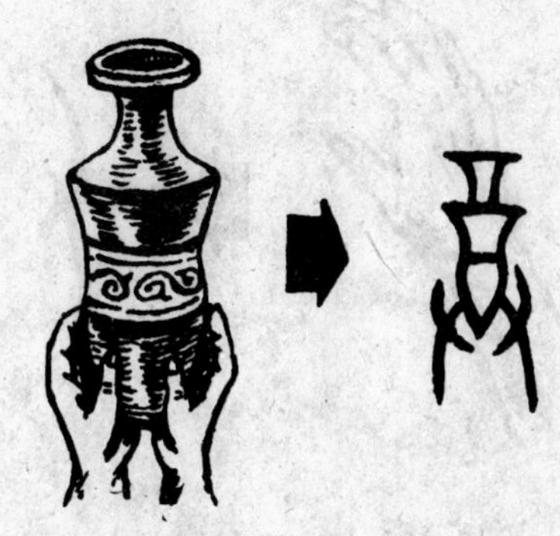

Its original meaning was "wine vessel or the ceremonial utensil used in sacrifice offering ceremonies." Its form in ancient writings was two hands holding a vessel of wine. From the idea "to offer wine with respect" it extended to indicate "respect," "noble," etc. It is interchangeable with 樽.

左 zuǒ

〔附〕 佐

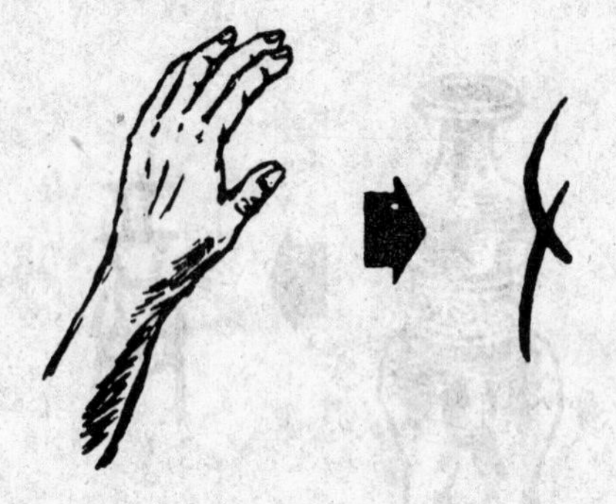

As a simplified semantic symbol, graphically it is the form of the left hand. In bronze inscriptions, it was in the form of 左, left, which also means "to support" and "to help." Later, when with the latter meanings it was written in the form of 佐.